Nearly Perfect

An American Success Story by
Farmer and Betty Meadows
as told to
Cindy Day

Nearly Perfect

Copyright© 2003 by Meadows Farms, Inc.

Printed and bound in the United States of America. All rights reserved. No part of this book may be reproduced in any form or by any electronic or mechanical means including information storage and retrieval systems without permission in writing from the copyright holder, except by a reviewer, who may quote brief passages in review.

ISBN: 0-9741858-3-3

2525 W Anderson Lane, Suite 540
Austin, Texas 78757

Tel: 512.407.8876
Fax: 512.478.2117

E-mail: info@turnkeypress.com
Web: www.turnkeypress.com

A Word from Farmer & Betty

The writing of this book has been a real adventure, like everything else that we get involved in. We have spent hours and hours making audio tapes and notes for Cindy Day, our co-writer. We scheduled time to do this at Snowshoe Ski Resort, Cancún, Jamaica, Nassau, Acapulco, Baltimore, Washington, D.C., Old Mill Park in Fredericksburg, and a park in Charlottesville, Virginia.

The feeling of reliving all our experiences and memories of the last fifty years is indescribable. It seemed we found ourselves feeling sixteen years old again, renewing the thrill of those first kisses and sexual encounters as a new bride and groom; and crying again and again over the sad times.

It has taken us two years to "do" this book. The hardest part was "cutting." Without omitting the things we wanted in, we probably would have ended up with a two-thousand-page book! We are sorry about the people and the memories we couldn't include in these pages, but they are no less in our own hearts and memories.

We could never have done it without Cindy Day, our co-writer, and Cece Whittaker, our editor. Many thanks to these great gals.

We hope, as you read our story, you enjoy it and find some "life lesson" you can use.

Love you,

Farmer & Betty

A Word from Cindy Day

Nearly Perfect ... in twenty-six years I have heard those words many times from my employer, benefactor, and friend, "Farmer" Bill Meadows. As I helped Farmer and Betty with their book, I came to learn that "nearly perfect" was much more than a state of health. It is a philosophy, a lifestyle, a passion, and an outlook. It represents more than just past accomplishment—it likewise refers to hope and possibility and commitment to today as well as all the unknown tomorrows. It is a joyful spirit that makes every day count.

Many thanks to Farmer and Betty for giving us an intimate glimpse of a "nearly perfect" life together.

Cindy Day

DEDICATION

As we dedicate this book, we immediately think of our children, Jay and Doreen, Kate and Rocky, and our grandchildren, Miranda and Monica.

Then, secondly, we want to honor our parents, Noel and Maye Meadows and Robert and Olive Lewis, as we know they gave us life and are mostly responsible for the people we became.

Thirdly, we honor our brothers and sisters; Berman and Phyllis Meadows, Gilven and Nila Meadows, Fred and Margaret Meadows, Nola Turner, Dave and Janice Meadows, Vic and Sara Meadows, Bob and Shirley Lewis, and Mary Lou and Roger Provencher.

Fourthly, to all of the wonderful people and events that we were forced to leave out of this book (which we have not forgotten). Only in the interest of space and time have we omitted so many memories.

Prologue

*I*t is 2:15 in the morning and I am wide awake. My wife talks enthusiastically of the night's events, as I unpin her corsage and set it on the nightstand. "Be careful, honey. I'm going to save that!" she reminds me, and I nod. Then, "What a great night!" she says happily. "I'm going to take a quick shower."

"Want some company?" I suggest, but she doesn't hear me. I think she's singing as she starts the shower water.

Alone for the first time in twenty-four hours, I consider this weekend in light of the fifty years preceding it, for this is our fiftieth anniversary. We are celebrating at The Greenbrier Hotel in White Sulphur Springs, West Virginia, as we have for the past ten years or so. But this time, it is different.

I believe I was eleven or so when I first saw The Greenbrier, well before Betty and I had ever dreamed we would celebrate our Golden Anniversary with a net worth of seventy-two million dollars. The grand hotel sat poised among the purple hills, like some sort of displaced royalty. Geographically, the hotel was located a mere fifty miles from Crab Orchard, West Virginia, yet we were as far removed from its splendor as the east is from the west.

Meadows

Our family pickup truck carried my mother and dad, as well as a payload of five children in its large cargo bed. When Dad swung the truck onto a side road, we sat back and enjoyed the view as the little town below got smaller and smaller. When Fred turned around to get Mother's attention, he let out a low whistle.

"Wow! Look at that!" he shouted, shaking my arm.

"What, Fred? *Omigosh!*"

Before us stood the magnificent old hotel, dominating the vast landscape in front of us.

"That's the White House!" my brother insisted, but I knew better than that. It was a palace, I was quite certain.

A few moments later, Dad pulled to the side of the road and parked. "Well guys, what do you think?" he asked with a chuckle.

We were dumbfounded, of course, and could only listen as my dad explained.

"This here's The Greenbrier! It's over two hundred years old! And in all those two hundred years, it's been just for wealthy folks."

We all nodded, appreciatively. That certainly made sense to us. Even at an early age, we were well-acquainted with the inequities of life and accepted them as a matter of course. It stood to reason that rich people could afford to do things that poor people could not.

"President Roosevelt stayed here a couple of times when he was in office, and I hear that President Truman was here just a few weeks back!"

"Wow! The President!" Gilven gaped at the hotel, through its wrought iron barrier.

"And not just presidents," my father continued. "Queen Elizabeth herself stayed here!"

My mother nodded with great satisfaction, and added, "Yes, indeed, with her children!"

"Could we stay there?" I wondered aloud.

"Certainly not, Billy! I told you, it's just for wealthy folks!"

"Well, can we at least get a closer look?" I implored, pressing my head against the black iron balustrade that encircled the sixty-five hundred-acre resort. "Maybe drive through?"

My father appeared to consider the idea carefully, then nodded thoughtfully. "I'll see what I can do, son."

Swinging the pickup truck back onto the road, my father brought us to a stop sign in front of a little house of some sort. A uniformed man stepped out and nodded curtly in my father's direction.

"Do you have your service pass? It says right on it to use Gate C."

"Oh, no, I'm not here to work," my father began.

"Then move this heap out of the way! This entrance is for guests only!"

My father nodded with understanding. "Well, sir, I can appreciate that, but I thought you might allow me to drive my family through for a quick look."

The guard seemed to take this as a personal affront. He sputtered for a moment, but quickly regained his composure. "Sir," he said, his voice steely, "you need to move along now. I won't ask you again."

"Well, thank you anyway, Sir, and good day," my father retorted, unabashed, and away we went.

Disappointed, we children sat grumbling in the back of the truck. "We just wanted a look," Freddie intoned softly.

"This here fence is about as close as you'll ever get to that place," my brother Berman predicted, as The Greenbrier faded from our view. But I didn't believe it. Not for a minute.

That was a long time ago. The years, so rich with memories, have passed in the twinkling of an eye, and I have been here many times. I am comfortable in this milieu, not intimidated in the least by the opulent surroundings.

The bed is turned down, with the customary chocolate mints on our pillows. Soft, thick robes are lain across the foot of the bed, along with Betty's negligee. I undress and stretch out across the crisp linen sheets, impatient for Betty to come to bed.

I close my eyes briefly, giving thanks to the Creator for my life and all my blessings. I cannot imagine feeling any more nearly perfect than I do at this moment.

It has been a weekend to remember. The boy from the coal camps, who still lives deep inside me, felt a sweet satisfaction when he reserved one hundred rooms for his anniversary party. We have thoroughly enjoyed mingling with the people who mean the most to us—our family, our friends and our professional associates. We have laughed and reminisced and played golf and danced.

Always a rock 'n roll aficionado, I have filled the evening with my favorite local band, The Hubcaps, who played their magnificent repertoire of rock 'n roll oldies at our twenty-fifth anniversary party. During dinner, and in between the Hubcaps' sets, a disc jockey entertains us with the likes of Nat King Cole and Tony Bennett, playing our favorite love songs of yesteryear. Betty and I danced as one, and though I danced

Meadows

with many of the guests, it is never as good with any other woman.

I introduced a few special people, and then our special guest performers—The Coasters—who wowed us with a fabulous floor show and brought back many a memory of the '50s and original rock 'n roll.

I did not want the night to end, but I knew at some point, the lights would come up, and the music would end, and the guests retire to their rooms. It was time for the gifts.

I looked out into the sea of guests, my heart filled with love and gratitude. I saw all who have made the trip, as well as the dim outlines of loved ones who are no longer with us. My emotions welled up in me and I searched for Betty's hand.

I have thought about the words I would say, knowing that there is not enough time to say all that is in my heart; how truly blessed my life has been with my four children, Jay, Cindy, Kate, and Rocky, my wonderful daughter-in-law, Doreen, and my two precious granddaughters, Monica and Miranda. I am thankful for my successful business, consisting of twenty-two nurseries manned by over seven hundred employees, now safely in the hands of my son, Jay, and bringing in over forty million dollars a year. After all this time, I am still in awe of our two million-dollar home with its seven bathrooms, considering that my life with Betty began in a two-room shack with no running water at all!

And there is Betty. She is my best friend, my lover, my everything, standing beside me as she has throughout my life. Words fail me, and I turned my attention to my gift for her, tears clouding my eyes.

"We have always loved art, especially sculpture," I began, and continued, describing a few of the pieces we have enjoyed over the years, such as the seven-foot eagle, suspended from our twenty-foot ceiling at the farm. "Betty has a favorite sculptor, Sassy, whom some of you are probably familiar with … " Moments later, I remove the velvet cover from the black marble sculpture entitled, "The Kiss," a piece whose creation was specially commissioned for my wife. Betty's eyes sparkled with pleasure as her hand stroked the cool surface.

Our guests were laughing and applauding enthusiastically. But Betty held up her hand and they quieted down. "No matter what would happen to me now," she began shyly, but looking into my eyes, "I would just always know that I had such a wonderful life and such a wonderful partner to have shared all the things that we have shared together. And I am truly grateful to have had such a loving life, and I think it's more wonderful because I have been so loved and been able to return that love. It has certainly been an adventure to say the least!" Her gentle voice trembled momentarily. But she went on, "I have a little

Nearly Perfect

something for you, too, Bill." She was grinning then, like the cat that ate the canary. "I couldn't bring it inside here with me, so would you all please indulge me and take a little walk to the front lobby?"

I looked quizzically at my wife, but she headed me off. "Come on! Quickly!"

We were caught up, then, in the throng of over two hundred guests heading excitedly for the lobby. Eventually, we took our places in front of a huge covered object.

"It's a really big sculpture! You know how Farmer likes big things!" I heard someone say.

"No—it's an ice sculpture of the two of them," someone else said.

Betty cleared her throat. "I'm not much of a speechmaker," she said, "but there was a time many years ago when the thing that mattered most was that we have a car, so that we could be together. In 1954, we bought our first car with money that we had saved, and I couldn't think of too many things that looked better than my husband in the driver's seat of a really special car. Forty-nine years later, I think I probably still feel the same way, but I'd like to find out for sure."

With a flourish, my bride tugged at the tarp that concealed my brand new ... Rolls Royce convertible!

There was an almost reverent hush, followed by excited murmurs, but I could only say, "Oh my heart!"

Betty laughed joyfully and said, "That's what I thought you'd say!"

I was speechless. We still had some time to take a little spin around the hotel grounds. It was magnificent! When we returned, our dear friend and former chauffeur, Stephen "Stevón" Hodges, took a few people touring. I returned to the ballroom hand in hand with my loving Betty, still in a state of complete euphoria. The time passed quickly and soon everyone had said good night. We wrapped our arms around each other's waists, and headed back to our suite.

It was a night to remember. It was the party to end all parties. So it was as I waited for my wife to return from the shower, that I took those few minutes to thank the Creator for all that I have in my life, my beautiful life.

There are many reasons why a man might choose to come to The Greenbriar, I thought to myself with irony—the service, the prestige, the Five Star facilities, but for me, it was something else. I remember looking through those wrought iron bars so long ago, and I know I came here *because I can.*

Then, Betty emerged, beautiful and seraph-like in her luxurious towel.

"Feel better?" I asked, when actually *I* suddenly felt quite a bit better.

Meadows

"Wonderful!" she breathed. "Do you want to turn the radio on and maybe drape a towel over the lamp like we did on a certain couple's wedding night?"

In our more than fifty years of loving each other, we have seen the best of times and the worst. We have grown up together, from those dizzying record-setting kisses in the darkened theatre or the front porch glider. We no longer break up at the drop of a hat, yet we still find love to be exciting and unpredictable.

My wife is more beautiful to me now than she was as a sixth grade tomboy, an eighth grade homecoming queen, or even as an eighteen-year-old bride. As awesome as our wedding night was, it doesn't hold a candle to the fifty years that have followed.

During those years, we have hugged and cried and kissed and slept and spent a *lot* of time in each others' arms! We have worn comfortable grooves into each other's lives—nothing else could ever fit as perfectly.

Before I could answer Betty, she had once again slid into my arms, molding herself to me as we became one. We swam in the sea of love, and came ashore breathless. In a hoarse whisper, my bride told me what I love to hear most.

"I'm so glad we're married."

I nodded and nuzzled against her. "Me, too," I whispered.

It was a night that was nearly perfect and it set my mind to remembering—so many wonderful, heartfelt, sorrow-filled, loving and perfect memories tumble together as I got ready for bed. I took a deep breath and traveled a little ways back in time …

*Noel Meadows and Maye Lily,
Bill's parents, 1929*

Chapter One

Boy Meets World

*I*t was 1935. I entered the world smack in the middle of the Great Depression as the third child in what eventually grew to become a seven-sibling family. Although hard times had hit our Crab Orchard, West Virginia coal mining town with a vengeance, somehow, the Meadows family continued to thrive and concentrate on the good parts of life.

Living that philosophy, Mother was delighted to learn she was pregnant for the third time. Despite hard economic times, she felt pure joy, unencumbered by financial considerations. But when she announced the news to her mother, Ma clucked her tongue and patted Mother's hand reassuringly. "It'll be all right, dear. Try not to worry."

Mother only laughed. "Mother, I'm not worried! I'm happy—I'm *really* happy!"

Maybe only Dad could understand how she felt. Their lives were filled with blessings; there would be plenty to share with another baby. Besides, they reasoned, the Depression would be turned around by spring. Living on faith in God and love for each other, they faced their future with hope.

As Mother anticipated my birth with great pleasure, she held out a secret hope for a girl; a kindred spirit to offset our testosterone-charged household. But, of course, in those days there was no way to know in advance. Still, some thought they could.

Meadows

"Lay down, Maye," my grandma urged her. "Let me balance this spoon over your belly. That's the only sure way to tell what you're havin'."

"*That* is nothing but an old wives' tale," Aunt Cosby said, coming clean with the facts. "There's only one way to tell what you're havin.' It all depends on how *high* you're carrying. Stand up over here, let me take a look at you."

Mother would smile at her well-meaning relatives and enjoy the anticipation all the more.

Crab Orchard consisted of only about three hundred families. Of those three hundred, the Meadows family could claim some sort of kinship with roughly one quarter. The close proximity to extended family lent an element of support that I have always recognized and been grateful for. In one way or another, throughout our experiences in life, Betty and I have nearly always found ourselves geographically close to that powerful force and blessing of family.

My mother was a truthful woman. I have no choice but to believe the story she often told me about the day I was born.

It was early evening when the front door swung open and Mother turned to see her coal-blackened husband filling the doorway.

"Noel!" she called cheerfully. "You're home early!" She ran to embrace him, discarding any thought of his grimy face and neck, arms, and trunk. "The children have already eaten. We can have some time alone together. Are you hungry?"

"Nearly starved!" he answered. "What do I smell?"

Mother took his hand in hers and walked him to the wood cook-stove. "Pinto beans and corn bread," she said. Attending the black skillet to the rear of the stove she continued, "and fried potatoes."

Dad's eyes lit up.

"Go and wash up," Mother said, "and I'll have it on the table in a jiffy."

Later as she washed up the dishes, Mother marveled at their good fortune for probably the thousandth time. The water running from the spigot was a luxury in Crab Orchard. She kept it to herself, though, never bragging or putting on airs, instinctively realizing that such a practice took the joy from living.

Moments later, Dad returned to the kitchen, shivering a little. "This March is coming in like a lion!" he said. Hearing no response, he looked over to where Mother sat at the table. "Honey?"

She sat hunched forward, her breath coming quickly. Her face registered

Nearly Perfect

pain, but not alarm. "I'm OK, darling, but before long … there'll be another little arrow in our quiver."

Dad smiled nervously. "Now? It's happening now?" he asked awkwardly.

Mother chuckled lightly despite the pain. "Not right this instant," she said, "but it's sure starting."

"Well who do we have? Who's going to help you, Maye?"

"Either Aunt Cosby or Aunt Sue," Mother answered, "or even Mother if she feels all right. We can get a hold of them in the morning."

Dad wasn't so casual about the timing. "Well, Maye, I'd feel better if we got someone right now. We can't be sure when the baby's going to get here."

"OK, Noel," she said. "But stop and tell the boys good night on your way."

As Mother smiled and eased back against the chair to rest a moment, Dad stopped in to see Gilven and Berman. Catching sight of him, they jumped for him, wrestling him to the bed they shared, laughing and tickling.

When Dad caught his breath, the smile left his face for a moment. "Listen, boys," he said, "in your prayers tonight, I want you to remember your mother. She's going to have the baby soon. Ask God to bring your little brother or sister quickly and safely. Hear?"

"We will, Dad," said Berman, both he and his brother suddenly sober.

Gilven nodded, his eyes wide.

"G'night, then, boys," Dad said, leaving each with a hug and a kiss as he did each night.

As Dad had suggested, winter was persistent that year, and even on the first of March, a deep chill hung in the air. Aunt Sue went out to find Dr. Whitlock, and returned with the news that he was attending to an emergency but that she'd left him a note. He did come several hours later, but explained that Mother still had a long way to go. "Looks like snow," he said as he turned to go.

Aunt Sue tossed another piece of wood on the stove. "*Feels* like snow," she said with a shiver.

As it turned out, the labor took hours and hours. Many family members and friends stopped by to see if they could be of some use, but my grandmother shooed everyone away—including Dad and my brothers.

"Ma," Dad protested, "that's my *wife!*" But he left anyway, leaving a kiss on Mother's sweat dampened forehead.

As the hours passed, Mother caught bits of the conversation, drifting into light sleep only to awaken to the rigors of labor, and drift off again. As time wore on, the pains came closer together, till it was time to push.

"OK, OK, Maye," my grandmother said, "that's it. Almost … OK … "

Then, suddenly Aunt Sue cheered, and Ma announced, "You have a brand new baby … boy!"

Mother cried out, her feelings a mixture of joy and relief as I made a grand entrance, accompanied by the resounding peal of church bells. She says she heard angels singing, and that all of the church bells in Crab Orchard began to ring as my lungs filled with air and I hollered my greeting to the world.

"That part's true," Dad always chimed in with a chuckle. "I mean about the church bells. It was Sunday morning, after all. The whole clan was on the edge of the pew waiting to find out whether Maye Meadows had a boy or a girl! Of course the bells were ringing!"

But Mother would just shake her head knowingly, and smile her private smile. "Well, maybe the bells just *sounded* like angels, but I'm telling you, son, on March the third, 1935, those bells were ringing for you!"

Betty's Parents, Robert Lewis and Olive Cole, 1934

Chapter Two

Beginnings

Betty's mother was already a married woman when her parents separated. Pained by the news, she took comfort in her own marriage. Betty's father, Robert Lewis, was a quiet, responsible man who had prospered in his elementary school years until the start of the sixth grade, when his father announced, "Boy, it's like this, we need you to work. We all need to pitch in." Robert watched his friends return to school that day through a veil of tears, as he stood waiting for the coal mine elevator to lower him down the shaft. He was eleven years old.

Robert was barely twenty when he married Olive, although he had been doing a man's job for almost ten years. Together, they began their life in Francis, West Virginia, in a dirty, two-room camping house owned by the coal company. The house was situated on a creek that was contaminated with household sewage.

But Betty's father worked hard, and her mother was a wonderful homemaker, making a cozy, clean home out of the dwelling. She cooked her family beans, potatoes, and corn bread, while sharing her dreams of a brighter future.

When Betty was three, she wasn't quite ready for the surprise she was about to have. Looking into the bassinet next to her mother's bed, she saw not one, but two little babies. Her mother had given birth to twins, Robert and Mary Lou. Apparently, the doctor and Betty's father had also been surprised.

"You are very important," the doctor had said to her. "A big sister gets to help out and have lots of fun with the babies!"

Olive did her best to carry on cheerfully, but the tiny house had become ridiculously cramped. She had always hated the coal camp. It was at that time Betty was introduced to the benefits of saving one's money. Her parents had gone without through the early years rather than fall into the snare of indebtedness to the company store as so many of their neighbors had. Goods at the store were outrageously priced, but offered on credit to the miners, so that when their paychecks came, they were already spent. The workers would then be offered the opportunity to become additionally indebted for their next week's groceries.

However, when Robert's check came, it belonged to him. He would take Olive and Betty in his old jalopy to a nearby town, or even into Beckley, where they would buy what they needed, at reasonable prices, for cash. The neighbors would stare, slack-jawed, as the Lewis family pulled up in front of the house and unloaded bags of groceries. Robert and Olive had been carefully planning and saving for the time when they could finally leave the camp. With the arrival of the twins, that time had come. In 1939, Robert had begun looking for a place to build a house. He found that spot right next to Betty's Grandma Net's house in Walkertown. He used his savings to buy it. By the time Betty was five, the family had their first "real home."

As has always been the practice in my family, the Lewis and Cole families and friends all pitched in to build that house. It was like an Amish barn raising. Cousins, friends and uncles all turned a dream into reality. Betty watched for hours on end as the magnificent new home took shape, seeming to grow from the ground like Jack's magical beanstalk.

Moving day couldn't come soon enough for Olive. She packed and organized things all day while Betty kept an eye on the twins. When the big day finally arrived, neighbors hugged and wished them well, some of them tearing up, sure that things wouldn't be the same without the Lewises. But throughout it all, her mother wore a look of happiness and anticipation that Betty never forgot. And when the last goodbyes were said, and everything piled into their car headed for Walkertown, Olive looked neither to the left nor the right, but straight ahead, pure joy radiating from her face.

Betty's new neighborhood was made up mostly of relatives; four of her mother's sisters and brothers had built homes near Grandma Net's house, giving Betty, Mary Lou and Bobby lots of cousins to play with.

The house was situated at the bottom of the hill with a creek running right past it that separated the house from the road. A footbridge carried the family across the creek to the road where Robert kept the family car. On the hillside, Olive developed a vegetable garden that she tended to with great care. The children pitched in when asked because they loved the fruits of their labors; homegrown beans in mid-winter, jams, jellies and preserves all year round, and many other homegrown treats.

Her mother was also an immaculate housekeeper, and as she had done before, turned the new house into a cozy home with a welcoming air. On Saturdays, Betty and Mary Lou would pitch in with the housework. On paydays, which came on alternate Saturdays, the women hurried through the housework and then they all drove to Beckley to pick up groceries and maybe do a little window shopping.

Before long, Betty entered school. She could never understand why some people professed to hate school, or even tried to get out of going. She loved every minute of it. And her mother saw to it that she was well outfitted, or as well outfitted as she could manage.

"Hold still, Betty," her mother ordered, a row of straight pins dangling between her lips. "I'm almost done."

Betty ran her hand over the stiff fabric that would soon be her new school dress.

"Do you like it?" Olive asked.

"It's nice, Mother! It'll be perfect!" Betty said. She didn't want to hurt her mother's feelings, but she was feeling impatient. She loved school so much that she had hated for it to come to an end that spring. But now it was *summer* and she wanted *it* to go on forever—she was ready to play!

Just then, Betty's cousins Patty and Margaret tapped on the screen door. "Hey, Aunt Olive," Patty said. "Whatcha doin', Betty?"

"Hey, Patty. My mother's making me a school dress. What do you think?"

Patty's face fell. "School? Yuck!"

"All right, you two," Olive said, "I'm done. Let's get this off." She pulled the dress over Betty's head and laid it on a chair, smoothing it out.

Betty would watch her mother sewing late into the night, when everyone else was asleep, but she'd never given much thought to the effort her mother put toward making sure she had nice clothes that were clean and fit well. Many of the children at school still wore tattered, dirty clothes, despite the respite from the Depression by then.

Patty and Betty saw their chance and headed to the creek for a nice swim until lunchtime. After lunch, Betty settled down on the front porch with her picture book.

Meadows

"The red ball," she read carefully. "The big blue car." There were only a few words in her reading vocabulary between first and second grade, but they were there to stay—to be joined by millions as the years went by. Betty always loved reading, and even today it makes up a big part of her life.

Sometimes her Aunt Oma would bring home magazines full of stories and pictures of movie stars.

"She sure looks different," Betty said, studying a heavily made up Vivien Leigh.

"She's a movie star," Oma explained. "They wear lots of makeup. I think Vivien's just beautiful." Oma applied her own makeup and mimicked the poses she'd seen in front of the mirror.

Betty would wonder if Aunt Oma knew her personally, but never asked.

"Betty!" Mary Lou called. "Mother said for you to play with me!"

Betty loved her little sister and always had, but it frustrated her that the only "game" Mary Lou ever wanted to play was "house." To Betty, such a game seemed to go nowhere. She didn't understand the rules or the object of the game—if there was one. She preferred scored, winnable games, like hopscotch, checkers, jump rope, Old Maid and jacks.

Her father had unwittingly compounded her frustration by creating an amazing backyard playhouse for the girls. It had a miniature kitchen, with table and chairs and little beds for the dolls. Not only did it enhance Mary Lou's desire to play house, it brought over every neighborhood girl—and their dolls. But Betty was a good sport, and even if she didn't actually get into the spirit of the thing, she'd bring along a book and read.

"Who do you want to be today, Betty?" Mary Lou asked.

"I'm Aunt Nellie, and I like to read," Betty answered.

"OK," Mary Lou said.

Some days, Betty managed to talk Mary Lou and the others into playing school, during which she would always be the teacher. But before long, she'd hear the boys outside imitating tommy guns and war sounds. "I'll be back in a little bit," she said as she quickly slipped away.

Betty's father had been a faithful coal company employee for many years by then, and as the saying goes, in a coal mine, you can't go anywhere but down. Robert Lewis had the notion, though, that hard, steady work would pay off, and one day it did.

He came home from work with almost a spring in his step that first night. "Olive," he said, "I think I've got my chance."

Betty's mother turned, her eyebrows raised. "You've always got a good one with me," she said smiling.

"Listen," he answered, setting aside her playfulness for the moment, "Bender says I can take the management course. Learn to do the supervisory skills. I'll get no time off of work to do it, so I'll be busy day and night for a while, but I think it'll be worth it."

"Will it get you out of that mine?" Olive asked.

"Some," he said, nodding. "Mostly, yes, I think."

"Do it!" she said enthusiastically. "I'll do whatever I can to help. You know Oma and Mother will pitch in if I need anything."

He smiled. "I was hoping you'd feel that way," he said.

Robert dug in. It must have brought him some deep joy to have arrived, so much later in his life, at an opportunity to return to education, which had been so harshly ripped away from him as a child. Ironically, the hard times that had forced him into work were suddenly providing him an opportunity to rise from the mines.

The coursework was detailed and complex at first, but as he labored through it, with Olive offering her own reading, writing, and comprehension skills, Robert found himself embracing his prospective role.

On the morning of the examination, Betty's father was ready. But *he* didn't know that. "Maybe I ought to run over that section on duties and responsibilities again," he said as he sat at the table, then stood, then sat again.

"You're going to be just fine, honey," Olive said. "Eat your breakfast."

And sure enough, that night, when the door swung open, Robert Lewis looked a little taller and a lot happier.

Olive ran to him. "You did it, didn't you!" she cried.

"We passed!" he said, taking her in his arms. "We passed!"

The times lightened up for Betty's family then. Although life had always been good, it had just gotten a little better.

Chapter Three

Water

While Betty's family got adjusted to their new home in Walkertown, I was learning some of the lessons life offers to young boys. One of them had to do with a great power in nature, water.

I knew that water was a serious matter. It was one of those "respect" issues my dad had always been so firm about. We children had a pretty healthy respect for it as well, though not as much as some people we knew. Our friends and relatives hauled water in buckets from a spring or stream, and were careful never to waste a drop. We had our wonderful running water, but even with that, we all used the same washtub of water on Saturday nights—and woe to the fellow who yellowed the water! Of course, Nola, my only sister, got to go first because, as mother said, "she was cleaner to begin with."

In 1941, when I was six years old, my family moved to Corinne, where my dad had been offered a job as superintendent of the coal camp. His responsibility was to oversee the housing and housing matters that came up within the whole coal camp.

At our new home, our coal was dumped into a coalhouse, which gave us bragging rights over the families whose coal was just dumped in a pile in the front yard. Our house was heated primarily by the big coal stove in the kitchen, where our family would gather in evenings.

In order to start the fire, we had to gather kindling wood, a job my parents assigned to one of us boys everyday. After we got a big pile of it together, we would help Dad with the cross-cut saw to get it into pieces small enough to fit into the stove. Even little Freddie took his turn with Dad and the saw.

Our house was close to the creek, commonly pronounced *crick*, which spanned fifty feet across, just a hair too narrow to be considered a river. Periodically, we would experience torrential downpours, making the current swift and the water level several feet higher than normal.

I loved to watch the rushing water carrying sticks and flotsam and jetsam to destinations unknown. I would imagine riding down the river in a little boat that never needed paddling. The aftermath of these storms brought plenty of kindling wood for us to gather after the water subsided.

It was after one such deluge that I hurried down to the water's edge and saw Davis Reilly dragging small logs and branches up into a pile on the shore. Davis was a teenager who worked alongside his dad in the mine to help feed the sprawling Reilly family. I didn't really know him, but had played on occasion with two of his little brothers. I yelled "Hey" to him, which he acknowledged with a barely perceptible nod. He was a young man on a mission.

I watched him closely, admiring his upper body strength, and the adult-like manner in which he carried himself. My admiration grew when I saw the terrific idea he had come up with for pulling in the wood. Davis tied a thick rope around his waist and a slipknot at the other end. With deadly accurate aim, he hurled the rope like a lasso, again and again, bringing in sizeable chunks of wood each time. He knew I was watching him, though he never looked my way. I was thinking maybe Fred and I could try something like that to surprise our dad. Wouldn't that be something!

I think Davis and I spotted the monster log at the same time. It bumped its way around a little curve in the creek, emerging larger as it neared us.

"Uh-oh!" I thought, grinning.

But Davis's expression was one of grim determination. He twirled the rope a little to give it momentum and flung it at the big log. But the rope didn't catch, and slid down into the whirling water. Hurriedly, he gave it another toss and felt the rope go taut.

I watched as his sinewy arms pulled hard against the rope. He appeared to strain with this one, probably thinking he might have met his match. But it would be quite a prize to take home and cut up. As I continued to watch, my amazement turned rapidly to horror. With the rope already tightly tied around his waist, Davis was losing the battle! His boots began to slide slowly down the bank as he struggled to free himself of the tether. With nothing to grab, to hold himself on land, he called out, "Help," tentatively at first. But when he realized he was helpless against the inertia, his plea came in earnest. "Help!" he screamed in a heartrendingly pitiful way as the enormous log won the battle, dragging Davis into the raging water.

The sight was staggering, but I raced toward him, trying to grab his hand before he slipped beneath the water's fury. Failing that, I began to scream as well, running to the closest house first, and then another, "There's a boy in there! There's a boy in the river!"

Quickly a small crowd gathered, including my dad, who scooped me up and held me for several moments. Mr. Reilly, learning that it had been Davis, began running down the length of the creek, shouting his son's name. I started crying.

Between my sobs, I found myself repeating the horrid tale over and over again, as I was continually asked what had happened. I could only remember that terrified look on Davis's face as his big, muscular body was pulled into the water like a reed, his hand outstretched in the direction of a six-year-old boy who could not save him. The vision of it hung before my eyes for weeks afterwards.

His body was found two days later, about three miles downstream, battered and bruised, and still tied to that log. It was a while before I felt like playing in the creek again. In time, my parents whispered that I had, "gotten over it," but, of course, I never did forget.

Betty's Grandparents,
John Kelly Cole and Jeanett McKinney, about 1920

Chapter Four

Three Little Monkeys

Betty's family regularly visited Grandpa Cole. His office was located on a prominent corner on the main street of Rhodell. A little brass plaque read: Kelly Cole, Justice of the Peace. Around the corner, on the side street, was another door. It was a plain white door, with its shade customarily pulled down over the window. Her mother would tap lightly and call out, "Daddy, it's Olive!"

"Well, look who's here!" he would call, opening the door with a flourish.

When he'd moved out of the house he had shared with Grandma Net, he had settled into the back rooms of his office. Over the years, he had turned it into a neat, comfortable little apartment.

A door led to his office, where his big desk was always covered with papers and law books. The children were not allowed to go in there alone, but Grandpa Cole would always take them in there so they could get a treat. A glass bowl on a little table held candy and gum for his clients. He would hold it high above their heads so they couldn't see what they were picking. His eyes would crinkle around the edges as Betty, Mary Lou, and Bobby jumped and laughed.

Before he led them back into his apartment, Betty would always stand on tiptoe to reach for the little monkeys that sat high on the shelf. Grandpa would reach them first and bring them down so the children could see them, and they would each pose, imitating one of the monkeys.

Meadows

"Children," her grandpa would begin, "it's just like the Good Book says. There's no need to speak ill of your neighbor. There's no need to listen to gossip. And there's no need to look at things that can't do you a bit of good. There's all kinds of evil in the world, and we need to protect ourselves."

They would all nod seriously, thinking of those little monkeys keeping evil at bay.

The Sunday ritual continued as Olive unpacked the basket she had carried on her arm. They pulled chairs up to Grandpa's little table for a lunch of thick sandwiches, applesauce, three-bean salad, and some of that fresh milk that everyone loved but Betty!

"Dad," her mother would say after lunch, as she looked through his things, "what have you got that needs mending? Any of these old things falling apart yet?"

Grandpa chuckled. "Just these," he said, handing her two pairs of socks. "Can't seem to keep them from wearing through at the heel."

Olive put the socks in her bag, and arranged a few goodies on Grandpa's table after clearing away the meal things. Then it was time for goodbyes. The children showered their grandfather with kisses before they left. Betty's memory of gentle, old Grandpa Cole is that of one of the loveliest people she's ever known.

Later, when the Lewises moved to Crab Orchard, Grandpa Cole would stop to visit them via Greyhound Bus on his way to and from business trips in surrounding counties. On one such visit, in 1946, he told his daughter that he wasn't feeling well.

"I think when I get into Beckley, I'll just go right over to the hospital, Olive. Something just don't feel right."

Betty's mother touched his forehead, as if he were *her* child. "Dad, let's wait until Robert gets home and we can drive you over. Sit down and just rest here a spell."

"No, honey, there's no point in getting everybody all anxious like that. I'll go on and let you know what I find out. I'm sure it's nothing."

Despite her best efforts, Olive was unable to convince her father to wait. Reluctantly she walked him out to catch his bus to Beckley and then alerted her kin that Grandpa was going to the hospital. When Robert got home, they all drove to the hospital, meeting cousins, aunts, and uncles already gathered there. Everyone was able to see Grandpa, whose only complaint at that time was about his sore feet.

"Well, Dad, I guess we'll see you tomorrow," Betty's mother said, giving her father a hug and a kiss. "Have sweet dreams." She smiled and ushered her children out of the room.

But the next morning, after she went out to phone the hospital, she returned quickly, her face red and damp. "I hate to have to tell you this," she said, struggling with her own pain, "but your dear, darling grandfather passed in the night."

It was little surprise to those who knew him to learn, in the days that followed, that their Grandpa had paid for and planned his own funeral, leaving no burden to his beloved children. He was truly a great man.

*Senator Robert C. Byrd's
Sunday School Class in Washington*

Chapter Five

A Byrd's Eye View

My parents had a fairly serious interest in politics, as did many of the working class people they associated with. Issues like tax hikes and bond referendums could have a noticeable impact on a man with a big family and small paycheck. And perhaps, for my father, the interest went a little deeper, having made friends with a young man by the name of Robert C. Byrd, who lived three doors down from us in Crab Orchard. Senator Byrd eventually rose to the position of one of the most powerful and respected United States Senators, serving as Senate Democratic Whip in 1971, then Democratic Leader in 1977, a post he held until 1988 and during which he also served as Senate Majority Leader. In 1989, he became Chairman of the Senate Appropriations Committee as well as President pro tempore of the Senate, in which he became third in line for the United State Presidency. Although he has served the Senate for close to fifty years, and has held more positions of leadership than any other senator in the history of the United States, in 1946, he was simply Mr. Byrd, my Sunday school teacher.

As Sunday school superintendent, my dad played a big part in selecting the teachers. Mr. Byrd was one of those "fine young men" whom my dad admired. After World War II, Mr. Byrd returned from his stint as a welder in Florida and decided to run for public office. My father managed his successful campaign for the West Virginia House of Delegates in 1946, and they became fast friends.

Meadows

Though he was a busy family man, with two little girls and a burgeoning political career, Mr. Byrd planned a field trip to Washington, D.C. for the entire church youth group.

"Can we go, Dad? Can we?" Gilven asked, speaking for the three of us older boys, Berman, himself, my younger brother, Fred, and me.

"Let me think on it, boys," Dad said. "I'll talk to Mr. Byrd a bit before I give you my answer."

As it turned out, the four of us joined up with about forty other boys two weeks later on the trip to the nation's capital. We all piled into the bed of a huge truck, outfitted with benches and covered with a big tarp. Dad had spoken to us quite seriously about how we were to deport ourselves away from our parents, leaving no doubt whatsoever in our minds on the subject of behavior.

Two hours out of Crab Orchard, we felt the truck come to a stop, and soon the tarp was pulled back.

"Bathroom break, fellas! Hop out and stretch your legs." Mr. Byrd was dangling the keys in his hand. "Who's first?" he asked. We had pulled up into the gravel yard of a tiny filling station with one toilet.

Several boys queued up outside the door of the restroom, but the rest of us formed a line along the perimeter of the woods, unceremoniously relieving ourselves in the manner in which many of us were most familiar.

"All right fellas!" Mr. Byrd admonished us. "You can't be doing that once we get to the city!" He retreated to the cab of the truck for a moment, returning with a huge thermos jug and motioned for us all to gather around. "Erma made us some Koolaid, guys! C'mon and get yourself a drink."

For the first time, I realized how thirsty I really was, and moved eagerly forward to take my turn. But when I reached the inner ring, I realized with horror that they were all sharing the few small cups there were.

Turning to the older and wiser Berman, I asked, "Now what? Everyone's drinking after each *other*?"

Berman's lip curled noticeably at the very thought. Then he had an idea. "Quick! Get Gilven. He's liable to take a drink before he even realizes it!"

The loathsome behavior was just something *we did not do!* "Get a new cup, honey," my mother would remind us when we were little. "We don't want to spread germs." As we grew older, mother's warnings became more dire. "I saw the Nichols girls at the gas station today," Mother might mention. "They were *sharing* a soda! And their mother had seen them … " A dismal shake of the head told us what we most certainly had already learned. People who drank after each other were just asking for trouble.

We Meadows boys made our way over to a hose, where we took turns slurping the tepid water.

Mr. Byrd waved us back over. "Have some Koolaid, boys! There's plenty!"

"Uh, no thanks," answered Gilven wistfully. "We prefer water."

Mr. Byrd appeared unconvinced but let the matter rest. And we spent a good deal of our trip thirsty.

But the trip was worth that bit of distress. Washington, D.C. was an amazing city! We had read in school all about the Jefferson Monument, the Washington Monument, the National Archives, and many other famous sights, but we had never dreamed we would visit them personally. The Lincoln Memorial was magnificent; the tall figure of Abraham Lincoln on the enormous concrete form awed me. When we reached the Washington Monument, we marveled at its height, as it majestically reached far into the sky.

But it was the Capitol Building itself that awed Mr. Byrd the most. "Look at this thing of beauty, boys," he said as we stood grouped at the base of the steps. "Everything we know today as law is legislated—created—in this building." As we stared at the round, sculpted construction, a light breeze drifted around us. "I hope someday some of you boys come to visit me here!" Mr. Byrd said with a twinkle.

Everyone laughed, not exactly sure what it was Mr. Byrd was getting at, but willing to play along.

On the truck ride home, we reflected on our visit to that incredible city. None of us, of course, had ever seen anything like it.

"Is that really where they make all the laws?" Gilven asked Berman.

"Mr. Byrd said so," Berman answered. "So I guess it is."

I just listened and thought about it all, listening to the rattles in the truck bed, and thinking I'd probably be back there one day.

As time went on, Mr. Byrd did exactly as he'd implied he would do. In 1952, he was elected to the United States House of Representatives, and headed to his new home in Washington, D.C. It was only a short while afterwards, after Betty and I married and moved to New Jersey, that Byrd asked my dad to move to Washington, D.C. to become his office manager and personal secretary.

With great anticipation, my parents moved their entire family to Northern Virginia, where they spent the next several years enmeshed in the Washington political scene. By then, Mr. Byrd had become Senator Byrd.

Interestingly, Senator Byrd and I have something in common other than our Baptist roots and modest beginnings in Crab Orchard, West Virginia. We

Meadows

are also both amateur painters, and enjoy creating landscape paintings. I especially enjoy practicing my art by copying the creations of other artists.

Earlier, Byrd had painted an extraordinary scene of an old mill, with its water wheel in motion, a dark and dramatic work of art, which he had presented to my grandfather, minister of the church we all attended. One of only two paintings the Senator has ever completed, the painting hung over the fireplace in my grandparents' home for many years until their deaths. At that point, I asked if I might have it.

I hung the canvas in my home, enjoying the knowledge that I had a painting by a U.S. Senator whom I had known personally during my youth. I thought about it only occasionally, when someone would specifically ask about it. I was caught off-guard when a representative of the West Virginia College Fund requested that I donate the painting.

To be honest, my first reaction was not exactly gracious. "I don't want to donate that painting," I groused to Betty. "That's part of my family's heritage. Don't you agree?"

"Well, I don't know. But you know, they may set it up with a little brass plate that says 'Donated by William J. Meadows.'"

"You think so?"

"Maybe. But either way, wouldn't it be nice for everybody to be able to see the painting?"

Finally, I decided to do what I did best (but *only* in painting)—I worked for hours copying the beautiful landscape that had brought us such pleasure over the years. That way, once I relinquished the original, if anyone asked about the copy, there would always be a story to tell.

Bill and Betty at sixteen-years-old, 1950

Chapter Six

A Tip Top Time of Life

Back in 1946, we were just grateful that Mr. Byrd was around to arrange that memorable trip to the capital. I felt a little like a world traveler until the feelings started to dull, as they always do. For one thing, there was a happening of some magnitude in Crab Orchard in 1946.

Freddie was the first to come home with the news that a new family had moved into the house we had all watched being built over the previous few years.

"Three kids. Two girls and a boy." He shared his information in the bulleted style of a newscaster.

I was mildly interested, though we had so many children to play with that three more didn't really matter one way or another.

Mother, naturally, shed a different light on things. "Why, those three will be thrilled to meet your great big family. And some little girls for Nola! Y'all go introduce yourselves."

Freddie and I headed across the yards to the new house and stared in wonder. We had never really thought in terms of the house being completed or occupied, and we were a little nervous as we stood on the front steps and knocked. A boy around Freddie's age answered the door and stood staring at us, just as we did him.

From inside, we heard a voice calling. "Bobby, don't just hold the door

Meadows

open. Invite them in, or you go on out."

The boy stood aside to allow us to pass into the hall, where we could glimpse boxes stacked here and there, as well as a mother and two girls unpacking dishes.

"Hello," said a smiling woman, who walked toward us. "I'm Mrs. Lewis and this here is Betty and Mary Lou, and that's Bobby."

We introduced ourselves, then invited the boy outside to play. He looked tentatively at his mother, who hesitated, then encouraged him.

"You go ahead for a spell, Bobby. We'll save you plenty to do." And with that, the three of us ran out the front door.

I had no way of knowing that those few brief moments would forever change my life; that, in fact, my new friend's sister would become my partner for life, redefining all I thought I had known about love. At that moment, I knew only that we had new neighbors, and that meant a new kid to play with. It was pretty simple.

We played often with the Lewis children. They blended well with our little community. Betty was nervous about starting in the new school that fall. She would be entering seventh grade, and I was going into sixth. As it turned out, it was a wonderful time for both of us. We both loved reading and occasionally would share good stories we found. We walked home from church together regularly and went to the 4H Club, which was big in our town, holding regular meetings on Saturdays. We took it all very seriously, and soon Betty was just as involved as the rest of us.

But one of the nicest outings we enjoyed was to our favorite spot, not far from the school. It was called the Tip Top. The Tip Top was Beckley's answer to the ice cream parlor. But for Beckley, it was an extraordinary answer! Run by an Indian couple, Tip Top served not only delicious ice cream, but a secret sauce that made its famed "Triple" an unforgettable experience. It was that Triple that kept all of us coming back, over and over again. In fact, many a child, when sent to buy lunch, decided to forgo the sandwich and milk for the more decadent Triple. I was pretty sure I'd scored some brownie points with Betty the day I treated her to her first Triple at the Tip Top.

For my part, Betty didn't need to score any points. She had made her home in my heart long before I knew about it—or before she knew either, probably. In fact, I guess I began to make an absolute pest of myself, knocking on the Lewis's door, asking for Bobby, then immediately asking him, "Is Betty here?"

Nearly Perfect

Finally, suspicion overcame my young pal. "Do you have a crush on my sister or something?" he asked.

I felt my face turn red hot, right up to the ears. "That's a dumb question!" I answered indignantly. "Really dumb!" I repeated, and walked away—without answering.

Sitting alone in my room, later that evening, I flipped open my black and white marble covered composition book, and turned to the page marked "GIRLS," where I had written so many names over the years. I remembered my criteria for this particular list. Cute *and* nice. Girls listed in my book had to be *both*.

I rested my chin in my hands for several long minutes, then pulled out my pen and made a huge "X" across the entire page. On the next page, I wrote, "GIRL: Betty M. Lewis." When Betty made the list, everyone else fell right off. It was a little scary, but exciting, too. Could this be love? Betty and I were twelve years old.

Though I was always surrounded by people, there was no one I cared to ask about this particular thing. It was so important and so big and so personal that, in fact, I couldn't imagine discussing it with anyone except Betty, and I wasn't ready for that either. For the time being, I could only savor the mixture of feelings I had, while spending every spare minute with the girl I might just be in love with!

Betty remembers it in her way. I kind of like the role I play in her memory.

* * *

One evening after dinner, Bobby ran into the kitchen and grabbed my arm. "We need you, Betty! The teams are uneven."

I looked anxiously at my mother, who merely smiled and shrugged. "You can't stay in the house all the time, sugar. May as well go meet the other kids."

Reluctantly, I followed my little brother into the soft evening light. Bobby, never a stickler for etiquette, motioned in my direction, saying, "This here's my sister."

And with that the games began.

We started a rousing round of Red Rover, and when Billy Jack Meadows headed over to our team, he aimed straight for me. I was next to his sister, Nola, and I knew he could break our grip easily. We braced ourselves, only to have Billy barely bump against our hands, then throw himself back like he had met a brick wall.

"Woah!" he groaned, then turned and grinned back at his team. "Oh, well!" he said, chuckling and easily placing himself between his sister and me.

Meadows

Immediately, my hand felt clammy as I could feel the sweat popping out. All I needed now was a nosebleed or something! I stole a glance in Billy's direction, then looked quickly away. He was so cute, with his curly, blond hair and his blue eyes. The next time I glanced his way, he smiled, and I managed to smile back before turning away, embarrassed.

Lying in my bed that night, I thought about the new neighborhood, with so many children, and so many names to learn. Maybe I would start with just one. Billy Meadows. I might be able to remember that!

It turned into a great summer for me. There was always plenty to do, and I couldn't help but notice that Billy was the natural leader of the pack. He was funny and nice, and everyone wanted to be around him. Best of all, he seemed to want to be around me. We became fast friends in the weeks that followed. He invited me to Sunday School and the Baptist Youth Fellowship, where I made a few more friends. When a new 4H Chapter was organized, many of our church friends joined, along with Billy and me. Since the meetings were at night, he offered to walk me home, which seemed very chivalrous to me. When he walked me home the second time, he held my hand. This time, I didn't perspire as I had during our game of Red Rover, but my heart pounded so hard I wondered if he could hear it. It was a very exciting time for me!

Chapter Seven

Risks and Rewards

I had a lot on my mind at that time—I guess we both did. I was preoccupied with the love of sports. I enjoyed watching just about any sport, but I didn't necessarily enjoy all the discipline and pain that went with contact sports, like football and wrestling. We all enjoyed shooting hoops and I was pretty sure I'd go out for basketball in ninth grade, so we all practiced whenever we could. But there was something special about running. I would get winded, and my legs would get rubbery, just like the next guy's, but it seemed if I could push myself on just a little beyond that point, my body would sort of revive itself. At that point, my mind would be free and the air would feel good on my skin. It felt like I could run forever. All too soon, the coach would blow his whistle, signaling the end of our warm-up time, and we would move into football or baseball or whatever sport we were currently working on. But it was never quite like running.

But in eighth grade, I had gone out for football and was placed as an offensive end. Though my love affair with sports was in the early stages, I knew already that the burly, gruff, one-armed Coach Earl was mediocre at best, as far as coaching was concerned, although he won all his games. I would often analyze his decisions and imagine how I might have done something better. When he went over a new play with us, I would later sketch it out in my notebook and make changes that I thought would improve it. I would look around at my teammates and imagine how they might perform in a different capacity. I didn't realize then, in ninth grade, that I was already laying the groundwork for what would become a lifelong passion for me as an adult.

Each day after classes ended, we would head over to the high school for our football practice. Sometimes it seemed like all I could do was close my eyes and hope for the best. I would look into the faces of the opposition and see clenched teeth and blazing eyes, and a sort of meanness I did not possess. But when practice ended and Coach Earl sent us to do laps, I forgot about everything but the running. My energy would return, as my beaten body seemed to come back to life.

It was on just such a day, after an especially grueling practice, that Coach Earl barely gave us time to swish our mouths with water before sending us around the track. The guys were all groaning, but I stepped out, ready for the familiar exhilaration to overtake me. During practice, I had caught several glimpses of an older boy who was running laps alone, pacing himself evenly, running with tireless grace. I wanted to look like that, and feel the way I knew he must be feeling. I moved along slowly until the boy passed me, then moved in behind him, picking up his rhythm and stride so that I always stayed the same distance from him.

After our first lap like that, he gestured for me to move in beside him. I was thrilled to run alongside a high school guy who obviously knew what he was doing on the track. Lap after lap, I kept pace with him, oblivious to my classmates' leaving the field for the day and heading home.

When I thought my legs were about to give way, and my lungs were on the verge of exploding, that wonderful second wind kicked in, and I felt that I was floating around the track. When we finished our eleventh lap, my running partner looked over at me, as though sizing me up. "Shall we break?" he asked.

I thought for a moment. I was sure if I took a break, I would not be able to get back on the track. But I thought of sitting down with some cold water, and said, "Yeah, why not?"

With that, my partner pulled out the stops and took off running at top speed. Too astonished to react in any other way, I matched his pace and ran with all my might until we made our last circle. As we willed our legs to slow down to a walk, he slapped my back, and said, "Nice run." With that, he grabbed his bag and headed off the field.

I stood there for a moment, my face stretched into an ear-to-ear grin. Murmuring to myself, "Nice run." I looked around and realized the school was deserted, and I had missed the late bus home. I walked to the highway and stuck my thumb out, scoring a ride after only a few minutes.

Walking in to a late dinner, I ate silently, thinking about the afternoon. Before long, my older brother Berman joined me.

"Hey, Billy," he greeted me, pushing his hand through my hair. "You know Pete Rush?"

"Nope," I answered, without looking up.

"Well, he just happens to be the Woodrow Wilson High School miler."

"And ... ?"

"And he said you gave him a real run for his money today!"

I looked up, wide-eyed. "That was *him?*"

"Yep. And he says, and I quote, 'Tell your kid brother to get his butt on the track team!'"

"Well, I'll be ... " I muttered, feeling that silly grin pulling at the corners of my mouth again. Berman paused only briefly in the kitchen doorway and looked back at me.

"That's swell, Billy. Really." Then he was off.

After dinner, I went to my room and once again pulled out my composition book. I had started a page I called "GOALS" back in the second or third grade. There'd always been something I wanted to do, or be, or try, and looking down the list, I could see I had met almost all of the goals I had set for myself. But by ninth grade, I no longer considered myself a little kid and I knew that my goals were likely to become more challenging, and more significant to me when I met them. And on that day, I had a new goal: Be a Track Star. I wrote the date next to it for posterity, then lay back against my pillow with my notebook face down on my chest, thinking about my run with Pete Rush.

The next day, a couple of the fellas gave me a ribbing about my prowess on the track, but more of them were passing around a story about my running a marathon with a champion, and so on. It was an awesome feeling to have people talking about me as though I were a hero. I couldn't wait to catch up with Betty at lunch time. I was all set to tell her about the day before, but when I caught up to her, the smile on her face told me that she had already heard. "Billy Jack," she said, "I am so proud of you!" She made me feel like a king.

Physical education class and sports were major focal points for me in high school. But on one afternoon, it wasn't sports that had me fascinated. That fall, we were wearing sweaters and light jackets to school, but while in our T-shirts in the locker room, I saw dark, ugly looking scratch marks on my buddy Stan's exposed inner forearm.

"Stan!" I exclaimed, "What happened?"

He rotated his arm slightly to give me a thorough view. "Like it?" he asked, grinning broadly.

It was then I realized I was looking at letters—J. C.—in a coarse, scab-encrusted tattoo on the inner side of his arm. "Who did that to you, buddy?" I asked sympathetically. I imagined a couple of bullies engraving some sort of mark of victory into Stan's skin.

"I did it!" Stan answered, chuckling at my ignorance. "Joanne Combs. J. C., get it?"

At that, Roderick Gallimore pushed up his sweatshirt sleeve and flashed his version of the tattoo. His arm wore "J" for Jeanette.

"What the heck!" I was thoroughly amazed. Then two other fellows I didn't know very well grinned and pulled up their sleeves and pointed at their gruesome insignia.

As we all headed out to the track to warm up, I pondered the ritual.

Not long after, in the locker room once more, I was shocked to see the mess on Stan's arm. "Criminy, Stan! What happened to it? Is it infected?"

"No! It's not infected," he said, slightly affronted. "Look at it. I *changed* it."

I stared at it and realized the "J" had been mutilated into an "N," and the "C" had been transformed into an "O."

"Nancy Olson," Stan said plainly.

"Oh," I said, "what happened to Joanne Comb?"

"I don't go with her anymore, and Nancy didn't like me having her initials on my arm!"

"Boy, Stan—your arm could be nothing but a set of tire tracks by the time we graduate!"

Stan wanted to laugh, but he shook his head and said, "Shouldn't be a problem for you, Billy Boy. Everybody knows there's just one girl for you. When you grow up, little Betty Lewis will be packing your lunch pail to take down in the mines!" He slapped me on the back with a hearty laugh, and jetted out of the locker room.

Later on, when I told Betty about our conversation, she smiled sweetly. "You never know what might happen in the future, Billy," was all she said.

I mulled over those words for the next few days. Stan was right about one thing; Betty Lewis was the girl I was in love with. And she'd likely be the only love of my life. Though we were very young, we fit like a hand in glove. I could not imagine that that would ever change.

I sat on my bed for a very long time before reaching for my bookbag.

Zipped safely in my pencil case was life's most deadly school supply—the compass! Fine for drawing circles, and measuring angles, better yet for carving in desks and tree trunks. On that particular evening, it would serve to "carve" a young man's arm.

I stared at the instrument, periodically touching its needle-like tip to my finger, amazed at how sharp it truly was. It was like the point of an ice pick! I shuddered a little, then clenched my teeth as I took my first real step toward making Betty Lewis an indelible part of my life—or my arm, at any rate.

I lightly scratched the letters into my skin to get a red outline. Then, I began to etch for real, as little droplets of blood rose to the surface. It got pretty messy and it hurt. But it was worth it. When I was done, I wiped my arm with peroxide and pressed a hankie on it to stop the bleeding. I admired my handiwork for several more minutes before remembering that I had one more step to take in creating the tattoo. Black ink!

Rummaging through my pencil case, I extracted an ink pen cartridge. I look grimly at it; cartridges were not cheap and certain assignments had to be completed in ink. But I determined that this particular use of ink was not frivolous. Using the compass to puncture the cartridge, I dripped the black fluid over my freshly lettered arm, and used the hankie to work it in. I added a little more just to be on the safe side, and then washed off the excess. I admired my new, black tattoo—B. L.

I turned off the light and lay down across my bed with an important thought in my mind. It was high time I kissed that girl.

* * *

One afternoon, before a 4H meeting, it had begun to snow. Of course, we immediately began to hope for a school closing the next day. Behind our house, there was a great sledding hill where half the neighborhood gathered after the slightest snowfall. Speeding down that hill, riding tandem up against Billy's back with my arms locked tightly around his waist, I discovered a whole new set of feelings that had no name. And feelings that I knew could never be shared with another living soul.

On our way home from our 4H meeting that night, we found that our little world had been transformed. The snow had fallen hard, covering everything. As we looked around, we saw the great heights of the white pines, their soft, fragrant needles, transfigured into white hovering angels along the pathway. Walking hand-in-hand with Billy through that wonderland was a magnificent experience.

As we stepped across a little ditch, I suddenly felt my foot sliding out from under

Meadows

me, causing me to throw Billy off balance as well. He extended both his arms in a frantic attempt to catch me, but I fell to the ground, pulling Billy on top of me. We lay there, face to face, afraid to breathe or blink. My body tingled all over, as the moment seemed to stretch out indefinitely. Finally, Billy got slowly to his feet, and pulled me up as well, his eyes never leaving mine.

"Are you all right?" he asked dreamily.

"I'm OK. You?"

"Fine."

He took my hand and we walked on wordlessly, until we reached my back gate. Turning toward me, he put his arm around my waist and kissed me. I was stunned, and could only react with wide eyes and a little gasp, at which point Billy promptly kissed me again.

The sensation was electrifying, and more than a little unnerving. When he released me, I ran straight into my house, and went directly to my room, where I lay in the dark, my head swimming with what I knew must be love. For the briefest moment, I saw my whole life spreading out before me, with Billy Jack Meadows at my side. I was fourteen years old and in the eighth grade, and he was thirteen, and in seventh, but I knew even then that I would marry that boy.

My feelings for Billy crescendoed over the following year, as we spent so much time together. I thought he was just the cutest boy on earth with his head full of blond curls and sparkling grey-blue eyes. He was always the clown—he loved being the center of attention! But as we spent more and more time together talking about the future, about life, about religion, I came to know his serious side.

He felt very strongly about some things, like what was right and what was wrong. His father had taught him that many times things were unfair, but still the right thing to do. It concerned him that people did not always do the right thing.

And he had big dreams. He wanted to be a millionaire with a big house with a swimming pool and beautiful landscaping and flowers everywhere. One thing I really liked about Billy was his positive attitude. He was always in a good mood. The only negative thing I ever saw in him was his lack of self-confidence. He thought he was "dumb." I really don't know why he'd come to that conclusion because he was full of interesting ideas and thoughts. He'd read quite a lot and could do just about anything he set his mind to. Perhaps it was because at one time, when he was real young, he couldn't talk plainly, and the kids teased him. His mother thought he might have had polio, but conquered it by the age of ten or eleven.

In a way, Billy was the exact opposite of everything that I was. I was very quiet, easily embarrassed, did not look for attention, did not have big dreams, was a good student and an avid book reader. But there was something that drew me to him. I truly loved being with him, talking with him, listening to his dreams and being his girl.

"All right, campers, listen up!" Miss Adams called, tooting on her little metal whistle and clapping her hands. Her blond ponytail bobbed up and down beneath her faux Indian headdress. In one hand, she held a rubber tomahawk, which she raised high to further emphasize her need for our attention.

"Navajos, grab your gear! You're in Lodge One. Cherokee, Lodge Two. Seneca tribe, Three. Mohicans, Four. All of you be back here in thirty minutes for the big powwow!"

Billy and I separated reluctantly as we headed toward our respective lodges. He and his friend Ernie and some others we knew had been assigned to the Cherokee tribe, so, of course, that's where I wanted to be. It was my very first trip to 4H Camp Greenbriar on the Greenbriar River. I was so excited about the whole thing, even after I noticed that some of the squaws in Billy's tribe were very cute. I barely saw him except for the tribal games, where he would be happily chatting in the center of a circle of people. He would always call out to me, and make me feel important, as I struggled to keep the green-eyed monster at bay.

Our leaders kept us busy all day, and by nightfall we would fall into our bunks, exhausted. After fifteen minutes or so of silence, the leaders would quietly rise and sneak out to who knows where, and we campers would gather on a couple of bunks to talk. My two best friends, Shirley and Eunice, were in my lodge. Into the wee hours, we'd talk about boys and our limited knowledge of sex. In those days, there were no school films or little pamphlets on "becoming young women" and I didn't know a single girl whose mother had "had the talk" with her.

"Do you know anyone who's 'done it'?" Eunice asked.

"No, of course not!" Shirley shot back vehemently. "Who would do that?"

"Well, married people do," I ventured.

"I guess they're willing to go through that if they want to get a baby," Shirley admitted. "I know it hurts a lot."

"How do you know that?" I asked, quite curious.

"Do you really understand what they do? Have you seen what boys have?"

"I've seen my brother's," Eunice said. "In the bathroom. He didn't lock the door."

"Oh, God!" I exclaimed, covering my face. How embarrassing! "I would die if that happened to me! I changed Bobby's diaper when he was a baby, but he doesn't even know I saw it! That little thing wouldn't hurt anyone!"

I didn't dare describe the strange way I had felt when Billy kissed me. I just said,

Meadows

as I usually did, "I wish Billy and I were married," after which my fellow campers promptly bombarded me with pillows. I was sure none of my friends thought about boys quite the way I thought about Billy.

That fall, Billy started junior high school. Each morning we would meet at one end of the lane or the other so we could ride the same bus to school. The long ride to town was another opportunity for us to hold hands and steal kisses while our bus driver, Angelo, turned a blind eye. All went well until Billy got kicked off for fighting. It was a silly thing, really, over someone playing "keep away" with someone else's cap, but we realized that Angelo, who had a high tolerance for necking, throwing paper wads, and shouting out the bus windows, would throw a fighter off the bus with no warning whatsoever. It was a sobering thought, but there were still quite a few times when Angelo veered sharply to the shoulder, and several of the boys, including Billy, were told to take a hike. The boys would clamor off the bus with big boastful smiles, but it was a different story when they dragged themselves down our lane after dark, only to hear an earful from their worried parents.

It was on one such bus ride that my friend, Peggy, made an important announcement. "My uncle's opening a movie show," she said. "And I can go for free whenever I want."

We stared at Peggy in disbelief. "A movie show? Where?"

"Right down behind the post office. He owns that block garage!"

This was great news in a burg where there was absolutely no form of commercial entertainment. The whole bus murmured excitedly.

"Cost you ten cents to get in. But like I said, I can go in for free."

That weekend, there were little signs posted here and there, announcing Duane's Movie Theatre, with shows at 7:30 on Friday and Saturday night. I wondered how I might be able to raise the money, but on Saturday morning, Billy invited me to go--his treat.

That evening, we joined the throngs of kids who filed into the cinderblock garage to sit on board and block benches and laugh at the antics of Abbott and Costello. Everyone was in stitches; everyone, that is, with the exception of Billy and me, who sat entwined in the back row, kissing as if our lives depended on it.

That little theatre provided much diversion through the crisp fall, and the cold, dark winter. With spring came more evening light and the chance to play outside after supper again, but things had become different. We had gotten older, and the hide-and-seek type games that had been enough before unexpectedly seemed a little juvenile.

When summer came, we rode bikes up to the Piney River to swim, and still went to the movies on a regular basis. I was so excited when we got our first flyer for the upcoming 4H Camp.

Nearly Perfect

"Billy, we're going to be in the same tribe this year," I vowed. "I'm not sure how I can do it, but somehow, we've got to be together!" Expecting Billy to applaud my bravado, I was puzzled by his silence. "Right, Billy? That'll be great, won't it?"

Billy turned his grey-blue eyes in my direction, and a little surge of anxiety rippled through me. "Betty, I've been thinking ... "

I know I held my breath until he finished talking. I did not protest as I listened to him suggest that we break up for camp week. I didn't cry, either, when he suggested we go out with other people. I made no comment when he assured me we would get married someday—to each other—but that for the time being we were too young to go steady all the time. All the while he spoke, I held my breath. Then, when he finished, I exhaled slowly.

"OK," I answered quietly. "We can do that."

Camp was not nearly so much fun that summer. I cried for Billy at night, and during the day, I would cast narrow-eyed glances at him as he flirted with an Italian girl, named Margaret Quinter. When camp was over, Margaret was forgotten, and Billy and I were together again.

We spent a lot of time that summer sitting on the glider on the front porch. Billy came over to my house almost every night. We could talk and kiss for hours. Sometimes we talked—sometimes we kissed.

We talked about our future, and planned what we would do after we were married. Sometimes we didn't talk, we only kissed, over and over. It was like we were kissing machines!

My new friend Ruth Ann loved to tease me about my great romance.

"Little Billy Meadows is a baby!" she would taunt. "What do you see in him?"

I hated to admit that her words hit a sore spot. I was going to high school and would be turning fifteen in a month. High school boys were a different class altogether. Ruth Ann even knew boys who drove, though we wouldn't be riding with them for another year or so.

As it happened, after school started, we did see less of each other. When we were together, like at 4H Club meetings, Billy would still take my hand and I would still imagine marrying him someday.

But we still had some growing to do, and that time it was I who suggested we date other people. We were so young and we needed experience with other people

"I want you to know who you want," I said very sincerely.

"I know who I want, Betty."

"We're young yet. I know who I want, too. But we need to be sure."

Billy nodded slowly. He'd accepted the idea, but I knew it hadn't pleased him much.

Meadows

When a dorky boy invited me to the Snowflake Ball at the Black Knight Country Club, I decided why not?

Janet Meador cornered me on the bus one afternoon. "I didn't know you and Billy had broken up," she said indignantly.

It had never occurred to me that he would really date anyone else. "Oh?" I asked, stalling.

"I didn't know," she went on, "until I saw him holding hands with that Joanne Combs! I was so ... surprised!"

"Hmmm ... " Joanne Combs was a pretty, blond friend of mine, who had dated Ernie, one of Billy's friends, a little while before. I doubted that it would amount to anything. Still, I considered, Billy did have this thing about holding hands, and I remembered that's how it all had started with me. Had he, I wondered, kissed her, too?

I grabbed a piece of notebook paper and scrawled out, "Billy, I need to talk to you. Will you walk me home on Sunday night? Betty."

As soon as I got home, I gave it to Bobby. "This is for Billy," I instructed. "Take it over there and wait for an answer."

Ten minutes later, Bobby returned with my note with the word, "OK," hastily printed at the bottom.

Sunday night came too soon. Billy and I walked home in awkward silence. My well-rehearsed speech had evaporated from my mind, and I finally broke the silence by blurting out, "I want to get back together."

Seeing his eyes grow solemn, I could not wait for his response. I quickly pressed close against him, kissing him long and hard until we separated a little to catch our breath. I thought for a moment my knees might give way, but by then, Billy's arms were snuggly holding me.

"I still love you, Betty," he said. "I know I always will."

"I love you, too," I said quickly. We embraced again, and said good night. My heart felt light as I realized how much I had missed Billy. "I wish we were married."

The Meadows children, 1947

The Meadows boys and parents, 1946

Chapter Eight

Manners

No matter how big we got, we were all expected to follow the rules. That was especially true in our own homes.

"Your daddy'll be home soon! Everybody get washed for supper!" Crowding around the tin sink, we splashed ourselves with a little water and hopefully satisfied Mother's critical eye. We did not want to do anything to endanger the approaching dinnertime. No matter how hungry we claimed to be, there were to be no snacks or samples. We waited for my father to come home, greet my mother, wash his hands and face, and sometimes change his shirt, then settle himself at the head of the table. Only then did we join him, as my mother began to bring the food to the table.

On that particular evening, we were all seated around a steaming pan of chicken and dumplings, eagerly awaiting the signal to eat. My father bowed his head and spoke softly. "Father, we ask you to bless this food, and the hands that made it. May we be truly grateful. Amen." Then he ladled out a portion onto his plate, and passed it to Berman. "Pass this to your mother, son."

After Mother and Dad were served, we served ourselves.

"Where is Gilven this evening?" Dad asked, after taking a quick mental roll call of those present and accounted for.

"He'll be along shortly. He stayed after." I volunteered. My older brother had a penchant for getting caught doing just the things that caused a boy to have to "stay after." None of us were angels, but as I said, Gilven had a penchant for getting caught.

"Ah," my father replied and continued eating.

Moments later, the door flew open with a bang. In blew Gilven, who slipped quickly into place at the table as if it were the most natural thing in the world.

Silence fell on our table. Not a fork moved, not a jaw chewed. We all stared in horror at our renegade brother, who seemed to have set civility back one hundred years in one fell swoop.

"What?" Gilven asked innocently. "*What?*"

My father cleared his throat and cocked an eyebrow, willing his son to understand without the use of words.

"Oh. Sorry." Gilven jumped up and shut the front door, then jumped back in his seat and grabbed his fork.

Another "Ahem" from my father and Gilven looked around, confused. Tentatively, he rose to his feet and said, "Sorry I'm late, Mother." But before he could take his seat again, my father shook his head, almost imperceptibly. A look of understanding crossed my brother's face, as he crossed over to the sink and gave his hands and face a perfunctory splash of water.

"Sorry about all that," he said. "Man! Am I famished!" He sank into his chair with great relish as he pulled the serving bowl close to his plate. Still, no one moved.

"Son, you have forgotten—"

"Oh, no I haven't!" Gil cut in. "Thank you, Lord, for this good food! Amen."

"—your hat."

Gil's hands shot to his head and grabbed his cap. Removing it quickly, he set it in his lap where it remained throughout the meal. The entire family let out an audible sigh of relief and began to eat again, hoping there would be no further disruption.

Dad was a reasonable man, generally soft spoken, slow to anger, and quick to smile or laugh. But he was a firm believer in good manners, and the strict enforcement thereof. And in Dad's book, a gentleman never, *never* wore his hat to the table.

Meals were an important time in our family; a time of talking, planning, sharing the day, enjoying the food, and appreciating our family. But in a large family, it simply wasn't feasible for every one of us to do exactly as we pleased without first taking the rest of the family into consideration. We knew, for example, that if Berman took as much meat as he wanted to, the serving plate might be empty by the time it reached Nola. Or, if we all decided to talk at the same time, we would have mayhem. Further, if we all decided to abandon the use of napkins and simply lick our fingers, we would be no better than a bunch of monkeys in the zoo.

On that same evening, Freddie was annoyed because he'd lost his baseball mitt somewhere. He wanted to use mine, but I didn't feel like letting him lose mine, too. As our meal progressed, Freddie leaned in toward me and whispered, "C'mon, Bill! I would let you use mine."

I responded by jabbing him with my elbow, and an "I said NO!"

My father raised his eyes. I immediately lowered mine and continued to eat. I knew from experience that those dumplings were delicious, but it took a little time for the heat from the chicken stew underneath to escape. I was doing my best to be patient and not burn my mouth.

A moment later, there was another nudge on my thigh. Fred was not giving up. I gave him a look, but didn't say anything. Then he started poking at my leg. It was too much for me. "Knock it off, Fred!" I nearly hollered.

At that, my dad had had enough. "Bill," he said firmly, "you may be excused."

I looked at my dumplings, just about ready to eat. "But Dad," I implored, "Freddie's been—"

"Son," he interrupted, "please excuse yourself now."

I left the table, fuming, but I knew better than to stomp off or slam a door. Arguing at the table was not acceptable behavior. Further displays of anger on my part would not be kindly received. But I was still hungry—and *furious* with Fred.

I remembered watching Betty and her sister, Mary Lou, argue one time over whose turn it was to wash the dishes. Mary Lou had gone to Mrs. Lewis, who declared it was Betty's turn. Mary Lou left the kitchen, but turned back with a smirky smile, to which Betty reacted with a venomous "I hate you!" Her little sister quickly replied, "I hate you, too!"

I felt a dread in my stomach. I would have been whipped for using that kind of language. And imagine hating my own flesh and blood! Why, they shared a room! What would happen now? I pitied the poor Lewis family, being torn asunder by the power of hatred. Was Betty really the wonderful girl I had supposed her to be?

We sat on the porch for a few silent minutes before I headed home. Finally, I could ignore the situation no longer. "Why'd you do it, Betty?"

Meadows

"Do what?"

"Tell Mary Lou that you hate her."

"It was her turn and she knew it!"

I stared at her in disbelief. At that moment, the screen door slammed and Mary Lou joined us on the porch. "Can I wear this sweater tomorrow?" she asked, holding up a fuzzy pink angora.

"OK, if I can wear your yellow blouse."

"Sure. G'night, Bill."

Once again, I was dumbfounded. "I thought you two hated each other," I fairly stammered. "What just happened?"

Mary Lou just laughed as Betty squeezed my arm. "You're funny, Billy Meadows. G'night!" I gave her a big kiss and said goodnight.

Well, I knew I didn't *hate* Fred. Couldn't even imagine saying such a thing to him. We were pretty good buddies most of the time, even if he *had* just cost me every bit of my dumplings. I sat out on the front porch, where I could hear my family's conversation without their knowing I was listening.

"You see," my dad was saying, "if we fuss and argue at the table, we'll be no better than heathens. My stars, imagine this whole group wearing hats and singing and arguing and licking their fingers, and chomping their food! Why, we wouldn't even be a family! We'd be a herd! People would buy tickets to watch us eat our supper, like a rodeo come to town!"

Everyone laughed. Even I had to snicker at the image he brought to my mind. I went back inside from exile, and stopped for a moment by the table.

"Sorry for the fuss, everyone," I said. "I'm going to do my homework now."

Bill's Teenage Friends--
Ernest Ballengee, Jack Riffe, Bill Meadows,
Carl Riffe, Bill Riffe and Teddy DeHart, 1952

Chapter Nine

Coming of Age

Manners were essential to good living, and as I said, we took great pains to practice them in the Meadows home. But we didn't grow up entertaining the notion that everyone prized proper behavior. And even if everyone in Crab Orchard had been perfectly behaved, there was still Mr. Reed.

"All right, come on, come on, come on!" Mr. Reed was bawling out orders like a drill sergeant, clapping his meaty paws together, and sometimes even blowing that ridiculous whistle he wore around his neck for bus duty.

I cringed as I walked by him, from neither fear nor respect, but more a deep-seated loathing. Mr. Reed was a bully.

"As if it doesn't take long enough to haul you students in from the mountains and the mines, I'm not going to stand here all day while you lollygag your way into *my school!*"

Of course it wasn't really his school. He wasn't the principal—just a biology teacher with a loud mouth and a grudge against the students bussed in from coal country. There were probably about three or four hundred of us; sixty or so from Crab Orchard alone. A lot of us, as I mentioned, were kin, and those who weren't were darned good friends. We were a tight little group and I don't mind saying I was a bit of a leader.

Reed seemed particularly irritable that morning, probably because the temperature had dropped unexpectedly in the night and no one had dressed for the chill. Mr. Reed stood stomping his feet, most likely to keep warm, though it added to his generally ferocious demeanor.

My cousin, Dwayne, was the "runt of the litter," and had learned to be a tough little mite in order to protect himself. When he walked by Mr. Reed, Dwayne shot the bully a dirty look. I thought Mr. Reed's eyes would pop out of his face. His hand shot out and he landed a sharp shove against Dwayne's shoulder, pushing him into two other students before he hit the ground. Dwayne bounced to his feet, with his dukes held high, but his older brother quickly whisked him into the anonymity of the school corridor.

We all darted past Mr. Reed and reconvened a little further down the hall.

"He can't do that!" my brother Freddie proclaimed.

"Why not?" Dwayne asked glumly. "He hates us. It's not the first time he's pushed one of the bus students down."

"But maybe it should be the last," I thought out loud.

"Waddaya mean, Bill?"

"Hey, Bill has an idea—listen to Bill!"

"Can we go get 'em Bill? There's only one of him! The odds are good."

I thought about it for a moment. And in those flickering seconds I saw my dad, and wondered what he might say. "Never be the one to start a fight, son." But also, "Stick up for your little brothers, or anyone who's weaker than you, boy." And "Now, Billy, respect for authority is an important principle for getting along," and, finally, "I'm so proud of you, son."

I closed my eyes for a second, willing my dad's image to a back burner for the moment. I needed to figure this one out myself. "We're gonna get him," I promised, and enjoyed the general murmur of agreement that rose from my little pack.

"Now? Can we do it now?" my little brother pleaded.

"Not you, Freddie," I said, "you stay out of this. You, too, Dwayne. Just us older guys. Who's in?"

My cohorts stepped forward, the mischievous gleam gone from their eyes as they considered what they were doing.

"Let's go, then." We retraced our steps toward the front entrance, where old man Reed was smiling, chatting with the last of the bus students, who came from town, and wore nice clothes.

His expression quickly changed when he saw us approaching him. "Hey, you coal kids, I thought I told you to get a move on. Now get!" With that, he swung his arms in front of him, a broad sweeping gesture that just happened

Nearly Perfect

to make solid contact with my chest. He'd given me a hard push, but I was ready. I stood my ground. And then, I did the unthinkable.

Drawing back my arm, I smashed my clenched fist into Mr. Reed's chest, and followed with a nice uppercut to his chin. It was then that I suddenly began to feel very alone in the matter. We had made a plan whereby *if* it seemed appropriate to hit Mr. Reed, I would do it first, then they would all join in—and my little brother, Fred, would remain in the auditorium. Glancing behind me, I saw that my compadres had lined themselves up against the row of lockers, clearly separating themselves from my little squabble with Mr. Reed. I immediately learned a life lesson; you can't always depend on your friends.

Mr. Reed staggered. I thought it was odd that my heavy-handed, well-directed blows had barely fazed him. But then I looked down and saw the cause of his imbalance, feeling both touched and fearful at the same time. There at the bully's knees was my brother, Freddie, arms encircling them, making a desperate attempt to bring the man into submission. There's another life lesson; you *can* depend on family.

In a matter of seconds, I felt myself being virtually lifted off the ground as Coach Pelish grabbed my brother and me by the fronts of our shirts and thumped us up against those lockers. "Have you lost your mind, boy? Hitting a *teacher!*

"Well, he pushed my cousin and he pushed me and he prob—"

Before I could complete my defense, Coach Pelish adjusted his grip and shoved me up against that locker again. "Enough, Meadows! Tell it to the principal. The rest of you, go on to class."

With that dismissal, he unceremoniously dragged my brother and me to Mr. Perogory's dreaded inner sanctum.

The phone call was made to my father's store, and the situation was explained. He was asked to come and get us, and keep us home for the remainder of the week. Freddie and I looked at each other grimly, not wanting to even speculate about our fates at the hands of a judicious father. We waited in silence.

When Dad arrived, his face was serious, and I think he might have felt ashamed of his boys at that moment. "This is very serious, Mr. Perogory. You can be sure that the boys will be dealt with most severely."

During the discussion of the incident, Mr. Reed said, "If this happens again, I'll beat the hell out of them." My dad, being a man who never used profanity, experienced an instant adjustment in his judgment of Mr. Reed.

"How in the world can you expect these young fellows to grow up respecting

Meadows

older folks if you stand there and express yourself in such a blasphemous manner?" he rebuked him. "What kind of an example is that?"

With that, my father took us each by the arm and led us out of the school. We rode in silence to my father's store, at which point, my father handed us each a box cutter and motioned to a shipment of groceries needing to be shelved. "We will talk later, boys. I need to think."

I'll never know what went through Dad's head that day, but despite my disappointment in my cohorts, and the unpleasantness of doing a great many penances over that weekend, I can't say that deep down I was very sorry for what I had done.

It must have been something in the air, but the episode with Mr. Reed was not the only incidence of trouble that year. Lots of the fellows were "feeling their oats."

"Hey!" Nancy Drovers cried out in mock pain, gingerly rubbing her behind. She had been "flicked" as she passed one of the boys on the bus. Interested onlookers laughed.

"Gotcha!" Oliver Harper laughed, and so did Nancy Drovers.

The physical education teachers had been selected as the ones who would talk to the students about this latest outbreak of inappropriate boy-girl behavior. But the talks just elicited giggles from the young ladies who seemed to feel that this type of attention was completely harmless. Everyone was doing it.

I leaned against my locker waiting for my buddies to meet me for lunch. We had all done our share of tail-flicking, despite the warning we had received. Just then, as Peggy walked by, I reached out and gave her a quick flick, meeting her look of consternation with a satisfied smile.

"Meadows! I saw what you just did! Don't you know you're already on thin ice?" It was none other than Mr. Reed. And there was no question that I was definitely on thin ice.

"What'd I do?" I retorted indignantly. "What are you talking about?"

"OK, trouble maker, now you're a liar on top of everything else. We'll just see what Perogory says about this!"

Great. Another trip to the office. It had been only two weeks since I had belted Reed, and there I was headed back in. There was no doubt that Mr. Reed had it in for me.

Catching Mr. Perogory in the reception area of the office, Mr. Reed nudged me toward him with a smug declaration. "I caught me another butt-flicker."

Mr. Perogory shook his head slightly, perhaps wondering if Reed's latest arrest would actually save the Western World from the threat of Communism.

Nearly Perfect

"We've asked you fellows not to do that," he said.

"I didn't!" I declared, albeit falsely.

"C'mon Meadows!" Reed chided, "I saw you with my own eyes."

"You're wrong." I knew I was back-pedaling, and my palms were getting sweaty, but I had told my dad I would stay out of trouble. And I had better.

"Great!" Reed said, "You're gonna take this coal boy's word against a teacher." He spat out the word *coal* as if it were the filthiest substance on earth.

Mr. Perogory shot him a hard look in reproach. Then he gave me a look of deep consternation. "I will ask the young lady in question. Who was it, Meadows?"

"There was no one! I didn't do it."

"It was that Smith girl, Anne," Reed said.

"Peggy," I corrected without thinking.

"Right then. I will speak to Miss Smith about the incident. Meadows, get to class. We will speak later."

I darted from the office in a blind panic. My temporary reprieve gave me just enough time to think of a plan, even if it were a lame one. I would simply ask Peggy to lie for me.

The cafeteria was emptying out as students began making their way to fourth period. I assumed Peggy would be called out of her class, probably in less than ten minutes. I had to reach her first.

"Peggy!" I saw her yellow sweater as she moved down the hall with a group of girls. She turned and saw me running toward her. "Wait up!"

"Oh great! *Now* what?" But she was smiling and I thought there might be a chance.

"Peggy, everybody knows Reed has it in for me," I began.

"And?"

"If I get in trouble again, I could get expelled."

"So what has that got to do with me?"

"You're going to be called to Perogory's office during fourth. Will you tell him nothing happened?"

"You mean lie? You mean pretend I wasn't insulted by the embarrassing thing you did? You mean … "

"Please, Peggy. You're my only hope … " and Peggy disappeared into her math class without giving me an answer.

A few minutes later, I crossed my fingers when I heard Peggy's name over the loud speaker. I had not expected to hear mine as well. I gulped hard as I felt my classmates staring at me sympathetically.

Meadows

Reed and Perogory stood shoulder to shoulder, and Peggy and I stood before them without looking at each other. Perogory cleared his throat. "Young people, this behavior has got to stop. We must make an example! Now, Miss Smith, I understand Mr. Meadows flicked your uh—flicked you during lunch today."

I looked at Peggy and could hardly believe my eyes. Her face registered shock, offense, disgust—and all very sincerely! "I beg your *pardon?* No one flicks me! I don't allow it! If that had happened, I would have been the first to let you know!"

Perogory shot Reed a look of contempt. "All right," he said to us, "you are free to go. Hands to yourselves." He turned to his side. "Mr. Reed, would you step in here for a moment?" The heavy office door closed behind them.

"Thanks, Peggy," was all I could manage.

"You owe me big," she retorted with a mischievous grin.

As several weeks passed, the fervor over Mr. Reed began to recede a little. We bussed students did our best to steer clear of him, even to the point of avoiding eye contact. Still, there were times when he would make disparaging remarks, or give one of the smaller guys a little push, if he were walking too slowly. We grumbled among ourselves, but always beyond Reed's earshot, wanting to avoid any further trouble for the most part.

So, I was really pretty surprised when I got hauled back into the principal's office first thing one Monday morning. There stood Mr. Reed, his arms crossed smugly. Mr. Perogory sat behind his desk, looking at some papers, but looked up at me over the top of his glasses.

"Mr. Meadows, it seems we have yet another problem, and once again your name is attached to this problem."

I waited expectantly, happy with the knowledge that for once I had done nothing wrong.

"So what's the problem?" I asked, trying my best not to sound fresh or belligerent.

Mr. Reed stepped toward me, and for a moment, I thought he might hit me. "The tickets, Meadows. We know you took 'em Friday night, and you're no doubt selling them on your little black market. But it's all over for you, pal."

Mr. Perogory held up his hand to quiet Mr. Reed, his eyes never leaving my face. "Son, this is a very serious charge. It's theft, plain and simple. And it calls for your suspension."

My mind raced in confusion. "What tickets? I don't know about any tickets!"

Nearly Perfect

"You took a roll of football tickets, Meadows," Reed answered. "They were on the desk in the physical education office, but mysteriously disappeared. You were the last person seen in that area."

"Please, Mr. Perogory, I didn't take anything. I don't steal. Let me prove it to you. Please!"

Perogory nodded his head thoughtfully. "Be back here during lunch tomorrow. See if you can come up with anything by then."

It was a grim day for me. My many mischievous antics had gone unpunished for the most part, but then, there I was facing punishment for something I truly had nothing to do with. What irony!

At practice that afternoon, I tried to shake off the gloom and put in a good afternoon's practice, but I guess Coach Pelish could see that my heart was not in it. "What's up, Meadows? You're not yourself."

"I *wish* I wasn't myself! I'd rather see me getting suspended than be me getting suspended."

"What?"

"Mr. Reed says I stole some football tickets. But I didn't, Coach!"

The coach thought about it for only a moment. "I know you didn't! You were dressed out for the game, and already on the field when I ran back inside for my clipboard. The tickets were still there then!"

"They were?" I asked, my load suddenly lightening. "Then you could vouch for me! Will you tell Mr. Perogory that it's all a mistake?" My heart beat joyously at the thought of being exonerated.

"Sure, Bill. Don't give it another thought. I'll speak to Perogory first thing in the morning."

The next day, I could feel Mr. Reed gaping at me as I got off the bus. I knew he was feeling tickled with his latest victory, so I turned and looked him squarely in the face, without flinching.

"It's not over yet," I said quietly, almost to myself.

"What'd you say, Meadows? Are you talking to me?" he asked darkly.

I didn't get to see Mr. Reed receive the news of my vindication, but I found that by that time, I'd really lost the stomach for the excitement. Besides, that year seemed to be unnaturally fraught with tension. There was also the whole episode with Mrs. Perkowski.

"Class, this is Mr. Machaski. He's going to be student teaching with me this quarter. We are very fortunate to have him!" Mrs. Perkowski looked pleased as punch with herself, and gave us her very best imitation of a smile.

Machaski looked like an all right guy, kind of young and clean-cut. He seemed a little nervous at first, but once he warmed up, he was pretty cool. I sized him up carefully, wondering whether he was smart, or had a good sense of humor. To my way of thinking, anything was better than Perkowski!

Just the week before, Mrs. Perkowski had called my parents to let them know that I'd been disruptive. She made it sound as though I had had fits in class, rather than cut a couple of wisecracks while she was teaching.

My dad, as usual, had little patience for someone who was disrespectful, whether it was to a teacher, or a peer. "Son, I don't care if you like the woman or not. That's not the issue here. She has prepared a lesson to teach you, and you are obligated to listen without interrupting her. That's pretty plain, isn't it?"

I nodded my head. I knew my dad was right, but I liked cutting up and the feeling of being a bit of a ringleader.

Ann Armentrout was one of those people who was always right. She read the lessons all through lunch hour and then got the answers right when Perkowski called on her. It was just that kind of student that always seemed to make teachers feel great—and I could not understand why. I wondered what it would be like to get straight A's and have the teacher use you as an example in a *good* way for a change. I got an idea.

"Hey, Betty, can you help me with my homework?" I asked. Betty was a great student and she had no problem remembering the right answers. "I need to pull my grades up in Perkowski's class. She's really leaning on me, and she talked to my dad about my being disruptive … "

"Sure, I'll be happy to help you out, Bill," she said, "but you'll have to put in a little effort yourself, too."

"Oh, I will," I assured her. "I really will."

Over those following weeks, Betty coached me in the evening, helping me use all kinds of tricks to remember the answers, and I started to get back some pretty good grades. Each time we had a quiz, Perkowski would come sniffing around my desk, like a bloodhound on the trail of an escaped convict. Understandably, it made me uncomfortable, but I was determined to hide my feelings. My studying was earning me those good grades, but I guess it was also earning me her suspicion.

Another part of our grade was composed of class participation, so I made sure to stick my hand in the air every chance I got—but nobody could outdraw Ann Armentrout. Machaski did his best to call on different people, so we all got a chance to show how ignorant we were compared to Ann.

When Ann finally did make a mistake, I almost didn't believe it. No one blinked an eye when she blatantly misstated some information. I even saw some students jotting down her pearls of wisdom, as Mrs. Perkowski nodded approvingly.

"Hold up!" I called out. "That's not right!"

Mrs. Perkowski glared at me, and Machaski looked at me as if I'd lost my mind.

"Sorry, sir," I said, "but she's wrong. I read that in the book last night. What Ann's talking about are the figures from the research they did at first, from the turn of the century."

Machaski picked up his book and started rifling though it, looking for the right information, as Mrs. Perkowski made her way to the front of the room. Though the class was quiet and in order, she smacked her hand on the desk and barked out, "That's enough, Mr. Meadows. That was uncalled for!"

The next morning—you guessed it—I was summoned to Perogory's office during homeroom. I could hardly think of a better way to start the day!

"Have a seat, Bill." I guess by that time we had gone beyond the need for formalities. "Mrs. Perkowski is very upset at the way you've treated the student teacher. Says you're even more disruptive than you are with her."

"That's not true, sir. I've been studying hard to bring up my grade, and for some reason, that makes her mad."

"Oh, come now, Bill. That's ridiculous. Any teacher would be glad to have a student work hard for her class. You make it sound as if she's got it in for you."

"It sure seems like it. I haven't been disruptive at all since Machaski got here. Ask him!"

Mr. Perogory looked thoughtful. "I think I'll do just that," he said. "Mrs. Bostick, can you send someone to get Mr. Machaski down here?"

A few moments later, Mr. Machaski stood next to me, grinning like we were big pals. "Hey, Bill!"

"Mr. Machaski, I understand that there have been some problems in class. With Bill."

Machaski looked baffled. "Bill, I wish you had come to me if you had a problem. We could've worked it out."

Mr. Perogory cleared his throat. "Uh, no, Mr. Machaski. I'm talking about Bill's causing a problem for you. Disrupting your class, being disrespectful. That sort of thing."

Mr. Machaski let out a little snort that fell just short of a laugh. "Bill? I'm afraid not. He's one of those students every teacher dreams of! Responsive,

Meadows

prepared, interested, participating—it's been just great having him. His grades really reflect the effort he puts into it, too."

Mr. Perogory blinked his eyes slowly, and I gathered from his expression that he was not very happy with the conflicting information he had received. "Very well, then. You may both go. Oh, Mr. Machaski, when you return to class, please ask Mrs. Perkowski to see me on her break."

We turned to leave and Machaski shrugged at me, obviously baffled as to where Mr. Perogory had gotten his information. So I shrugged too, and off we went down the hall together.

Bill, sixteen-years-old, 1951

Chapter Ten

Play Ball!

While school did provide me with a variety of challenges, one of my favorites was in the field of sports. I never lost my fascination with running track, and had done pretty well. I had ended that year with enough track wins to take me to the state track meet in Charleston. Coach Ross Earl had been behind me all the way, and finally we faced that last race together.

The track was made up of hard-packed cinders, the white lines created just that morning, poured from paper sacks of lime. I hoped it wouldn't feel too different under my feet for me to hit my pace. That would be important when I was running against the best of the best.

The race started out fine, and I had a nice place, about a quarter of the way down the pack. Just past our first turn, I saw an opportunity to move to an inside track. I changed my pace a little to get in sync with some people I would need to pass, and then I made my move. It happened to be at the exact moment that Jerry Gilders had chosen to make *his* move. The impact was stunning as we hurtled into each other. I slid across the cinders on my knees, then rolled to keep from being trampled as sixteen eager runners made their way past me. I knew better than to cry as I dragged myself painfully to my feet.

A firm hand on my shoulder caused me to turn my head. The coach gave my shoulder a little squeeze.

Meadows

"This hurts pretty bad," I said between breaths.

"I bet it does," he answered. "The question is, do you think you can get back in there?"

I didn't have a quick answer.

"Just run, Bill, that's why we're here," he said. He clapped me on the shoulder again, and I limped back onto the track and willed my aching legs to move. They did, slowly at first, but then gathered speed, moving ahead, as I relished the feel of the air speeding past my face. Stride by stride I narrowed the distance between the pack and me, amazed when I passed the last man running. Then, one by one, the other runners fell behind me. Next, I began to close the distance between the lead man, Ralph Henderson and me. We had run against each other before, and he was good. But on the last leg of the race, Ralph was way up ahead, and we were not too far from the finish line.

I looked briefly at the sidelines, and there, I saw my coach. He was smiling, and when our eyes met, he gave me the thumbs up signal, as though I were already the winner. Suddenly, I knew I could still win, and I pulled out all the stops and went for it full steam ahead. And it was darn close. Ralph grabbed me in a bear hug and could only say, "Man!"

I managed to huff out congratulations as coach put his arm around my shoulder. "Nice job, Meadows. Real nice."

We were both disappointed, but I knew that day that the coach was proud of me for hanging in there. I felt a little proud myself.

The feeling of pride remained under the surface, and as I prepared to enter the tenth grade, I thought of the opportunities that lay ahead. In the fall, I would go out for football, and of course I'd be running track again in the spring.

I had mixed emotions when it came to football. I was fascinated by the game strategy, the how and why of each play, how each position functioned; but I was not especially interested in all the bone-crunching physical contact. I actually considered myself somewhat lucky to be second string. Of course, when it came to practice, it didn't matter too much whether you were first or second; you had to go through the drills regardless.

I was an average guy with a medium build, and I shuddered at the thought of some of those larger and older guys lumbering down the field toward me. I was really too small to play defensive tackle, and I suppose I didn't look especially enthusiastic on that one particular day.

Coach Wiseman gave me a sardonic laugh. "Hey, fellas, looks like these coal miner boys don't want to play ball today." At that point, I was temporarily playing defensive tackle.

Nearly Perfect

Fifty years after the fact, I can still remember how those words made me feel. I had heard those kinds of remarks before—remarks designed to make small men feel big; slurs intended to make good, honest boys ashamed of their fathers' hard work, embarrassed of the very heritage that kept the whole region moving … those words made me angry, and resentful, and made me want to hurt someone.

On the very next play, I went between the tackle and the guard, and grabbed the quarterback. My face was wet as the hot angry tears splashed down my filthy cheeks. And I played my heart out. I played that way through the next five or six plays, 'til my anger was spent, and my eyes were dry. I remembered that day.

When it came to the actual game, I didn't mind dressing in my uniform and sitting on the bench soaking in the logistics of the game. I certainly wasn't expecting Coach Wiseman to bark out my name.

"Meadows! Nate can't go back in—get in there and take his place!"

I glanced at the clock in disbelief—a minute to go, and I was to step in as blocker—quite a stretch from quarterback, my regular position. Sometimes life made no sense. Unfortunately, it wasn't the time to figure all that out. At that moment, I stared into the eyes of the opposition, six inches taller than me, and probably fifty pounds or more heavier. His expression tended to give the impression he had plans to get our ball carrier. I wasn't up on all of the psychological tactics that seasoned players practiced, but I knew I couldn't show fear. I looked into the eyes of the big defensive tackle and gritted my teeth.

At the snap, I roared into his left shoulder, and had it not been for him tangling his feet with mine, he might have gotten right past me. But instead, as the ball went up, soaring in the direction of our wide receiver, my opponent went down, an expression of shock and dismay on his face. But I didn't take time to gloat. As soon as it registered that I'd done my job, the crowd seemed to burst into life. The buzzer sounded, and just then, the scoreboard flashed twenty-one to twenty—Touchdown! Woodrow Wilson High took the game. The euphoria was something I would remember for the rest of my life.

In the locker room, there was a grand commotion. It died down suddenly when Coach Wiseman stepped inside, clipboard in hand, a smile on his face. "Men, that was some kind of game out there! I don't know that I've ever seen the likes of it. I am one proud coach today." His smile stretched from ear to ear and with one accord, we burst out in a deafening round of applause and cheering. Coach shook his head in amazement, and turned as if to leave, but stopped, raising his hand to restore order. "There *is* one other thing. Meadows! Front and center!"

Self-consciously I moved to the foreground, where Coach clapped a heavy hand on my shoulder. "Boy, that was without a doubt, one of the finest blocks I've ever seen, and I've been doing this a long time now!" He smiled, shaking his head again in disbelief, and left the locker room.

There were about ten seconds of dead silence, then the whistling, cheering, and applause resumed, and the congratulatory slaps rained down on me like hailstones. I was a hero, and it felt great!

My brother, Fred, and I spent hours and hours playing baseball. He was a catcher and I was a pitcher. We loved the game and spent lots of time in the summer, playing on the adult men's league. I loved to pitch and Betty loved to come see me play. There were times I would pitch nine or more innings. There was no concern about protecting my shoulder, then, and I would definitely pay for it later when my rotator cup was completely destroyed and shoulder surgery interrupted my physical activities for about six months.

Many times, especially in the last ten years, I've had high school students approach me and say, "Farmer, what lottery did you hit? I know you live in a thirteen thousand square foot home, seven bathrooms, twenty-two televisions in there, nineteen telephones and so on and so forth, so what lottery did you hit?"

Well, it's really a terrible situation when our young people feel that the only way a person could be successful in life is to hit a lottery. One of my first comments to them is the old adage, "Well, you know, the harder I work, the luckier I get."

I really don't know that that's all of it, of course. But I do know that when you've had someone in your life that has made a positive impression on you, helped you, shown you personal encouragement, and for whom you have great respect, that that's the lucky part of life. I was very lucky in that way. Few people have been as fortunate to have enjoyed the opportunity to know and be inspired by someone like Coach Van Meter.

Coach Jerome Van Meter was the head football coach as well as the basketball coach of my high school in Beckley. He is now one hundred and four years old and in a nursing home in Beckley, but he's still walking, but with a walker; still sharp, and a good thinker. He's still somewhat outspoken when inspired, and he attends almost all the alumni activities.

The man had a profound impact on my life. First of all, he was a very winning coach. In fact, I think during the three or four years I played under his supervision, he lost only one ball game. As a young man, I was truly impressed by that. It helped me develop a determination to always be a winner myself.

Nearly Perfect

He and his wife both worked at school. They did not have any children so his life was centered equally around his wife and the players that he coached. Football took precedence in his life.

I remember that on the first day of football practice each year, Coach Van Meter would explain to his team that the number one thing we were there for was to win. He'd talk about winning from the very beginning. And that certainly rubbed off on me! He said that he was not and never had learned to be a good loser. Of course there's a difference between learning how to be a good loser and being a good sport after you have lost. He certainly was always a good sport. But he was hurt and hurt deeply the few times that he had to face losing. He taught me that you don't smile, you don't laugh, you don't have a very good time for a day or so after you've lost in any type of activity.

I remember teaching that to my boys and even after I had stopped teaching them and was working with Little League Football, I would always call the parents in before I'd get the team started. I would explain to them that I was a good coach, show them my record, and almost guarantee that we would win every ball game—which we did during the couple years I was doing that.

One of the mothers asked, "How do you go about teaching them to be good losers?" I told them that if, by chance, we were to lose a ball game, then I would have to get one of them to come and talk to the boys because I never had learned how to be a good loser. I suggested that maybe she or her husband could come down, and talk to the boys a couple times a week while we were practicing, and tell them how to be good losers. But I told her that I would totally fail in that, and I think that that is from (a little bit of outgrowth of) playing some important games with a coach who just knew that he was going to win them all. Winning came so frequently because he was so properly prepared, and of course that's the reason why 99% of the time I have been successful.

This concept carries over into business and all of my other endeavors as well. Being prepared is always primary, but also contributory is the fact that it is such a terrible, painful thing to lose. I have tried to assimilate this idea into the raising of my sons and my daughters; that losing is such a gosh awful thing, and that if they ever adjust very well to losing, then they need to get out of that sport, because they're learning something that isn't a good thing to learn.

So Coach Van Meter was a strong winner and believed in it, and that was a wonderful thing that I did learn from him. But he also had a nurturing quality, although it was considerably more subtle.

Meadows

No one ever questioned anything the coach would say, which was reasonable considering his record. But one time, after studying a play he put out, I could see where I thought something was wrong with the mechanics of it. I didn't say anything right away, but I kept thinking it would work better the way I had in mind. Finally one day, I got up enough nerve to edge up to him while one of the other coaches had taken over for a minute and I said, "Coach? Coach, if I could just mention one thing about this play … "

He seemed to be listening, and I said, "If we could only split our offensive linemen a little bit more, then we would be able to split the defense a little bit more, and on our dive plays, it'd be more likely to work. Then maybe we could work without having to block much."

He said, "Well, I certainly do appreciate your comment, but I've spread out so much now, nobody'd ever be dumb enough to spread 'em out anymore, because then we *could* do what you're talking about."

"I just thought maybe sometime at the end of the game," I said, "when we're winning by our usual three or four touchdowns, we might just try it."

"Maybe," he said. "Maybe."

Well, the next week in practice one day, we went to the huddle, and I heard him explain to all the lineman, "Take another six-inch split longer than what you are already between each lineman, and see if we can get away with Coach Wiseman's defense over there."

So the offense split, the defense split right with them, and we ran all the way through two or three times. Then he said, "You all get ready, we're going to try this next Friday night."

After that game, he said, "Thanks, Meadows. You're a thinker out here. Sometimes some people think a lot better than they play."

"Well, thank you Coach," I said. "I'm glad that I can do something since my playing ability is not tops out here."

One afternoon, he said to me, "I want to tell you, young man, you need to be a coach someday. You're not going to make it to college level playing football. We all know that. You know that, but you certainly can coach college level some day."

That's probably one of the main reasons I ended up as a coach—and coached ten years and lost only three ball games.

This took place around fifty years ago. Another course of action that distinguished Coach Van Meter back then was his practice of going to big colleges and asking along the lines of , "Can I come to your fall practice, summer practice, or spring practice? Any time that it doesn't interfere with your team?"

Nearly Perfect

In this way, he would find out all the new things that were happening in football. There were no other high school coaches taking the time to do that. One time he went as far as Oklahoma.

When we had the next practice, he didn't necessarily go straight through the way he had observed the other teams, but maybe mostly that way and then he would add his little changes.

Woodrow Wilson High School now offers an award to alumni. They call it the Golden Eagle Award. It goes to someone who has shown the most progress in economic endeavors, and it was ten years ago that I received it. At that time, we were worth around twenty-five million dollars. It was when I was called in to receive the award that I was fortunate enough to see Coach Van Meter once again. There he was, in his middle 90s, and he still remembered me—not as a player, but as a potential coach.

"I'm glad to see, son," he said, "that you're doing all right in business. What ever happened to your coaching skills?"

I said, "Well, Coach Van Meter, I enjoyed coaching for ten years—almost more than anything I've ever done in my life. And I sure do appreciate you recognizing me and giving me encouragement in your own way."

I think in my teaching career and in my experiences with employees, I've come in contact with thousands of people over the years. I hope that as I get up in years, I, like Coach Van Meter, can remember and have a little positive influence on the people who have crossed my path.

Betty at age eighteen, 1952

Bill at age eighteen, 1953

Chapter Eleven

The Big Surprise

"Don't go in the living room," Betty's father told her one evening as Betty came through the door. Her mother was setting dinner on the table. "Why not?" she asked.

"It's a surprise," he answered. "Now don't go in there!"

I'm sure Betty, Bobby and Mary Lou ate their dinners very quickly that night, and as soon as they were through, before the dishes had even been cleared, a knock came on the back door.

"Is it time?" called Jason Long.

"Just about, Jason. Come on in. You wait here with Olive." And Mr. Lewis went through to the living room. They could all hear him humming silently to himself, as their anticipation rose all the more. Meanwhile, several more neighbors tapped expectantly at their back door.

The Lewis children were beside themselves with curiosity. When their father finally gave the word, they were the first ones to shoot into the living room. There, Mr. Lewis stood in front of a little table that had been draped with a tablecloth. When the entire group was properly assembled, he pulled off the cloth with a theatrical flourish. Mouths dropped open at the sight of Crab Orchard's very first television set.

Mr. Lewis quickly turned it on. All eyes were glued to the blue-black images of Milton Berle and his guests. So was the beginning of a new era

Meadows

for our little town—and for Betty and me.

I went over to the Lewises' house almost every night to watch a little television with Betty and her family. We sat close to each other on the floor, our legs occasionally bumping into one another, but otherwise not touching. If she offered to go into the kitchen for cold drinks, I'd go along to "help." But once we got there, we would kiss deeply, until Betty would push me away, worried that her father would walk in on us. She'd whisper, "I wish we were married," and I'd quickly respond with, "me too!" Then we'd go back out to the living room, usually remembering to bring the cold drinks with us.

Betty's father created a little recreation area in their attic that same summer. It made a great place to play games or listen to records. We learned to dance there. First the Jitterbug to Glen Miller's "In the Mood," later rock and roll. It turned into one really nice summer, with great times and lots of friends around.

* * *

I was looking forward to the start of school again, as usual. Things were off to a great start until September 26, when I turned sixteen. It was my friend, Ruth Ann, who reminded me of the significance.

"You're so lucky!" she gushed enviously. "Car dates at last!"

I thought about Bill and the fact that he wouldn't be driving for quite a while. I would miss out on a lot if I waited for him to be old enough to take me places. I started to feel as if I were sacrificing a lot for him. Added to the occasion of my spotting him in town, surrounded by girls, including townies, who were generally too good for the bus kids, I began to feel resentful.

"I think we need to talk," I said to him one afternoon. I went on to explain that I had felt very upset seeing him talking to all those girls, and that at the same time, I wondered how it was going to be with all my friends going on car dates and me having to wait. It was an extremely emotional moment, and overall emotional time period in our lives.

Ultimately, it was because we felt so seriously so young that we felt we needed to break up. But the break up periods didn't last long. We knew we loved each other, and that we belonged together, yet instinctively, we knew we had to see other people. But for all of our efforts, we remained hopelessly in love. Each time we reunited, we would talk about how terribly we'd missed each other. Then we would discuss our future together, with Bill painting such vivid pictures that I could imagine everything he described, as though it were happening just then.

"I want a big house, Betty. Not a mansion, necessarily, but something really nice. And a swimming pool, just like the governor has."

"With flowers all around the edge," I chimed in.

"Flowers and trees and a little rock wall … "

"And two children," I added, for posterity.

"Yep, two children—a boy and a girl. I'll name my boy Rocky Meadows!"

"Oh, Bill! That's funny!" I laughed, but then I saw that he was serious. "But real nice," I added quickly. "And you know I want my little girl to be Lucinda (after the beautiful young native girl in the movie Mutiny on the Bounty)."

Bill kissed me chastely. "It's going to be a great life," he assured me.

That March, Bill finally did get his driver's license, along with a long list of dos and don'ts, no doubt hard-earned by his older brothers Gilven and Berman. Mr. Meadows let his three driving sons use the delivery truck from his grocery store, and many great times were spent with a group of young people going for barbecues at Pete and Bob's Drive-In or loaded in for football games.

It was a rare occasion when Bill had the truck to himself, but when he did, we went parking. We would kiss for hours, feeling like we would burst from the euphoria of it, but always using self-control to keep ourselves in check.

Then, one night, Bill took me to a new place he had found. It was very secluded, and we didn't see any other cars even looking through the trees to the road beyond. It was there that we graduated from necking to petting, provoking even more of the dizzying unresolved feelings we had been dealing with for so long.

Breathlessly, I whispered, "I wish we were married, Bill," and for the first time, he whispered back, "We may as well be. You know we'll always be together. Why do we have to wait?"

It was the first time we had ever talked about sex. I was very anxious and exhilarated at the same time. "We can't keep doing this, Betty," Bill went on, "it's not healthy."

"We probably should just go ahead and do it," I ventured, wondering if I had finally succeeded in shocking Bill.

He was very quiet, and I could almost imagine a little angel on one shoulder, arguing with a little devil on the other. "We'll do it next time I get the truck," he decided.

We kissed some more, and then headed home, hardly talking. Neither of us brought up that discussion again, but three weeks later, Bill asked me if I would like to go out for a ride on Friday night, alone. We both knew what that meant, and an awkwardness between us opened up as we rushed toward a new step we were not really ready to take.

When Friday arrived, I felt shy and nervous. I could hardly speak as we drove out to our parking place. We began kissing right away, and continued as we always had, for a very long time. At last, Bill dug into his wallet and pulled out a condom. I had never seen one before, but understood the necessity of the contraption. We both sat looking at it, perhaps knowing that it signaled the end of our innocence.

With shaking hands, I began to open the little package. Just then, Bill took it away from me. "I changed my mind," he announced resolutely.

I felt rejected and embarrassed. "What?"

But Bill pulled me close and whispered sweet words I'll never forget. "I love you, Betty Lewis. I aim to make you my wife someday. I don't want to spoil all of that by doing something stupid now. Let's go home."

Abruptly, Bill backed the truck out of our necking spot and turned toward Crab Orchard. I felt myself beginning to cry a little, but I was smiling, too. He loved me. He wanted to marry me. He wanted to save that special thing for our special day.

Bill and Betty's Wedding, August 6, 1953

Chapter Twelve

Moving Forward

1953 was a difficult one for me. Bill was in his last year of high school, and we planned to get married when he graduated. I signed up for a semester of secretarial classes at Beckley College. At the end of the semester, I got a job with an accounting firm, making one hundred and fifty dollars a month.

Meanwhile, my friend Janet, who was still in high school, seemed to enjoy telling me about Bill. "He sat with Carol Sue Stone at lunch," she'd report, or "He walked Margaret to homeroom; I heard him talking to Elsie at the lockers."

I would burn with jealousy, but didn't dare mention it to Bill for fear that he would think I was spying on him. Instead, I began to make little comments about getting engaged. I figured this would make an irrefutable statement to all those high school girls who found my boyfriend so interesting.

"Seen any nice rings, lately?" I might ask, jokingly, to which Bill would respond, "Not yet, but soon!"

"How about proposing to a girl?" I would suggest, to which he would say the same, "Not yet, but soon!"

He always seemed so good natured, and I didn't really mean to pressure him, but I wondered if he would ever make it official between us.

One night, as we sat smooching in our spot, and I asked, "When are we going to get engaged, Bill Meadows?" he responded, "Right now!"

Meadows

He reached into his pocket and pulled out a ring, smiling broadly. Sliding it onto my finger, he said, "It's official. We're engaged, and you won't get away from me again!"

For once, I was speechless. I laughed and I cried, and kissed him over and over again. But after a while, I began to wonder how he'd managed it.

"It's so beautiful," I said, holding the sparkling diamond chip close to my cheek, "but how did you ever afford it?"

"I saw it in the jewelry store, Betty, and I knew it was time and I knew it was right. So I decided it was also time to sell those pigs."

"The 4H prized pigs?" I asked, amazed.

"Those are the ones," he answered, smiling without an ounce of regret.

I hugged him all the more, feeling such joy at the beautiful token of love and commitment. Years later, on our twenty-fifth wedding anniversary, he would bestow me with a magnificent diamond ring that I wear lovingly on my ring finger today. But I still wear the little diamond chip he gave me that summer night, right next to it, on my pinkie. And I have to say that it means even more to me than the fourteen-thousand dollar anniversary beauty.

When he delivered me to my front gate that night, I couldn't wait to tell my parents the good news. They were quiet for a while until my mother finally cleared her throat.

"I know you're excited, honey, but you're still awfully young."

I was too excited to let their grim reaction dampen my spirits. It was really going to happen. Wishes really did come true!

But there were hurdles to cross, as well. Bill fretted about what he would do with his life. He thought of starting his own business. Maybe a barber shop, he thought, like his Uncle Walton. At that time, the country was engaged in the Korean War, and people were reluctant to hire young men for fear that they would be drafted, so starting a business sounded like a logical pursuit. Bill wasn't worried about the draft. He and some of his friends had joined the National Guard, figuring that they would then be the last ones drafted.

But when the time came for Bill to attend the two-week National Guard training session, I was miserable. Though I had my job and my girlfriends, I didn't think I could make it for two weeks without Bill.

"Please," I begged him, "isn't there some way I can go with you?"

Bill was sensitive to my feelings and very tender during those last days.

"I wish we were married, Bill. I don't want to wait. Can we elope before you go to camp?"

Bill was hesitant. "No, Betty, you deserve a real wedding. When I get back."

Nearly Perfect

"You promise?" I asked, cheering up for the moment. "We can get married when you get back?"

"Yes, yes, I promise," he vowed, kissing away my tears. "We'll get married when I get back."

I stood waving, wiping away more tears, as Bill's bus pulled away. But then, I got to work! I had two weeks to arrange everything, and the first thing I did was look at my calendar. August 6, 1953. That would be three weeks after his return from camp.

I walked straight over to Reverend Donnelly's office door.

"Well, hello Betty! What brings you here today?"

"I want to reserve the church, Reverend! For August sixth. Bill Meadows and I are getting married that day, and we'd like you to perform the ceremony."

Reverend Donnelly stood up and pumped my hand enthusiastically. "Why that's wonderful! And I'll ask Edna to play the organ, if you like!"

I watched as he penciled our names onto the church calendar, my heart beating wildly. This was the real thing!

Heading home, I decided not to tell anyone just yet, though I was certain that it would be out soon enough after the pastor's pianist, Bill's Aunt Edna heard the news. No one was at home as I sat down at the kitchen table with the thick Sears & Roebuck Catalog open before me. Thumbing through the tissuey pages, I came to the section I wanted. Wedding dresses. Nervously, I compared the details of the pictures as well as the cost of each gown. Circling the dress and veil I'd chosen, I carefully wrote down the catalog numbers. Next, I flipped over to loungewear and selected a filmy, white negligee like one I had seen movie stars wear. Then, feeling generous, I turned to the men's section and picked out a bathrobe for my future groom. My hands shook as I wrote out my order and sealed the envelope. Then, I had only to wait.

As the two weeks neared completion, I was very nervous as to how Bill might react to the plans I had made. I hoped he wouldn't be angry that I had gone so far without him. I fervently vowed that he would never regret marrying me. If only I could work up the nerve to tell him!

* * *

While Betty was back at home, and I was in training for the National Guard, I had started to have misgivings about promising to marry her so soon. I knew she and I belonged together—there was never any doubt in my mind about that, or as to how much we loved each other. My big stumbling block was the fact that I did not have a job. I was bound and determined to support my future wife, and I knew I couldn't do it at that time.

As I rode the bus back to Crab Orchard, I was nervous about how Betty might react. I had told her four or five times before when we would get married. I felt like a heel, knowing I would have to disappoint her again. I pictured her pretty face there waiting for me at the bus, and I knew that I'd have to wait just a little bit to break it to her, as much as I wanted to get it over with.

* * *

I was overjoyed to finally see Bill again. I hugged him tightly right there in public at the bus stop. I suggested we have a romantic little dinner, to which he readily agreed.

We talked happily through dinner, as I constantly searched for just the right moment to break the news to Bill. Finally, we were finished eating, and it was then or never!

"Bill, remember before you left you said we could get married when you got back from camp?"

"I sure do," Bill said, "and soon we will! But Betty ... "

"I know—August sixth!" I said.

Bill looked startled. "What do you mean?"

"I set the date for August sixth," I said, letting out my breath.

"Well, you see, Betty, about setting that date, I'm not—"

"I got the flowers—"

"I think I need to—"

"—the church, Reverend Donnelly, Edna and everything!"

Suddenly Bill was very quiet. The order of flowers could be cancelled, dresses could be put on hold, but in a small town like Crab Orchard, once the church was reserved for a wedding, there was no turning back. "Well," he said, "so it's all settled then."

"All settled," I responded, my jubilation fading quickly.

"That's good, real good," Bill answered weakly.

* * *

As it turned out, my misgivings were not meant to be aired. By the time I got home, my bride to be had already planned our nuptials. It was a time to be joyful, and I did my best to feel that way, trying not to let her down. But the fear of being an out-of-work husband was not in any way assuaged.

She could see my internal struggle, and as always, Betty was very concerned and very supportive. I think it was then that she made a prophetic and truthful pledge. "Bill, I know this might be hitting you hard all at once like this. But I just felt it was the right thing to do." She paused and looked shyly into my eyes. "I made a vow to myself, and I'm making the same one to you. I promise you, Bill, you will never regret marrying me. I will be the best wife, mother, and friend I can be. I will treat you like a king. I promise."

I saw the depth of feelings in her eyes and I knew she meant what she was saying with all her heart. I believed her and began to feel a little easier. And to this day, I can honestly say, I never have regretted marrying Betty.

*　*　*

The next day, Bill went and got himself a job as a ditch digger, where he labored for a week or so until they moved on. Discouraged, he wondered still how he would ever support a wife. I was optimistic, as usual. I had a good steady job, and went out and rented us a little two-room house from Bill's Uncle Willard, that had no running water or bathroom. We furnished it with hand-me-downs from various friends and family, getting everything in order for our married life.

Everything was set for the big day, with Mary Lou, Janet Meadow, JoAnn Combs, and Ernie standing up for us. Bill's Aunt Edna, who played the organ for the ceremony, also prepared punch and finger foods for a reception at our little house after the wedding. It was really going to happen!

On my wedding day, August 6, 1953, I got my hair done, then treated myself to my favorite lunch at the counter of G.C. Murphy. Each time I did anything, like eat lunch, or walk to Murphy's, or browse in a store, I would say to myself, "This is the last time you will do this as a single girl."

It was a very dreamy day, right up until the time I walked down the aisle to stand at Bill's side. There, I realized that my darling husband-to-be was very much on the verge of losing it. He was pale and perspiring, and his knees were knocking audibly. I caught his eye and smiled confidently. He smiled back, and moments later, we were finally married.

More than anything, I wanted to take my new husband to bed and unravel the mysteries of love together. Our friends finally began to leave, much to my relief, and we were alone at last.

"We're really married!" Bill said incredulously.

"And tonight's the night!" I added nervously. I opened my little overnight bag and pulled out my negligee, then hurried shyly to the closet to change clothes. When I

Meadows

came out, Bill was smiling, with his arms wide open for our first married embrace. He had taken a throw rug and lain it over the lamp to soften the glare of the light and set a romantic mood. The radio was playing softly. Overwhelmed, I fell into his arms and he lowered me gently to the bed. A bed that was full of rice. And cracked corn. And who knows what other horrible, scratchy, uncomfortable things.

"Oh my gosh!" I hollered, angry and indignant. "That's not funny!"

Bill looked flustered as he began pulling the sheets off the bed, and brushing the grain onto the floor. "It's all right, honey. Really," he soothed me, and I was somewhat mollified until I heard laughter floating in through the open window.

"Phyllis Deal!" I screamed, certain she had spearheaded this little project. The laughter receded into the distance, and the night fell silent.

Bill smiled and held his arms out once again. We kissed passionately, and crawled into the bed once again. Our kisses were fiery, but even our love couldn't explain the smell of smoke in that room.

"Bill! The lamp!"

The rug that had helped dim the lights for atmosphere, was then providing additional ambiance of a blazing fire. We scrambled out of bed and grabbed towels to beat the fire out. Several frantic moments later, the fire was out with no real damage to speak of.

Bill sat on the edge of the bed, shaking his head. I moved closed to him, and he pulled me onto his lap. "Do we dare try again?" he asked sardonically.

I answered him with a kiss that I had been saving since that very first time we had played Red Rover; when my hands had turned clammy. It was the kiss a bride reserves for her groom. A kiss that tells a story, asks a question, and solves the mystery of love once and for all. It was a kiss that never again went home to a cold empty bed declaring, "I wish we were married."

After a few minutes, I whispered, "I am so glad we are married." A little while later, I whispered again, "I Am So Glad We Are Married!"

The morning after our wedding, we got up early. Bill's brother, Gilven, had lent us his car to take a trip to Virginia Beach, Virginia. We were both so excited to be taking the trip. I had always wanted to see the ocean, and wondered how it would feel to stand next to such an incredible, unending vastness.

There we were, eighteen years old, newly married, and for all intents and purposes, had never been anywhere. We had decided on Virginia Beach after Bill's Aunt Edna suggested it. She and her husband, Elliott Deck, routinely went to Virginia Beach for summer vacations. Aunt Edna helped Bill get the reservation set up at a little motel called Tourist Haven, which has long since been demolished.

It was such a thrill to anticipate having a real honeymoon. I had never dreamed we'd be able to go, and, of course, adding the prospect of seeing the ocean for the very first time made it all that much more thrilling.

That morning, we left bright and early, but we didn't make very good time. Somehow, we managed to find ourselves parked in secluded areas two or three times, reinforcing the ideas we'd shared the night before about being glad we were married. It was a memorable trip before we got there.

But when we finally did arrive, I was startled and even frightened at the massiveness of that great body of water. It took my breath away. I can still remember the sensation of inhaling the salty air, hearing the unfamiliar roar and power of the waves, and feeling the spray on my skin. It was overwhelming. I have lived in fascination with that great beauty ever since.

In every way, the two newlyweds with only a few dollars to share had a truly wonderful honeymoon. Our time was spent enjoying the wonders of married life, sharing beautiful, sunny days on the beach, fishing in the shade, and making sweet love in our little room in the Tourist Haven Motel.

Even as we drove away, our honeymoon endured, as we laughed and talked the whole way, planning what we would do in the great life ahead of us. I had loved Bill so much before we were married, I didn't see how it was possible to love a man any more than I did. But on our honeymoon, I found that my love for him grew deeper and stronger every day.

Bill and Betty at nineteen-years-old, 1954

Bill and Betty with first car, 1954 Chevrolet

Chapter Thirteen

Getting Starting

"Bill, where are you going so early?" My sleepy bride turned over, looking tousled and disappointed to see that I was dressed and halfway out the door.

"I'm going out to get a job, Betty. I need to get out there before all the jobs are taken!" With that, I kissed her on the forehead, and headed out the door with absolutely no idea where I was going. On our wedding day, we had exactly fifty dollars in the bank. I thought it might be a good idea to start adding to the collection. I headed down our little lane, and walked toward town, thinking hard about what our future might hold.

A car pulled over and a couple of my buddies leaned out to greet me. "Where you headed, Bill?"

"Job hunting! I'm a married man, you know."

"Yeah, yeah, we know," the driver said. "Hey, they're hiring laborers on that new section of West Virginia turnpike. Ralph Carter is superintendent. He might could give you a job."

"Thanks!" I hollered over my shoulder, starting off at a jog toward Ralph Carter's house. Ralph was just backing his '43 Plymouth out of the driveway when I flagged him down.

"Hey, Ralph, can I catch a ride over to the turnpike? I'm looking for a job."

"Sure, Bill. I know they are looking for six or seven more laborers this week."

Meadows

At the job site, he took me over to meet Greg, the job foreman, who represented the Latrobe Construction Company from Pennsylvania. Greg shook my hand, sized me up and said, "We'll give you a try."

I started that morning, and was proud as a peacock when I arrived home close to dark and told my wife I was a working man.

Next morning as Betty headed for the bus to go to work, I jogged the two and a half miles to the work site. Though it was almost September, it felt like July, and I gave it one hundred percent. If Greg asked for volunteers to stay late and finish something up, I was always the first to my feet. Some of the older guys would shake their heads at me.

"Sonny, you'll burn yourself out! Pace it, kid. Besides, you're making us oldtimers look bad."

I also took a lot of ribbing about the contents of my lunch pail. My loving wife seemed to be of the mind that every inch of space in that pail needed to be filled. Each day, I would open it to a cornucopia of edibles—two or three overstuffed sandwiches wrapped neatly in waxed paper, an apple, a banana, a thermos of coffee, some cookies, and a jar of fruit.

"Whatcha got today, Bill?" the guys would ask me as I laid out the contents. I accepted the good-natured jibes in stride, secretly filled with pleasure over the care my bride took in all that she did.

In a short while, my hard work paid off. I was thrilled when Greg called me aside to give me the news that I was being promoted to carpenter's helper. "You've done real well, Bill. It's time for you to move ahead! You go out and get yourself a nice hammer, and be ready to learn something new. This is a good opportunity for you."

That afternoon, I couldn't wait to tell Betty my news. When she arrived home from work, I immediately told her we were going to go into town to celebrate.

"What is it, Bill? What's happened?"

"C'mon. Let's get dad to drive us in to Beckley. I'll tell you on the way."

Betty and I sat hand-in-hand as we rode in my dad's car. Her face lit up as I related the conversation I had had with Greg.

"It's union work, Betty," I said. "Do you know what that means? I could be making five, maybe six dollars an hour! Can you imagine?"

"I'm so proud of you, Bill! I knew you would do good with whatever you tried!"

"Thanks, honey. Now all I have to do is buy a hammer."

"Don't you have a hammer?"

"Not a good one. Just that old one I borrowed from Dad."

Nearly Perfect

"A hammer is a hammer, isn't it? What difference does it make?"

"It makes a difference to me. I want a good tool to do a good job."

Betty was quiet as I began earnestly examining the hammers at the corner hardware store, feeling their weight and grip, and taking a few practice swings here and there.

"How about this one?" Betty suggested. "It's only three dollars."

"Betty, I'm not interested in the cheapest one. I want to get a good one," I said. I picked out a handsome model with a deep cherry-colored handle and smooth steel head. "Something like this."

"Bill! That's six dollars! I'll have to work a half a day to pay for that!"

"I know. But I'll only have to use it for two or three hours and it will have paid for itself!"

Betty looked doubtful as I laid the hammer on the counter and carefully counted out the money to pay for it.

As we left the store, Betty turned toward our home.

"Wait, honey," I said. "How about our little celebration?"

"What did you have in mind, Mr. Moneybags? Caviar and champagne?"

I kissed the little worried frown knitting Betty's brow together. "No, honey. I was hoping you might squeeze a nickel out of that little pocketbook of yours and treat me to a Coke at the tavern."

Betty changed course. "I'll go to the tavern," she called over her shoulder, "but it's your treat!"

By then, it was October and the weather had cooled considerably. I began to consider the winter months, and what I might do to earn money while work on the turnpike shut down. Betty's salary would certainly tide us over. We lived frugally, and saved whatever we could. We ate many meals with our parents, or ate bologna or peanut butter sandwiches. Our childhoods had been filled with stories about families who had bought things on credit and lived to regret it when the Depression came. Our parents had avoided that pitfall and encouraged us to buy only what we could pay for. We began to save for a car, resisting the urge to finance one as so many of our friends were doing.

Our first snow came shortly after Thanksgiving. Ralph gave us the word that the project was officially on hold until spring. I was a little glum, but I knew I would figure out something or another.

That night, Betty and I lay snuggled up in bed talking about our options. Every so often, Betty would interject, "This house is freezing." I was cold, too. It seemed as if we had spent an awful lot of our young lives huddled around coal stoves for warmth.

Meadows

The next morning, Betty began her weekly housecleaning, which she attacked every Saturday morning, just as her mother had. Floors were scrubbed, rugs were swept, and lemon furniture cream brought a shine to our old hand-me-down pieces. Betty moved through the place like a whirlwind, but even her activity couldn't seem to keep her warm. She wore heavy socks and gloves, and periodically went and hovered by the stove.

"Tell you what, Betty. I'm going to build you the biggest, warmest fire! This place will be toasty and you can sit and read in comfort without having to be right on top of the stove."

Betty smiled. "That would be great, Bill. I don't mean to complain."

As Betty completed her housework, I stoked the fire 'til I had some nice golden flames. Though it was designed primarily for coal, I thought a little kindling wood might help things along. Sure enough, within half an hour or so, the temperature began to rise pleasantly. Betty dropped onto the sofa with a satisfied sigh.

"This is great, Bill! Come sit beside me for a minute."

I joined Betty, and felt the chill melt right out of my bones as the room warmed.

Betty reached down and pulled off her heavy woolen socks and wiggled her toes a little. "Ah ... luxury!" she said dreamily.

I pulled her feet onto my lap and began rubbing them. "This is nearly perfect." After a while, I said, "I'm going to run down and see my mother, all right, honey?"

Betty gave me a big hug. "Thanks for the wonderful fire, Bill. You go on. Say hello for me."

As I stood in my parents' living room, chatting with my father, I was startled by an urgent pounding on the door.

"Fire!" came the cry as my dad threw open the door. "It's Billy's house!"

We threw on our coats and headed into the icy day. A thin curl of smoke was just barely visible across the tree tops, but I knew. My heart was in my throat as I thought of the big fire Betty had been so grateful for.

We arrived just in time to see two men dragging out the cedar chest, piled up with Christmas gifts Betty had wrapped in the evenings after work. A few piles of clothes lay about the yard amid the clusters of onlookers. I found Betty and ran to her, too late to do anything but watch those flames take down our first home and everything left inside.

We stood there, her barefoot, in the snow, our arms around each other and tears streaming down our faces. A fire truck had been summoned by a man

Nearly Perfect

who had caught sight of the flames all the way over at the tavern. I watched the glaring red light splashing across Betty's sorrowful face. I was completely helpless. Tightening my grip around her, I could only say, "It'll be all right." I wondered how in the world anything could ever be all right again.

My buddy, Ernie, pulled up in his car. "Get in," he said, motioning. We climbed into the back seat, numb with emotion. I looked at Betty's feet, realizing for the first time that they were bare. I tried to warm them by rubbing them.

"I'm all right," she said. "Let's ride over to my parents' house, OK?"

I agreed, wordlessly. By the time we arrived, the Lewises had received word of the fire and were putting on their coats to head out.

"Oh my God, Betty! Billy! Are you kids OK?" Betty's mother was openly crying, while her father stood rubbing his hands together helplessly.

We stood there shivering in the snow. The Lewises pulled us inside, wrapping us in blankets and bringing us hot tea. That night, Betty's parents gave us their room to sleep in and they bunked with Mary Lou and Bob. We lay side by side, in shock, I guess, not speaking, not moving, just shivering involuntarily from time to time.

Then, just when I figured Betty had drifted off, she moved close to me. "It'll be all right," she whispered. "We'll get it all figured out."

I wrapped my arms around her, relieved, and bursting with love for that amazing girl.

We celebrated Christmas and New Years, splitting our time between our two families, enjoying the festivities while pushing down the pangs of doubt about our future livelihoods. On January second, I returned to my hunt for work. I was not very optimistic. I had met with a lot of resistance before due to the draft, and it was no better that day. I sat miserably on a bench, thinking what a millstone I was around Betty's neck. She had promised I would never regret marrying her—but would *she* regret marrying *me*?

I knew that the Army was not an option. I had a tiny hole in my left eardrum, for which I would automatically be classified 4-F, but relating this information to prospective employers hadn't helped at all. I needed to show it in writing. I began to get an idea.

I broached the subject with Betty one night as we lay talking in bed. "I've really thought about this," I said. "If I volunteer for the draft, I'll go through all the steps, but then, when they get to the physical, they'll find out about my ear. They'll stamp my draft card with a big 4-F and I'll be able to prove that I'm not draftable. That'll get me a job for sure."

Meadows

Betty was not enthusiastic. "Bill, I don't want you to even think about volunteering. I couldn't bear it!"

"I won't be drafted," I assured her, chuckling. "I promise. They won't want me. I figure I could then get a job, save every penny, and then go to a trade school."

"Trade school?"

"Yep. Maybe learn barbering, like Uncle Walton. We could start with one shop, then a whole chain of barbershops. We'll be rich by the time we're thirty years old!"

Betty's eyes sparkled. Like me, she loved to make plans for our life together. "It sounds wonderful, Bill. All except the draft business. If this whole thing blows up in your face, you'll end up in Korea. And I might end up a nineteen-year-old widow."

We lay there without speaking, each lost in our own private thoughts, until I felt her hand twine together with mine. "I'll think about it, honey," she said softly before drifting off to sleep.

After two more weeks of fruitless job searching, I was more despondent than ever. Betty came and sat behind me, rubbing my neck and stroking my hair. "Go ahead and volunteer," she said. "It's a good plan."

I fell asleep that night thinking of a big red sign that said: Bill the Barber. I slept soundly for the first time since the fire.

Next day, when I told Ernie about my plan, he said, "Hey, I've been thinking about going into the Air Force. I'm signing on for four years."

"Well, Stan and I are going into Beckley tomorrow," I said. "Why don't we all go together?"

So, on January 25, 1954, the three of us caught the bus into Beckley to volunteer. Ernie and Stan talked back and forth about the war and what they'd do and learn in the service. I thought only about Betty, Barber College, and the life my wife and I were going to move toward that afternoon when I got my 4-F.

"This is it!" Ernie said as we came to a storefront with a picture of a soldier in combat gear. "After we're done, let's all meet at the back steps."

I stood in line for the U.S. Army recruits to fill out paperwork, and then go on to the physical exam. The doctor approached each of us as we stood shivering in our skivvies. When it was my turn, I stood silently as the doctor leafed through my papers.

"National Guard, eh?" he said approvingly. "Well, that's good enough for me!"

In a sudden state of panic, I motioned frantically to my ear. "Sir! I have a bad ear! I have a hole in my eardrum!"

"Can you hear me?"

"Yes, sir, but I know I can't pass a physical with this problem!"

"Now, don't you worry, son! I won't say a word about it. Uncle Sam will never need to know you have a little ol' hole in your ear. You're in the Army now, William Meadows!" And he clapped me on the back cheerfully and moved on to the next candidate.

An icy weight settled in my chest and my knees felt weak. Within a few hours, I had been weighed, measured, shorn, and outfitted for a whole new life. I was in the Army, and I didn't know how I would ever tell my wife.

It was dark and close to 7:00 p.m. when I finally got back to Betty's parents' house. My wife met me at the door expectantly, her eyes searching my face for anything to allay her fears. "Bill! I was so worried when I didn't hear from you, and you didn't come home!"

Gently, I took her by the elbow and guided her into her sister's empty bedroom, easing her onto the bed next to me. "It didn't work out, Betty," I said gently. "The doctor didn't even look at my ear. He just signed off on my papers, and I'm in the Army. I leave in the morning for boot camp at Camp Pickett in Virginia." I stopped, and held my breath, waiting for Betty to react. It didn't take long.

"Bill, *no!*" she cried. "You can't leave me. You promised. You said this would never happen!" She was clearly horrified, sure that the worst would happen.

"Betty, I have no choice," I explained as soothingly as I could. "There's no turning back. I know you'll be safe with your parents. Boot camp's only twelve weeks, then we'll be back together. You can go wherever they send me. I know they won't send me to Korea," I said, wondering how in the world I could make her believe that.

Betty dissolved into sobs, and I knew she was feeling an anguish she couldn't describe. I felt it, too. I only hoped things would be better in the morning.

In a while, Betty came to accept my fate. I, however, was a different story. "I *hate* this place!" I whispered to Betty during one of my rare phone calls home.

"Bill Meadows!" she said, mocking horror. "You said *hate*! You never say that word!"

"OK, OK," I said, but I was miserable. "There is nothing good about life in the barracks. Nothing." I missed my beautiful wife, her soft warmth, her

Meadows

kisses, her cooking, everything that had meant home just three short weeks earlier. Before the fire.

"Gilven's going to drive your parents and me up on Saturday," Betty said. "Isn't that great?"

"Great—yeah, if I live that long," I said. "I'm sick as a dog."

"You still have that awful cold?"

"Yeah, and the cough syrup they give me doesn't do anything but taste bad."

"Oh, honey, this is temporary," Betty reassured me. "After boot camp we'll be together again. Meanwhile, maybe you can learn something in the Army you can use when you get out."

It amazed me how the tables had turned since the early days. Back then, she'd been shy and hard to reach, lacking confidence, while I was the bold, happy optimist. But that day, Betty was cheerful, secure, working two jobs, and saving her money—and trying to cheer *me* up.

"I miss you, Bill," she said. "I can't wait 'til the weekend."

"Me, too. I still think we should buy a car."

"Well, we can, I think," Betty said. "We probably have enough money."

"That way, I could come home every weekend."

"Do you have a particular car in mind?" she asked.

"No, but I'll look at the ads. I'm thinking along the lines of a Chevy."

That weekend, when my family arrived, we checked into two little motel rooms. I hugged my wife, then my parents and brother. Then I had Betty in my arms again. "Do you think you could excuse us?" I implored them. "We need some time alone."

It was a wonderful visit, but as most visits like it do, it ended way too soon. On Sunday afternoon, Betty looked at the clock. "Oh no," she fretted softly, "we'll be leaving in three more hours." Shiny tears moistened her eyes.

"It's all right, baby," I said, trying to be strong for her. "Just a few more weeks. Be tough for me, Betty."

Not long after came one of the hardest goodbyes of my life.

Betty wrote to me everyday. Her letters were full of news and good cheer, as well as passion and loneliness. I would inhale her fragrance on each envelope before tearing hungrily into it. Sometimes, there was a can of cookies or a jar of preserves; something everyday that told me I was on her mind. I tried to put my feelings on paper as she had, pouring my heart into the inky scratch marks on paper, hoping that she would know all the love that went into each word.

One morning, as I went about my duties, my drill sergeant handed me an envelope. "Weekend pass, Meadows," he said.

Nearly Perfect

I opened the envelope to find a card with my leave printed on it. I couldn't believe my eyes. I had watched the other fellows receive passes, and immediately make plans for a trip to the city where they would pass the hours with strange girls and liquor. All I could think about was whether it would be faster to take a train or a bus to Crab Orchard.

I boarded a train Friday evening, thinking only of Betty and the expression on her face when she saw me. I had decided to surprise her rather than let her know I was coming, and I was very excited. Many hours later, I tiptoed up the front walk of the Lewis home and let myself in through the open door. It was 2:00 a.m. The steps to the second floor were blessedly quiet that morning, keeping their creaks to themselves. I slipped into Betty's room, shivering slightly in the unheated night air. Eagerly I peeled off my clothes, dropping them in a heap on the floor, and felt my way over to the bed. I slipped in between the covers and felt her long bare leg below the hem of her gown. I reached to her, to pull her close, and planted a wet kiss on the back of her neck.

Suddenly she shot up in the bed and screamed at the top of her lungs. "Betty! Betty! There's something in our bed!" It was Mary Lou! Betty was there in an instant, swinging her pillow wildly in defense of her little sister, who had decided to bunk with her to share the warmth. While I cowered beneath the blanket, Mary Lou had run for the switch on the wall. All of the sudden, light revealed two frightened girls and an embarrassed, naked soldier.

The bedroom door slammed open against the wall as I found myself staring into the determined eyes of Betty's father, who held high a crowbar to battle unseen night demons. We stared at each other for several long moments, then, comprehending, we all began to laugh. Mrs. Lewis and Bobby, who appeared a few seconds later, wore looks of utter confusion that only added to the hilarity.

Sooner after, we were all settled—my wife and I alone together for the second time in two months. We made the best of our time. Within a few minutes, Betty whispered, "I'm so glad we're married." And so was I!

The next morning, I felt we should take a look at cars. Because Betty and I believed in saving money, and had seen the benefits of defying credit from youngsters on up, she had shored up quite a bank account. Between working two jobs, and spending absolutely nothing on herself other than bus fare, lunch money, and basic necessities, she was able to show a two-thousand-dollar balance.

"I know I can make it worth our while," I said to Betty, "if you're sure you agree we should get a car."

"Of course—that's been the plan all along," she said.

That day, we found a top of the line, baby blue Chevy Belair, with a price tag of eighteen hundred dollars. We held our breath and took the plunge. At least, we thought, that would leave us two hundred dollars in the bank. Later on, we drove into Crab Orchard in style!

It was only a few weeks after that that I got my orders. We were going to Fort Dix, New Jersey. At that point, we had six hundred dollars to our name.

"New Jersey!" Betty cried. "Oh, Bill, don't you know what that means? Europe! We're going to be sent to Europe! I've always wanted to go abroad!"

"I don't know about that, Betty," I said, although that's what I had heard as well. "They just told me New Jersey." As a young person, and a newly married man, I felt I loved Betty more than any man had ever loved a woman. The thing I dreaded most was the thought of our being away from each other. That effort had been extremely difficult for me during basic training, and it dwelled on my mind constantly. The thought of a separation came on me like a ton of bricks. I worried that if I were shipped overseas, she would have to stay home, and I'd be on my own, thousands of miles across the ocean.

I had checked with cousins and friends in the service who told me that if you stayed in the states, you could keep your wife with you. So every night, I prayed that I would stay in the states so that Betty could join me after basic training and we could be together. But when I got the orders for Ft. Dix, which I knew to be the shipping out place for European posts, I got a terrible, overwhelming sick feeling inside. I felt that I was on the verge of a nervous breakdown; that I would actually die if I were shipped overseas. It was funny because all of the other guys sent to Ft. Dix were delighted at the prospect of going to Europe.

The Army gave me a week furlough before I was to report to Ft. Dix. I could only think about some private time with my wife, and thought hard about our options. There was really no place around for a married, homeless couple, and I found myself longing for those first few months of married life.

"Camping?" Betty repeated, sounding as though she thought I'd lost my mind. "Why on earth would we go camping?"

"To be together. Alone." My family had camped many times and we had all the fixings for a trip into the woods. "C'mon, Betty. I need to be alone with you."

Perhaps she read it in my eyes, or perhaps her own heart pleaded with her sensible mind to acquiesce. Whatever the case, she relented, and we packed up for our romantic camping getaway, stopping along the way to buy hot dogs, soda, and marshmallows.

It was late afternoon when we arrived in Hinton, and made our way to a spot on the banks of the New River. I set up the tent while Betty gathered a pile of wood so we could cook our hot dogs over a fire. By the time it was dark, we had a roaring fire and could smell the meat as it popped and leaked its juices into the flames. After dinner, she snuggled in close to me, and I enveloped her in my arms. We began to talk about everything we hoped to do in our new life together. Jobs, the move to New Jersey … everything had a place in the tapestry we were weaving. We began to kiss and decided to move inside the tent for the night. It was a romantic night, and we fell asleep in each other's arms, listening to that crackling fire and the night sounds of the country.

I woke with a start. It was very quiet and pitch dark. Something had touched me in the night. Betty's hand reached out and grabbed my wrist, pulling me back down beside her.

"There's something out there," she whispered, making almost no sound at all.

She wasn't telling me anything I didn't know. I felt around for a weapon, but just then felt the thing again. It moved against my feet at the base of the tent. It was as though ice water had suddenly filled my veins. I didn't believe for a minute that I could move, but I knew it was one thing I most assuredly *needed* to do!

Inching forward on my hands and knees, I mustered all the strength that was in me, and flung open the flaps, fists clenched and extended, hollering like a banshee at the unknown intruder. It was irrefutable. My face was only inches away from something huge, dark, and alive. I felt myself recoiling involuntarily as a puff of hot, fetid air streamed toward me. I looked into the terrifying face of an enormous bear; a bear who then lifted its head and bellowed, "*Moooooo!*"

I pulled myself back into the tent, my eyes like silver dollars. "It's a cow," I gulped. "Just a cow." I began to laugh almost hysterically, and hugged Betty who was still stiff as a board. "It's OK, honey," I told her over and over, laughing every time I thought of our big scare. But Betty didn't seem to find it humorous. In fact, we didn't get very far in discussion about the incident, and later that day, as the sun began to set, she looked me in the eye and said, "I think I'd like to go home now, Bill."

When I finally received orders, every other man I knew was sent to Europe—but I was assigned to spend my two years at Ft. Dix, New Jersey. I spent many a night thanking the Creator for that special blessing.

Within two weeks, I had an apartment in Lenore, and my bride with me, which made me exceedingly happy.

Private William Meadows, 1954

Betty waiting for secretarial job at Campbell's Soups

Bill celebrates 20th birthday, Fort Dix, NJ, March 3, 1955

Chapter Fourteen

Adventures in New Jersey

I heard a light tap at the base of the staircase, then my landlady, Jean, called up, "Are you ready, honey? You wouldn't believe the traffic on Monday mornings! You've got a lot to get used to!"

I called down, "I'll be right there!" My nerves were jangled at the thought of applying for a job in that strange place. Our landlady had offered to take me to Camden, New Jersey to apply for a job at Campbell's Soup. The ad called for a clerk typist. My mother had told me that my secretarial course would open doors for me, and she'd been right. But I was still nervous at the prospect of applying for work in what felt like a foreign land. Even the expressions were unfamiliar to me, like "Oh, fer Gawd's sake!" and "Yous guys."

Jean drove me right to the building, gave me directions on how to catch my bus home, and headed off hurriedly for her job. I took a deep breath and went inside.

That evening, I couldn't wait to tell Bill about my new job. I opened a ten-cent can of Campbell's tomato soup, but instead of throwing out the can, I rinsed it out and put a little bouquet in it, and set it on the dinner table.

"Dinner's ready!" I announced.

"Hey, flowers!" Bill said. "Is it a special occasion? What did I miss?"

"You didn't miss a thing," I said, "but your wife now has a new job—at Campbell's' Soup!"

"Congratulations!" Bill said, genuinely pleased. "I'm so proud of you. I guess that explains the elegant vase?"

Meadows

It took me three or four days of telling myself, "that wasn't so bad," and "things will get better," and "nobody likes a job at first" to realize that I simply could not stand my new job. I was in a secretarial pool, which meant that any number of people, using their rough-sounding northern accents, might be snapping out orders at any given time. It was loud, confusing, and totally unacceptable, despite the high four-dollar-an-hour wage.

I confided in Jean on Saturday morning while we sorted laundry.

"Well how's about that?" she said. "Just so happens a job opened yesterday over where I work in Morristown, at RCA. It's for an assistant librarian if that interests you."

"Oh, that sounds so much better than what I'm doing now!" I said, almost breathlessly. "I'm going to resign on Monday, and I'll ride in with you on Tuesday."

"Not so fast, doll. A bird in the hand is worth two in the bush, you know what I mean? Get the second job before you get rid of the first one."

"Thanks for the advice," I said, "but I'm quitting the Campbell's job whether I get another one or not! I can't take another day of it."

As it turned out, the following Tuesday, I started in my new job at the RCA engineering plant. Basically, I was a file clerk, but the environment there was so much more pleasant than at Campbell's and I was learning something new. I applied myself to the job and was rewarded with the prospect of double-time when asked by one of my supervisors to work on Saturday.

"Think of it, Bill! For eight hours on Saturday, I'll make close to fifty dollars!"

Together we sat with a yellow pad, figuring out how much we'd be able to save during our two years in New Jersey. We kept a strict budget for food and entertainment, and looked for any chance to squirrel away a little more into our savings.

Not long afterwards, I saw something in the local paper.

"Bill," I said one evening, "they're hiring down at the drive-in theatre."

"OK," he said. "What does that mean?"

"Why don't we go apply together? We could make some extra money and we would be together—and at the same time, see all the latest movies."

"When are we going to have time for that?"

"In the evenings. And if we worked at the drive-in, we'd be together, and have a good time also."

Bill agreed and that Saturday, we ate popcorn and watched "April Love," starring Pat Boone, in between getting sodas, sweeping and wiping down counters at the snack bar. We had a great time, and it turned out to be a much better way to earn savings—together!

*Bill, Betty, and Fred
at Marshall University*

Six Members of Crab Orchard Family Enrolled in Marshall

Chapter Fifteen

Small Town College, Big City Lights

New Jersey did seem very different to us, and it took some getting used to. But by 1955, we had definitely begun to enjoy some plusses along the way, like that time Betty's mother and dad came up to visit.

"C'mere, Betty. I want you to hear something!" I touched the round dial on the big brown AM radio one more time, trying to get the best reception. "Hurry up, Betty, I don't want you to miss it!"

Betty came out of the kitchen smiling broadly as she dried her hands on her apron. "Bill Haley!" she laughed, and grabbed my hand for a quick dance to the final chorus of "Rock Around the Clock." "Oh, Bill, I can't wait for the weekend! Mother and Daddy will be so surprised when we tell them where we're taking them!"

"They'll be surprised, all right," Bill said. "I just hope it's the right thing to do. I'm not sure they're as big Billy Haley and the Comets fans as you think they are, but I guess we'll know soon enough."

"Well, I didn't exactly say *fans*, did I?" Betty said. "But I do think it will be exciting for them. They haven't traveled much, but everybody's heard of Steel Pier. And everybody's heard of Bill Haley—it'll be terrific!"

And Betty was right.

"What! Steel Pier! What on earth for?"

They'd heard of it. But Betty's usually acquiescent father became very animated at the thought of traveling over to the seashore to see a rock and roll band. "I could see making the effort for Patsy Cline or Loretta Lynn, but I don't know that I want to do this … "

Betty's mother elbowed him while maintaining her smile. "It sounds lovely, dear," she said, "and who knows when we'll have another opportunity?" She aimed her last few words in the direction of Betty's dad.

The next day we piled into our Chevy Belair and made our way to the Atlantic City Boardwalk. Betty and I had gone there several times during our stay in New Jersey, so we knew where to park and how to get around. We'd never spent much money on our own trips, but since it was a special occasion that night, we had worked out what we'd spend on it in advance. We wanted it to be a memorable night for us all, including a nice dinner at a seaside restaurant.

We strolled the boards until Betty's mother looked a little tired, and we took a seat on a bench facing the ocean. "I've never seen the ocean before," Olive said quietly. Betty reached over and touched her mother's hand.

"You should have seen me when we went to Virginia Beach on our honeymoon, Mother! I was scared to death at first."

Betty's father was simple in his approval. "This is good."

And it really was good. We ate like royalty, or so it seemed, then made our way to the Steel Pier in time to hear the opening act. When Bill Haley's group hit the stage, playing their hit tune, "Rock Around the Clock," the crowd was ready to move. It was truly the essence of rock 'n' roll. The very boards beneath our feet seemed to reverberate with the wild new rhythms. No one could stand still, as the music compelled even the most timid feet to begin tapping.

Betty called into my ear just over the sound, "Look at Mother and Daddy."

I felt warmed and happy to see them holding hands and kind of moving to the music. Putting my arms around my bride, I tilted her cheek upward against mine, and pointed to the sky. "Now, that's a beautiful moon!" I proclaimed.

Betty looked at the tiny crescent lying on its back like a sly smile. She turned her head to counter my observation, and her lips ran smack into mine.

"Gotcha!" I smirked with satisfaction.

"Bill Meadows, you don't have to trick me to get a kiss!" she laughed and gave me another sweet kiss to make her point. It was a wonderful night, and I hated for it to end.

The drive home was quiet. Mrs. Lewis quickly fell asleep against Mr. Lewis's shoulder, who quickly fell asleep as well. Betty nestled against me, recapturing the music with a whispery hum.

"Bill?"

"Yes?"

"We're not going to Europe."

"Oh?" I ventured, wondering where she was leading.

"You know, remember how I used to think New Jersey meant we would end up in Europe?"

"Yep, you're right. We're still in New Jersey."

"But not for long, I guess—how much longer do we have?" she asked. "Is it four months to go?"

"Three and a half and counting!" I answered enthusiastically.

"Then what?" Betty asked.

"I guess we'll be headed back home," I said. "Is that what you want?"

"Oh, Bill, I don't care where we end up! I'm just wondering what we're going to do."

"Oh. Well, that's a good question. I've been giving it some thought."

"Really? What do you think you want to do next?"

Those words sent a tiny shiver up my spine. Without glancing in her direction, I knew Betty's eyes were riveted on me, filled with trust and anticipation. Though we hadn't exactly planned our two-year stint in the Army, it had worked out nicely. We were together, we had seen another part of the country, and we had saved a little money besides. But all we had really done was delay the inevitable. I was still a married man, and in a few short months, I would be unemployed again.

I cleared my throat, stalling only for a few short seconds.

"Remember how I talked about becoming a barber, like my uncle? He raised a huge family on barbering money, so it must pay pretty good."

Betty was silent. I nudged her a little and felt her head heavy on my shoulder.

"Betty."

"Oh, sorry, Bill, I can't believe I dozed off! What were you saying?"

"I said 'Wasn't it a wonderful night?' Just think, Betty, we saw Bill Haley and the Comets at the Steel Pier!"

"That's really better than Europe, isn't it?" she murmured before falling back to sleep.

The truth is, I had done plenty of thinking about our future, but I really wasn't coming up with much. I imagined we would be back in Crab Orchard, but then what? I knew I wasn't cut out for mining. I had seen it rob the youth from a young man's face. I had seen the widows and orphans left behind when the mine turned against the miner. I had seen the men left breathlessly disabled by the lung disease that claimed so many. Crab Orchard was a mining town. A one-barber, mining town, I might add. I promised myself that the next day I would get the newspaper and see what kind of jobs were available in the area. Maybe we wouldn't go back to West Virginia after all.

Betty's parents left for home early that Sunday afternoon. They talked excitedly about the things they had seen and done, and thanked us heartily for the outing to the boardwalk. "Betty, you'll probably miss all of this when you come home!" Betty's mother said. "This is a pretty exciting place!"

Betty smiled, and I wondered if she really did want to go back, or if she could be happy any old place.

Later that evening, we sat reading at the kitchen table. My mother usually called on Sunday nights, and I looked forward to hearing her voice, and telling her all about our weekend. When the call finally came, it wasn't from my mother, but Gilven.

"Gilven! Wow!" I said. It was a rare occasion to catch my brother at home—and he never had any interest in visiting on the phone.

"Hey little brother, what's happening?"

"Good! We're doing real good. What about you?"

"You'll never believe it, Billy! I'm a college boy!"

"College? What in the world!" Wild thoughts careened through my mind as I tried to make sense of Gilven's statement. He was certainly smart enough; he had managed to sow wild oats in practically every West Virginia field without ever getting into any serious trouble. But right about the time his luck was ready to run out, he had quit school and joined the Army. My parents had faced his decision with grim determination, my father declaring, "Maybe he'll get himself straightened out," while my mother merely dabbed at her eyes with a hankie. But suddenly that maverick brother of mine was going to college. It didn't make sense.

"It's the GI Bill! Has anyone talked to you about it yet?"

"No, I can't say they have. What does that mean?"

"Well, we're the GI's, and this here GI Bill is President Eisenhower's way of thanking us for serving our country. He's going to send us to college!"

"You didn't finish high school, Gil—how are you gonna ... "

"I know that, but I took my equivalency test already, and I passed. It's like graduating, I reckon, and it means I can go to college."

It was slowly beginning to sink in. Was the rebel of the family really going to be the first one to get a formal education? It hardly seemed possible.

"That's swell, Given. I'm real proud of you."

"I knew you'd be happy," he said, "but I want you to come, too."

"No way! I'm through with school."

"OK, then tell me what you'll be doing six months from now."

I gulped, not knowing how to respond to that one. "I'm working on that, but I sure won't be going back to school. I can tell you that for sure."

When Mother got on the phone, I could tell she was bursting with joy. "Can you believe it, Billy? Your brother's going to college! We are all so proud!"

I related the story to Betty. "In a few weeks, Gilven will start at Marshall College," I said, "down there in Huntington, West Virginia." Gilven, of all people!

Betty placed her hand over mine with a degree of intensity. "Do you want to go, Bill?"

"Well, no, of course not! I may not be too bright, but at least I'm smart enough to know I'm not cut out for college."

But, that was not the end of it. The thought of college—free college—weighed on my mind over the next little while. The guys on the base had begun to talk about it, and several were already making plans for school when their tour of duty was up. When I brought up the subject with Betty, I was surprised at how receptive she was to the idea.

"We're young, Bill. This is the chance of a lifetime. What do you have to lose?"

"I don't know, Betty. School was hard for me. I was so relieved the day I graduated."

"But you *did* graduate! Gilven didn't graduate, and he's ready to give it a try."

The idea moved between us day after day, like some kind of aimless tumbleweed, growing in size and picking up speed along the way. We talked about "if" and before long, we were talking more along the lines of "when." Then, one day, Betty laid a stack of mail in front of me. The top envelope bore the return address of Marshall College.

"What's that?" I asked, nudging it suspiciously.

"I sent for some information and an application for you. Just in case," Betty answered. She had an innocent smile on her face. "We were talking about going home next weekend. Maybe we can make a side trip over to Huntington?"

So that's the way the whole thing started—one day I was dead set against college, and the next thing I knew, I was filling out an application and touring the campus. You can probably guess the rest. Six months after my brother, Gilven, I followed suit.

We left New Jersey armed with a plan—much to my great relief! I had signed up for a double major in Social Studies and Physical Education, in secondary education. It was a dream, really. Never had I imagined being a teacher and a coach! And to top it off, Betty agreed to sign up for a semester for moral support—it wasn't that hard to get her to go to college! She stayed on after the first semester, majoring in Library Science. She'd planned on getting a job after the first semester, but the GI Bill provided us with housing in the married student barracks on the Ohio River flood plain and a one hundred thirty-five dollars per month stipend for our expenses. A flood plain is basically an area that you can count on being flooded two or three times a year. In that area, we had the opportunity to live rent free in a tiny, but neat trailer-like dwelling along with many other students. Together, we had saved nine thousand dollars during our time in New Jersey. So we were getting along just fine. Our entry into undergraduate school would begin in January, 1956.

Bill and Betty graduate from Marshall University

Chapter Sixteen

College Years

Betty has some great recollections of our college years. I enjoyed them, too, of course, but for my wife, I think it just may have been one of the happiest times of her life. I'll let her tell you.

* * *

Although I truly believed I would be happy wherever I went as long as I was with Bill, I was glad for the decision he had come to regarding college. I had confidence in him and in our great future together. I considered the opportunity a true godsend. I pictured myself doing a few years of office work somewhere, followed by motherhood and being a housewife in maybe a small town like Crab Orchard, where our children would walk to the 4H and BYF meetings as Bill and I had.

Though many women were attending college in 1956, it was far more important to have an educated husband. I had always enjoyed school and was looking forward to the business classes I had signed up for, knowing that gathering that knowledge would place me above the secretarial "pool" and into the domain of the private secretary. But when Bill first asked me to join him as a student at Marshall College, I was completely surprised.

"Oh, no, Bill," I said at first, "I mean, I don't know—it never entered my mind!"

"Come on, Betty. You love school," he said, knowing it was true. "And you're a natural. I need your help!"

Needed my help? Well, he hardly needed to say another word. We could take our basic requirements together and study at night. And I could be a college girl—something I had never dared dream of until that moment!

"I would love to go to college with you, Bill! If you think we can afford it," I added.

Bill pulled me to him in a bear hug and kissed me ardently to show his gratitude. But there was no way he could feel as grateful as I did. We were truly blessed!

In a few short weeks, I became accustomed to Bill's study habits.

"Betty, did you read this thing? It doesn't make sense," he would say. Bill was a visual learner—a phenomenon that would take another forty years for educators to study and recognize. But I didn't need any major study to be conducted in order for me to see that my husband viewed the world in a unique way. He could verbalize the most far-fetched concept so that it would materialize before my eyes. His words could draw me in to a picture that moments before had existed only in his mind. But something as verbally conceptual as the poetic rhythm of iambic pentameter remained about as much of a mystery to him as Stonehenge has to the rest of the world. It was in deciphering the concepts that I came in. I would try to think of a way to help him memorize the ideas and concepts, which in time became a part of him.

I loved our college years. Each new thing I learned opened another window, or took me down another pathway, so that my mind was never at rest. I would learn something in psychology, and it would relate to something else I'd learned in another class, such as English Literature. It was as though tiny pieces kept sliding into place, forming a mosaic of all that I knew, leaving spaces for all I had yet to learn. I had chosen the field of Library Science, with a minor in business. The love of books had been imprinted on my being before I had ever realized it, and my life would be greatly influenced by the things I read. I loved coaching Bill along, hoping that some of the pleasure of learning would rub off on him.

We were surrounded by young couples, living and studying exactly as we were. And they, too, were making the most of it. The atmosphere was a little different from what you might see at the average college, where partying and rebelliousness play major lifestyle roles. We were very serious about our education.

"Have some ice tea, Bill," I said, pouring us each a cool glass as we stepped out onto our little wooden stoop. Several other couples had taken a few minutes off to enjoy the day, too.

My cousin, Carl Riffe, threw open his door and shouted to the neighborhood at large, "Anyone for softball? Couple of innings?"

"Sorry, I've got a chemistry test tomorrow," came one reply, followed by similar responses from others.

"How about Friday night, then?" Bill called out.

"Yeah, now, Friday's good," said the chemistry student. Quite a few others chimed in as well.

After only a few moments, everyone disappeared back into their homes, ready to resume the rigors of studying.

I stretched out on the couch, supporting my textbook on my abdomen, while Bill sat with his books spread out on the kitchen table. "Listen to this," I said, and I commenced reading a lengthy passage from the "Introduction to Philosophy" book. When I had finished, I shook my head in wonder. "Can you believe that, Bill? What does that remind you of?"

"Carney's ninth grade biology lectures," he answered.

"Bill!" I laughed, tossing a pillow at him. "Carney was boring! This is so ... so alive. Doesn't it make you think?"

"It makes me hungry. Will you make some popcorn?"

"You're hopeless," I said as I went to the kitchenette to make a snack.

"I saw Gilven today," Bill said, "and guess what he told me."

"What's that?"

"He said Berman and Phyllis and Pammy are moving here—Berman's going to college, too! That'll be you and me, Gilven and Nila, and Berman's family—all together!"

"That's great news! I can't wait to see little Pammy. And Phyllis is great to talk to. Pretty soon your whole family will be here!"

Those words proved prophetic. By the following year, Nola and Fred had come, and we left the barracks and rented an apartment for the four of us. We loved being in such close proximity to family, as we'd known growing up. We spent a lot of our free time on outings together in one combination or another. The brothers loved fishing, of course, on the Ohio River, and we girls would often go along with a hamper of food, packed with cold fried chicken, biscuits, and lemonade. We would spread out our blankets and read, study, or just enjoy each other's company. The river was alive with the sounds of clanking barges passing through the locks, and the locks opening and closing. We could hear the boatmen shouting to each other. Sometimes I thought of Tom and Huck rafting down the Mississippi.

"Betty, how can you study by that noisy river?" Bill would ask. "It's so distracting I can't concentrate."

"I like it!" I said. But I didn't have the words to describe the peacefulness and *fascination I felt from the shimmer of the water, and the squawking gulls, so far from home. I loved the banter of the people, both on the water and on the shores, strolling in couples and groups. It was soothing yet exciting at the same time. And maybe a little distracting, but it sure beat studying at the kitchen table!*

* * *

It was a blissful time, I have to agree, with family all around and very little pressure other than to make the grades. But Betty definitely got into it more than I did. One morning, I watched her packing an old quilt into her bag, along with two books and a thick binder.

"You sure you don't want to come, Bill? I could make us a sandwich for later ... we could work on that biology stuff."

"Naw, you go on. I'll be fine. See ya later!"

I watched her bounce happily out the door, feeling maybe the slightest tinge of envy. The girl was absolutely crazy about college. Me—I just couldn't see it. I was holding my own, but never felt particularly confident. It seemed as though I had to work harder than most people for those A's and B's, and studying brought me little or no pleasure. I didn't doubt that going to college had been a good decision, but why did it have to be such a struggle?

Betty's optimism and joy made me grateful that she was my wife. She buoyed me up through those tough times, giving me the encouragement I needed to keep going. Though she probably would have enjoyed being what they call a "professional student," her consideration for me propelled us in the direction of year round college. This allowed us to get our degrees in much less time than the traditional four years.

As we entered our final semester, we started looking for jobs, sending out resumes and letters of inquiry. We waited patiently for offers to start rolling in. Meanwhile, we got advice and tips from our student advisors. We were both very excited when the first letter came—an offer for Betty to be a teaching assistant at Duke University! The offer included an opportunity for her to pursue her Masters Degree. She read the letter over and over, laughing, and hugging it to her chest.

"Bill, I can't believe it! Can you?"

Well, I definitely could believe it. Betty was so bright and so talented that I could picture her doing anything she set her mind to. I was certain other offers would follow. The next week, however, I got my first response, telling me that there was a glut on Physical Education teaching positions. The county in which Duke University was located could not use me.

"Don't worry about it, baby," I assured my wife. "If you want to go to Duke, that's where we're going. I can do anything. I don't have to be a physical education teacher necessarily. I'm flexible."

"No, Bill! You worked just as hard for your degree as I did for mine. We both deserve good jobs. We'll see what else comes along."

The next few weeks brought more offers for Betty, and more discouraging news for me. My advisor had no encouraging words, either.

"Bill, it's not uncommon for the job market to go in cycles. And it's really tough to predict. Three or four years from now, teachers will probably be scarce again. But I've talked to colleagues all over, and it looks like physical education and sports programs are not being expanded right now. There's just nothing out there."

Meanwhile, my brother, Gilven and his wife, Nila (not to be confused with my sister, whose name is Nola), had graduated and taken teaching jobs in Fairfax County, Virginia. Gilven had always been "fast" and talked to us excitedly about the bustling urban lifestyles in the county of Fairfax, where he lived.

"Come check it out, little brother. This place is incredible! And everybody's hiring. There's plenty of jobs up here."

It sounded like a great place to visit, but it was hard to imagine Betty and me, two country people at heart, adjusting to the rigors of city life. Our chance to visit came soon enough, when Betty was granted an interview for a position in the Fairfax County school system.

"I just don't know, Bill. I guess it won't hurt to talk to them, and, of course, I would love to see Gil and Nila. But it just sounds like such a busy place."

I was inclined to agree with Betty. Aside from Gil and Nila, my mother and dad had moved up to nearby Arlington, Virginia, too, when Robert C. Byrd had been elected to Congress. Dad served as Byrd's office manager for several years. But I also thought about my brother's claim of plentiful work opportunities. As the weeks crept by, I began to doubt very seriously that a teaching job would come through for me. I needed to look in another direction. "Let's check it out, anyway," I suggested. "And you're right, a visit with family would be nice."

We had been in Huntington for three years, so that drive back north in 1959 caught us off guard. The traffic and pace were frantic.

"Gracious! This is as bad as New Jersey!" Betty said as we got close to the nation's capital.

Meadows

But we found our way to the Board of Education Headquarters just fine. It was where Betty was to interview.

"Good luck, baby," I said. "I know you'll knock 'em dead."

Betty wore a neat suit and looked nearly perfect. She squeezed my hand. "I'll look for you out here when I'm done."

It was almost an hour later when Betty reappeared under the portico and waved for me. She wore a big smile and jumped into the car, kissing me gingerly.

"I take it the interview went well?" I ventured.

"I think so. I have a good feeling about this—they said they really wanted me!"

"That's great, Betty. I just knew that would happen. If it looks like something you want to do, I know I can find something up here, too."

"I'm sure you can, Bill. I have a good feeling about that, too."

Later that night, we lay together on Gilven's pull-out davenport, whispering in the darkness.

"It's loud here," Betty said.

"I know. So many cars and trucks," I agreed.

"And you can't really see the stars. It doesn't get that dark here, does it?"

"Gil and Nila seem to think it's just great."

"This isn't the type of town where your kids walk to Sunday night service, is it?"

"No, but Gilven says there are still some real country places a little further west … "

"Did I tell you what they pay up here?"

"How much?"

"Teachers start off at thirty-two hundred dollars a year! That's twelve hundred more than they get back home."

"That's a lot of money."

"A whole lot."

The following Monday, we returned to our academic life, talking occasionally of the trip to northern Virginia. Exams loomed on the horizon, after which college would finally be over (from my perspective). It was hard to believe. I spent many hours deliberating on my future, remembering none too fondly my time as a carpenter's helper, and those weeks as a ditch digger. With my degree, I figured I'd find something decent until the next hiring season for physical education teachers.

The letters arrived ten days after the interview. I brought the mail to the

Nearly Perfect

kitchen table and stared at the envelope for Betty with a Fairfax County School Board return address. Laying it on Betty's side of the table, I whispered a quick prayer. "Lord, if my wife wants that job, please let her have it!"

The one behind it had an identical return address emblem. Except, it was addressed to me. To me? My fingers fumbled over the paper, but then, reluctantly, I laid it aside. This is Betty's big chance, I told myself. This is not about me.

"Hi Bill!" Betty called. "You beat me home today!"

"Come here, Betty. You got some mail," I said.

Betty squealed with excitement when she saw the envelope. "Oh my gosh! It's from Fairfax County!"

"Well, open it, baby! This is exciting."

Betty tore open the envelope and unfolded the letter, murmuring as she read the words, half to herself, half aloud. Finally she slapped the letter on the table with a big smile. "This is it!" she said jubilantly. "They offered me the job! Listen, 'This is to inform you that we are able to meet all your conditions ... ' This is great!"

As usual, Betty's enthusiasm spilled over on to me, and I pulled her onto my lap, enveloping her in a hug. "I'm so proud of you, girl. And they met all your conditions—you must have driven a hard bargain."

"Not so hard. There was really just one thing. Hey, open your letter."

"Oh, OK—I can't imagine what they would have to say to me, though. Maybe they'll put me on their substitute teacher's list."

"Sure, maybe."

I opened the envelope with disinterest, and scanned down the page quickly.

"What does it say?" Betty asked.

I looked up into her dark, gleaming eyes. Her expression was inscrutable but somehow I knew she knew. "They want me to work in a new Physical Education Program. They're going to be opening up the county's first what they call "intermediate school." The construction's not even finished yet." I pushed the letter toward Betty. "They *heard* I was looking for a position in physical education, Betty. How in the world did they 'hear' that? I didn't even apply there!"

Betty had moved over to the refrigerator, and was busily shaking ice cubes into two glasses. I moved in behind her, encircling her waist. Betty brought a bottle of Coca Cola from the refrigerator and held it up gaily. "Let's have a toast, Bill! To our future!"

"Betty? Do you know something about this?"

133

"I may have mentioned your name when I interviewed."

"Am I the 'condition' that was met?"

"Yes," she said brightly, "as a matter of fact, you are. And I don't feel a bit bad about it, either! A year from now, they'll be thanking *me*! They are darned lucky to get you."

I held my bride at arm's length, looking at her with new eyes. She was smart, she was tough, and she was one hundred percent behind me all the way. She had put her own hopes on the line for me, and she'd won.

When we headed off for Fairfax County, Virginia, we had two thousand dollars in savings. We might have had less, but since our parents gave us canned food, and we only went to two movies (a thing we love to do), "Moby Dick" and "Dr. Zhivago," we managed to hold onto a pretty good nest egg to carry with us to the big city.

Start of Bill and Betty's new life in Northern Virginia

Chapter Seventeen

The Life of a Physical Education Teacher and Football Coach

The word *pounding* did not do justice to what my heart was doing that first morning of my new job. I could almost picture the thing throwing itself against my chest wall, hell-bent on putting himself out of his own misery. It was a lot more than pounding.

Betty, on the other hand, seemed cool and composed. She cooked us a nice breakfast in our new little apartment, packed us each a bag lunch, and gave my collar another good pressing when it refused to lay correctly. I tried to do the same, but every two or three seconds, I glanced at the clock.

"I think it's time to leave," Betty said.

"Oh, so it is!" I answered, trying to act nonchalant. I'm not sure if I was fooling anyone. But one way or another, we were both off to our first day of school.

Our destinations were about thirty-five minutes apart. I dropped off Betty at Robert E. Lee in Springfield, Virginia, then took the time on my return drive to work to reflect on our journey to that point.

Having collected few personal belongings during our six years of marriage,

Meadows

Betty and I packed up, rented a U-Haul and headed to northern Virginia. We were excited to meet our new challenges head on; what we thought of as our first "real jobs."

I felt a hard little knot in my stomach whenever I considered the fact that I had secured my position only by Betty's very desirable qualities. I took a page from her book that day and decided that I would never give my superiors any cause to regret hiring me. Besides, I was confident that I could do a good job for them, and I was grateful for the chance.

I reported to Glasgow Intermediate, in Bailey's Cross Roads, Virginia. The school was still under construction. I took a few moments in my car, watching my new co-workers exit their cars and head inside. I was relieved to find that I had dressed similarly, and that most of them carried lunch bags, too. I decided it was time to go in.

"May I help you?" the woman behind the desk asked warmly.

"Uh, yes, it's my first day. Bill Meadows."

The woman looked at me quizzically, then began perusing an official-looking ream of papers. Her eyes followed her painted fingernail down the list of names, as she shook her permed head of locks from side to side.

"I'm sorry—is it *Bell*? I don't see your name here, Bell. Mr. Lloyd is so good about giving me information on new teachers. Let me just go and ask him ... " She wrote down *Bell*. "Now you last name, would that be M-e-d-e-z? Or is it M-e-t-e-z?"

"It's Medez," I said. "M-e-a-d-o-w-s. First name, Bell. B-i-l-l."

"Oh my gracious!" the woman laughed. "Bill Meadows! The new phys ed teacher! I'm sorry! I guess I'm not used to that accent!"

And *that* was my introduction into the wonderful world of teaching.

That first night, Betty and I had plenty to talk about. "People up here are all so busy, Bill!" Betty exclaimed.

"Maybe that's why they talk so fast," I suggested, "they don't have much time."

"The head librarian was very friendly to me," Betty said.

"Everyone was nice to me, but they kindly joked about my accent a little. I guess there was no harm done."

"We're getting a huge shipment of new books in tomorrow!"

"The school is going to be real nice when it's done."

And it went on. After dinner, we decided to walk down to the drugstore for a scoop of ice cream. "Come on," Betty cajoled, "we can use the exercise."

Once outside, though, we looked around in dismay. Our building sat amidst a sea of asphalt and concrete. Although a little concrete path led from the Wilston Apartments down to the main road, to get to the Seven Corners shopping area, one needed to cross a busy four-lane highway.

"Wanna go shopping?" I asked my wife with a wry smile.

"Now you know the answer to that!" she said. "I have about as much chance of making it across that highway as a turtle trying to cross the highway. No thanks!"

It was an odd, almost overwhelming sensation for both of us, having spent so much of our lives in rural areas and small towns to suddenly be surrounded by the city frenzy and its accompanying cacophony. Bright lights and flashing signs came from every direction—even a trash dumpster bore the brightly spray painted letters of someone's name. It was a rude awakening for us.

We followed the sidewalk around the complex, circling several of the buildings and a playground, before returning home.

"We never did get any ice cream," Betty sighed.

"I guess we'll have to make it another night," I said.

Before our first weekend, we were already talking about taking a little trip home. Both of us longed for some other life, down another path, not chosen. However, Gilven and Nila had other plans for us.

"We want to take you guys to a nice restaurant on Saturday night," Gilven declared magnanimously. "Ya know, there are a lot of nice seafood places down along the Potomac—Hogate's, the Flagship."

"That's right," Nila chimed in. "And on Sunday, we thought we'd take you for a ride. Everyone around here does that on Sundays. We can show you some sights."

I looked at Betty and nodded slightly. Maybe that's how they stay sane, I thought. "That sounds nice, Gilven. Maybe we'll wait a week or so before going home."

Betty smiled. "We didn't really see much when we were up here before for the interview. I think I'd like to take a look around."

It was a lovely weekend, and Betty and I hungrily gulped in all the new scenery. Saturday evening along the Potomac River gave us a glimpse of the monuments at twilight, and our after dinner stroll, a chance to see the lights of Virginia, and the airport after dark. They were all quite different than the sights we were used to, but still beautiful in their own way. Our Sunday drive took us a few miles in a westerly direction, where we were immediately drawn to the dark, blue curves along the horizon.

"Bill, look!" Betty pointed eagerly ahead of us.

"Mountains! Just like home." Though we were still forty miles from where the hills actually started, Betty seemed to find comfort in the familiar view. I put my arm around her and squeezed her shoulder. It was going to take a lot of getting used to, but there was a good start.

On Wednesday, when I picked up Betty from work, I had some good news to share. Always a social person, I had been a little intimidated by the sophistication of my co-workers, and wondered if Betty and I would develop some friendships with people who were so different from us. But on that day, one of the other men casually mentioned a get-together at his house after work on Friday. "Just to unwind, you know? And get acquainted with the new people, like you. Nothing fancy—very low-key."

I was very excited about the prospect of actually getting together with some people outside of work. Something about Betty's expression, though, told me that she didn't share in my enthusiasm.

"I thought we might go home, Bill. We didn't go last weekend, and next weekend is homecoming, so we won't be going home then."

"Now, honey, I want to go home as bad as you do, but I think this is important for us. You know, connections are an important part of life, and right now we're not very connected."

Betty was quiet during the rest of the ride, staring out the window in what I mistakenly took for acquiescence. That evening after dinner I turned on the radio, and twirled Betty away from the sink and into my arms. "Let's dance," I whispered in her ear.

We danced on the bare, parquet floor of our tiny living room, melting together as one of our favorite slow songs came on. I was filled with contentment as I held my wife, and thought back over the years since that first attic dance. "I could do this forever," I murmured romantically.

Betty stopped. "Bill, would it be just terrible if I didn't go with you Friday night?"

Jarred out of my romantic state of mind, I had to stop and collect my thoughts. "Go where?" I asked.

"The party, for the teachers," Betty said.

"What do you mean, 'if you didn't go?' What's to keep you from going?"

"I don't want to go, Bill. All those strangers, and me being such a backward hillbilly ... "

"We're *not* hillbillies, Betty," I started to argue, but something in her eyes told me not to force the issue. I held her at arm's length. "It's not so important. We don't have to go."

"No, Bill, I want you to go. I think you should."

I pulled her close again as another song began, but my mind was no longer on the dance.

By Friday, a lot of the teachers were talking about the party, and I wished fervently that Betty would change her mind. But when I picked her up from work that afternoon, nothing had changed.

"You go on," she assured me after dinner. "Don't worry about me."

I felt a distinct twinge of guilt at the thought of going out alone on what was traditionally our date night, but Betty was resolute.

"I brought home three new books this weekend," she said, "and I just want to take a hot bath and do some reading. I haven't read much on my own since school started." With hugs and kisses, she sent me on my way.

John, our host, had a house in Broyhill Park, with a finished basement, complete with wet bar, the newest thing in home entertaining at the time. The lights had been turned down low and guests with drinks and plates of food circulated.

"Bell! Bell Medez!" I turned to see the school secretary, Mrs. Ammons, approaching me with a big smile. "Just teasing, Mr. Meadows," she giggled, giving my arm a squeeze. I smiled, a little bewildered, uncertain of how to behave. John and his wife, Peggy, introduced me to several of my colleagues whom I had not yet met. Everyone was warm and friendly, perhaps feeling the effects of a little alcohol, which I had never experienced.

"Dance with me, Bill!" called Sally Nelson, one of the girls' physical education teachers. She was a little older and a little taller than I was, but obviously loved to cut a rug. We danced several times, jostling into other couples on the tiny dance floor. When we finally stopped to get some refreshments, another member of the faculty named Barbara nabbed me.

"Oh no you don't!" she said. "My husband won't be caught dead on the dance floor. I'd like to at least dance once tonight."

Glancing at my watch, I was astounded to find it was 12:45 a.m. Though Betty and I hadn't discussed a time, I didn't expect to be out so late, and hoped she wasn't worried about me. With quick goodbyes and thank yous, I made a hasty exit, hoping that Betty had gone on to bed and wasn't losing sleep wondering where I'd been.

* * *

I heard the key in the apartment door, but resisted the urge to jump out of bed and throw myself into Bill's arms, begging him never to go off and leave me again. Instead, I lay perfectly still, until Bill eased into the bed beside me. Then I murmured and turned in his direction, "Hi, baby. Did you have a good time?"

Bill whispered, "It was fine, but I thought about you the whole time."

Satisfied, I gave his body a warm hug and drifted off to sleep.

The next morning, Bill and I slept a little later than usual, but when he came to the breakfast table, he was cheerful, and full of news about the party. I could tell he had had a good time, and I felt a little pang of regret that I hadn't gone with him. Still, when Bill came home two weeks later and told me there was another party, I declined again. That time, I was not so apologetic, nor was my husband as he left for it without me.

The following Saturday, Bill and I took our usual trip to the supermarket, and I was quite surprised when two pretty, young women greeted him as they maneuvered their carts through the frozen foods.

"Jean, Natalie, this is my wife, Betty," Bill said. "Betty, Jean and Natalie teach at the school."

The ladies were cordial and mentioned that they hoped to see me at the next party. "Of course, you may have to stand in line to dance with your husband," Natalie laughed, good-naturedly.

I laughed, too, but not especially good-naturedly. I was concerned about what might be happening to the two of us. We were close, and so much in love, and usually so much in agreement, that we had hardly prepared ourselves for the grown-up dilemma of having two completely different--even opposing--ideas.

I thought back over our short marriage. I had been so eager to marry Bill that I had us both convinced that we were ready at the age of eighteen. I knew there would be some things that Bill might miss out on with his single friends, but I made a vow that I would never give him cause to regret marrying me. I knew that he was completely satisfied with married life, and with me as his wife, but I couldn't help wondering if this party situation had potential to cause a problem for us. Then, more than ever before, I found myself thinking of the safe, protected life we had lived back in West Virginia.

The following week, after we had cleared off the dinner dishes and prepared the table for a card game, Bill disappeared and returned with a small paper bag. "Look at this, Betty," he said, handing it to me.

"Sloe Gin? What's that?" I asked unscrewing the lid and inhaling deeply. I pulled back with a grimace. "It smells like cough syrup." I gave it back to Bill.

He smelled it to, and said, "Yep, it's Sloe Gin. Liquor."

"Sakes alive, Bill, where did you get a thing like that?"

"From Charles, the custodian over at the school," he said. "We were getting in our cars at the same time, and he just handed it to me and said, 'Have you ever tried this?' and I said, 'no,' and he said, 'go ahead, take it.'"

"So you brought it home?" I asked.

"Yeah, I thought we could try it together."

Bill and I did not drink, but there he was, smiling expectantly. I thought about the preceding couple of weeks and how scary it was to seem to be pulling in two different directions. "Sure," I agreed, "let's try it."

Then Bill produced another bag which contained ginger ale. "You're supposed to mix it with this," he advised, as he poured the liquids together and added ice cubes. We clinked our glasses together and Bill said, "Down the hatch!" We both laughed and took a sip. It went down cold, but left a little warm patch somewhere in the middle of my chest. It tasted like a spicy cherry soda, and we both agreed it wasn't so bad.

"It's not something I would want to do all the time," I admonished, and Bill readily agreed.

"Of course not! I just though we could see what it was like!"

"Well, now we know."

"Yep, now we know."

"Sloe Gin, huh?"

"Right, because it goes down easy."

"Bill, that's s-l-o-w. This is s-l-o-e ... let's see here ... " I reached for my dictionary and in a few seconds found out that a "sloe" was a fruit, similar to a plum or cherry. Bill was unswayable. "Well, whatever it is, it goes down slow and easy, that's the important thing."

Soon after our introduction to liquor, Bill and I decided to venture into Washington with our close friends, Ron and June Matalorage, for an evening on the town. We dressed up for the first time in weeks and went to Blackie's House of Beef, renowned for its prime rib and fine steaks. When the waitress asked if we would like a drink, Bill ordered Singapore Slings. I nodded my approval. "Pretty fancy stuff, Bill! I've never heard of that!"

And like so many other firsts in our lives, we had our very first cocktail together in a restaurant at the age of twenty-five.

Over dinner, we talked about our life in Virginia with the traffic, and the concrete, and the parties, and the tourists. "Betty," Bill said, "I don't ask you to do things that make you uncomfortable. I have been respectful of you, I believe. But I would like to take you to a party, and dance with you, and show you off to my colleagues, and kiss you right in front of everyone if I feel like it. Maybe you feel like this is an unreasonable request, but I would really like you to consider what it means to me."

Meadows

    I looked at my handsome husband, and I remembered those teachers, Jean and Natalie, whom we'd come across in the grocery store. They'd gone all out on their appearances just to go out for groceries on a Saturday morning. It was then that I made my decision. I don't believe I was jealous, but it was smart thinking that made me tell my husband that I would go to the next party with him. I told him, in fact, that I was looking forward to it.

    A week later, we were off to our first party together, and I took great pains to look my best. I knew I was successful when I came into the living room and my husband said, "Wow!" It was a great night for both of us. I had a Sloe Gin Fizz and felt a little more comfortable talking to people whom I didn't know. Bill, of course, needed nothing but an opportunity, and he was off and running. But he never forgot who his date was. We danced all evening long, and I got a chance to see first hand how the other women reacted to him. I liked the feeling of being the one in the new physical education teacher's arms. There was no place I would rather be, that night or any other.

Bill, teacher and football coach, 1959

Bill, third in front row

Chapter Eighteen

Born to be a Teacher

Backtracking a little, it was about two or three weeks after I had started teaching that I began to realize that I was probably going to be the best teacher in the building. That was because once we got through with the orientation--the paperwork and getting acquainted and all, which was difficult and embarrasing for me back then--I very quickly saw something. When I went into a classroom, and stood at the front of class very quietly, it very quickly came to order. I started with about forty boys in physical education class, and their coming to order and giving their attention so completely made me realize that I was fully in control.

I had done some student teaching during which I was told by the supervisor and the teacher that I certainly had a good career in teaching ahead of me and I was going to be an outstanding teacher.

"How do you deduct that?" I asked the supervisor.

"Well because of your control—you're very demanding, and you're always going to have control of the classroom," he answered.

And I realized after three or four weeks there that the other teachers would come into the teachers' lounge and they'd be talking about "Johnny this and Jack that and Billy this," and how difficult their students were. I can tell you, they were already sweating the disciplinary aspect of it. And I had everything under control, myself. It was something I guess I was born with, to some degree.

But I also realized that having full control and being in charge is instrumental to the practice of being a good teacher. Learning can take place only after the leadership is established. To that extent, I was automatically headed in the right direction with the most difficult part of teaching.

The second thing most important in teaching is that you gain the respect of the class. There again, I gained, within two weeks of total discipline, the students' total respect. The respect goes hand in hand with your feelings for the students—you have to express your genuine appreciation for the guys and gals, and recognize somehow those vibes between you and all the young people in your class.

Incidentally, I use the terms "young people" and "students," but never say the "kids" in my class. The reason for this is that one day, after about two years of teaching, I took a little survey about what students disliked about teachers most. It turned out they did not like to be called kids. As soon as I found that out, I never again called a young person by that term.

I feel that the third important element of teaching involves the teacher's ability to make learning a pleasure. You need to always be having fun when you're learning. If the subject is not fun, or at least somewhat interesting, learning is probably not going to occur. An example of this involves math teachers who are excellent mathematicians, who could be excellent teachers. They know their subject matter very well, but they really have never figured out how to teach their subject in such a way that makes it fun for the students.

Certainly, the physical education part of my teaching provides a good opportunity to make learning fun. Sports can be fun. But when you have large classes, such as those in physical education, and they get converted to health classes, you can find yourself with maybe as many as fifty boys in one class. The health part of physical education is probably the most boring subject that one could ever teach! I realized that going into it. When you're challenged with subject matter like that, you need first of all to accept that you've got a boring subject to present; a health teacher has to face the facts. It was a challenge I believe I was able to meet.

An example of how I tried to overcome this involved a unit study on snakebites. I would explain that you put a tourniquet up above the spot where the snakebite occurred, that you take a sharp instrument and make a little X, then simply suck the wound to get the venom out, and then spit it on the ground. After I explained all that and had their attention, I would say, "And by the way, do you guys know what you do in case you get a snakebite on the butt?"

Usually, everybody got real quiet and then I would say, "Well, that's when you find out who your friends are." And they'd all laugh. Of course this is an old joke. There were always two or three who'd already heard it, but I'd ask them to hold off on answering in front of those who didn't know.

On my way to work during health class days, I would look over the chapter I was teaching before I arrived that day to get me current on the subject matter. I would keep a yellow pad with me—everything in my life centers around yellow pads—and I would list six or seven stories or interesting facts I could bring up that were relevant. I found that halfway through the class, the students were wide-eyed and attentive, anxious not to miss a word that Mr. Meadows (later on, Mr. Great, as I came to be known) had to say.

They'd leave my classroom invigorated, a lot of learning having taken place without their even knowing it. I think of that as the mark of success for a teacher; to make sure learning takes place. But I prefer to leave them with the impression that they didn't have to work during the class.

I used to have parents that would say, "My son says you play all day in health class; do nothing but have fun!"

And I answer them, "I sure work my butt off to be able to make it seem that way."

I spent my share of time in teachers' lounges. Often, some of my colleagues would be discussing, for instance, math class or history class. And they seemed to like to say that seven out of ten students had failed their test. They liked to say how parents complained how tough they were. So I guess we all have different goals and objectives, but I think as far as education is concerned, learning should always be fun if at all possible.

I felt that to a certain extent, the teacher himself (or herself) needed to share the burden of being interesting. Not just the material, but the actual character of the individual. To that end, I decided that my image could use a little tweaking. I wanted to appear as confident as I felt. I worked on becoming a sharp dresser, and carried myself with a no-nonsense gait. I thought about some of the negative concepts that a teenager might have, and gave some thought as to what might be the complete opposite.

"Good. Nice. Fine. Happy. Carefree. Enthusiastic. Optimistic." I tried out various words on Betty. "They all depict some aspect of being positive, but none of them is really great," I sighed. "I need a really great word I can use to help these guys squeeze the best out of everything. Something like 'great.' Yeah, 'great.'" I smiled to myself.

The next day, I used the word great four or five times in each class, then managed to squeeze it in quite a few times during practice. I told them I felt great, let them know a play was great, told them how great winning would feel, and congratulated someone on a great idea. And I actually did feel pretty great!

I took a good deal of ribbing about my affinity for the word great and a few people even began to call me Mr. Great. My newfound optimism seemed to almost be viewed as a challenge to some of my co-workers.

"How was John Carrido in health class today, Bill? Was everything great?"

Despite the good-natured teasing, I had to admit there were a few, like John Carrido and four or five others that made it tough to really love teaching all the time. They were the "bad boys" whose reputations often preceded them by several years as they made their way through the various schools and teachers. I knew things wouldn't truly be great 'til I found a way to reach them, too. But I didn't especially like them, I realized. They were rude and disruptive, they took away from my class time, and they didn't care about the school. I just plain didn't like them. None of the other teachers did, either.

But was it possible, perhaps out of sheer will, to love the unlovable? And what might happen if that were to occur? I remembered Old Man Reed who hated the bus students, and sourpuss Perkowski, who disdained success coming from my direction. Was I guilty of that same sort of favoritism with some of the players and my better students? I hoped not. At any rate, I made up my mind to win at this endeavor, and would go about it as I did any other challenge. I was going to like John Carrido, or die trying!

The next morning, I parked in the staff parking lot, as usual, and as I approached the back door, carrying several heavy boxes, I nearly tripped on John, who sat hunched on the stairs, wearing his usual sullen pout.

"Great!" I exclaimed. "Just the guy I was looking for. Someone told me you know a little something about engines." It was a stab in the dark, but I had seen the grease under his nails, noted his Briggs & Stratton cap, and once seen a car magazine slide out of his desk.

The tiniest of lights sparked in his eyes, but he kept his inflection flat. "Yeah. I might."

"Great! I think I have a little problem. Can you have a look?" The truth was, my car was running nearly perfect, and not very old at all, so I had to think fast. I had stalled out the previous week, and so I asked John about that as I led him to my car.

"When I was at a traffic light last week, she died out on me. What does that mean?"

John popped the hood. "Easy. Just need to adjust the idle a little." He reached into the carburetor and turned a couple of screws, then instructed me to try the engine.

"Great, John. I think that did it! Thanks!" We walked back up to the building together, and I'd almost swear that John seemed a little bit taller.

"Hey, how's a fifteen-year-old kid know so much about cars?"

"I'm sixteen. Got left back in fifth grade. My dad was a mechanic before he died. That was fifth grade, too."

Once inside the school, we headed in different directions, but I called after him, "Thanks, John."

He didn't turn around, but I heard him holler. "No problem, Mr. Great."

That was the beginning, and over the next ten years there were plenty of Johns in my life. My job was to win them over, make them my allies, love them, teach them something, and give them a little confidence to face the big, bad world.

I knew that sports offered a sense of belonging to people who might otherwise fall between the cracks. Most of the players had a nickname of some sort. The names were not cruel or embarrassing, but fun and enjoyable. This gave the guys a sense of camaraderie. Another of our team-building traditions was the giving of the five fingers. I found a competitive streak in almost all the boys I encountered, and noticed them often pitting themselves against each other, even when it wasn't officially part of our practice.

One afternoon, one of the fellows challenged another to see who would complete his lap around the track first. When they'd finished, I asked what the winner got. "Nothing, I guess," the winner laughed.

"When one of us brothers lost at something, we gave him the five fingers," I remember aloud.

"What's that?"

"It hurts! Believe me! One guy smacks the other one right here," I motioned to the tender inner thigh area, "and you have to be able to see a mark from all five fingers, or you do it over."

The next afternoon, as the team began to take their laps, my quarterback called out, "Loser takes five fingers, agreed?" Those boys flew through their laps, but one man finally did come in last. He laughed as one of his teammates kneeled before him like a footstool. Cocking his leg up, he rested his foot on his friend's back, while I made a great production out of readying my five fingers. When I laid my mark on that boy's leg, you could see five fingers *and* a ring! The boy howled and rubbed his leg,

Meadows

while his teammates laughed and hit him on the back. The five fingers caught on from that day forward, so that hardly a week went by that I didn't lay one on someone. For some reason, taking the five fingers was seen as some sort of badge of courage, and the boys took great pride in taking it without flinching.

As that year wore on, I couldn't help but notice that one of my boys didn't really seem to be fitting in or getting any closer to anyone. This was different than the John situation, because this boy didn't make trouble. He just sort of hung back, and didn't seem to mingle. And he was the only boy who still hadn't gotten the five fingers. I wondered if that might help him to fit in, even a little. It was worth a try.

Mark, the name of the boy in question, had a hard time doing pushups, which I often required at practice. He lacked the upper arm strength necessary for the exercise, but usually he gave it his best try. On that particular day, I announced that five fingers went to the boy who quit doing pushups first. Mark grimaced as the team hit the ground, and I watch him shakily raise himself up four times. Five. Six ... and no more.

"OK, Mark!" I announced, "You get the five fingers!" The team began to whoop as Mark put his leg up and took the smack as if it were nothing. Then he raised his arms and bellowed, "*That felt good!*" The entire team roared with laughter.

The following afternoon, I was summoned to the office before practice. Mr. Lloyd greeted me sternly, then he introduced me to another man. "This is Pierre Salinger, Press Secretary to President Kennedy. He is Mark Salinger's father."

"I'll cut right to the chase, Mr. Meadows," Salinger began. "My boy comes home with a handprint across his leg. Says you smacked him. I say 'What for?' but he says he has no idea. I ask him did he do something wrong. Mark says he's pretty sure he didn't. So I guess I don't understand how and why discipline is administered in the Old Dominion. I can only tell you this—if you so much as lay a finger on Mark Salinger, you'll be washed up as a teacher. Do I make myself clear?"

"I believe so, Mr. Salinger. You want Mark to be given preferential treatment."

"I want no such thing! But I certainly don't expect a teacher to haul off and hit him for no reason!"

"Mark is different, Mr. Salinger. He doesn't fit in with the guys, and that makes it hard for him to really be part of a team effort, even though he has great skills. School is almost over for the year, and Mark was the only one who'd never been given the five fingers. I honestly think yesterday was the first day Mark ever felt like one of the gang."

Salinger was quiet. His shoulders sagged noticeably. "I've tried to give him everything. I just want him to be happy."

"Acceptance is something you can't give him, though. Only his own peers can do that. And they did. Yesterday."

A moment later, Mark and two other boys walked by the office, laughing and talking animatedly. But when Mark caught sight of his father, he did a double-take and came back toward us.

"Hey, Dad. What's up? What are you doing here?"

"Nothing in particular. I just wanted to stop by and meet the man who left such a memorable imprint on you. I thought maybe I could learn this five-finger thing."

Mark and his father laughed, and I wondered if that was something they could learn to do together. Sadly, though, I suppose all of us failed Mark somehow. He ended his life some years later when he jumped off the Golden Gate Bridge.

Bill creatively thinking about never before tried football plays

Farmer and Betty's second mode of transportation

Chapter Nineteen

Coaching Football

From my days at Woodrow Wilson High onward, I have always loved the idea of coaching football. Like good business, it mixes good thinking with good strategy and the right ingredients for success. Once I got into the game, I found it must have been a good match for me, because over the ten years I coached, my team lost only a total of three games.

Although I did a lot of coaching as a high school teacher, I got to really spread my wings once our business got off the ground and Betty and I were able to take frequent vacations to the islands. One of the practices I enjoyed was spending time in Puerto Rico just before the start of the football season.

I would go out on Dorado Beach in Puerto Rico early in the morning. I'd pick up a branch and draw a circle with an X through it. That would be my center. From there, I'd draw the right guard, the right tackle, and end, and then go over and do the same on the left, getting the whole offensive line set up. I didn't stop there. Next I set up the defensive line and then all the backs till I got every body on the field. Then I'd go about setting up the plays I had in mind by drawing lines between the players. Maybe I'd have the right halfback dive through the line, but give the fullback the ball and have him dart between the tackle and the end.

I'd play around with it for a while, and around about 7:00 am, I'd have the

Meadows

plays ready that I wanted to try. At just about that time, the kitchen help of the Cerramarra Hotel would be about ready to finish up the graveyard shift. That's when the strategy session turned really fun.

"I'd like to hire some of the fellows from graveyard shift to run some football plays for me on the beach," I told the head man.

The look in his eyes gave me the impression that either his English wasn't good or he thought I was a nut case.

But I clarified my offer. "I'll pay them twenty dollars apiece to do it," I said.

That he understood, and from that point on, I had no shortage of players to test out my plays. I was quarterback, which gave me the opportunity to be in the midst of the action—a more hands-on kind of research. We took the plays slowly at first, and gradually increased them to real speed. In this way, I was able to make the adjustments that might be necessary in spacing, or timing, or even placement.

Back home, that last week before the season, I'd chalk out the plays on the basketball blacktop and have my players run them. This was a good way to get a jump on the other teams. And getting a jump on them was important. It's no secret that I wanted to win. And as I said, we did that most of the time.

I don't think winning came to my teams from making them watch game films or pounding the basics of blocking, tackling, passing and kicking into their heads—although I'm sure that information was important. I think we won, though, because of three practices I followed: 1. I made the players *believe* they could win; 2. I showed them what it *took* to win, and 3. I used creativity.

The last reason is most responsible for our wins. I prepared creatively. In fact, I did this so much so that the opposing teams never knew what in the world we were going to do next. Maybe we would use a double reverse pass, or our unique eleven-man defense. That was a new one to most people. In fact, once, when were playing against a larger school, we used the eleven-man defense. After we sacked their quarterback six times and backed them up sixty yards, our opponents were not only confused, but demoralized as well.

Their coach, who had established himself years before as a star player in a major college, took me aside. "Coach Meadows," he said, "you're wasting my time. This is not traditional defense. This is just not the way football is played."

But I had no reason to defend myself. One of the main secrets to winning in anything is doing something different—the unexpected. Being unconventional is more or less a trademark of mine. I might not have had the most talented, most skilled players on any given year, but one thing I can guarantee

Nearly Perfect

is that the opposition never knew what we were going to do next.

Another example of the creative plays we employed was called "Coach Wants a Touchdown." This is how it worked. The flanker, who was the fastest player, would line up two yards out from the right end. When the ball was snapped, the left end was to run down and break across, taking with him the defensive back. Then, the flanker would sprint straight across to the opening, defended only by a linebacker. No linebacker was ever fast enough to keep up.

The play almost always worked, not only because it could be deceptive, but also because I would not call it unless the flanker could show me on paper that he'd made the reception one hundred times during the week before and after practice—not *during*, but before and after.

Since it was such a sure bet, I didn't use it unless I needed it. Late in the championship game, we had a tie score. All during the game, my quarterback, John Nettles, was saying, "Come on, coach, call the play—Coach Wants a Touchdown." I decided the time had come, and called a time-out. When John jogged over to the sideline, he asked, "Now, Coach?"

"Now," I said. "Coach Wants a Touchdown."

John smiled and ran back to the huddle. Our flanker, Mike Tretick beat the linebacker by a wide margin, and caught John's perfect spiral. He'd made that catch at least seven hundred times before and after practices. His reception resulted in a touchdown and we ended up taking the championship.

I'm sixty-eight years old now, and very successful, but I don't feel like I've actually gone to work in the last forty years. As I've said before, and I'll no doubt say again, I don't undertake anything that isn't in line with what I consider to be exciting and what I believe I can succeed in.

In coaching football, just as in business, it never looked like work to anyone around me, because to me, it just never felt like work.

I ended up leaving coaching and teaching when I was at the pinnacle of my career, still absolutely crazy about what I was doing. Those were some of the best years I can remember.

Chapter Twenty

Finding Home

*I*t was a sweltering Sunday in August, 1959. Our little apartment in the Sleepy Hollow subdivision in Falls Church, Virginia held the heat like an oven.

"They're here," said Betty. "Are you ready to go?"

Fortunately, my brother, Gilven, and his wife, Nila, had a dependable car and knew their way around the area. They often invited us for a Sunday ride, and we accepted gladly. We lived on a shoestring budget, aggressively storing most of our earnings and spending very little on diversions like movies and amusement parks, and certainly not car or home purchases.

But a Sunday ride was free, fun, and cooler than our apartment, not to mention the good company we enjoyed. Sometimes, we would visit a cool shady haven like Glen Carlyn Park in Arlington, or Holmes Run Park, not far from where we lived. More often than not we would head over to a nearby crossroads called Tyson's Corner. There was very little to see there; a meat locker, some mud dunes where people rode their motorcycles and dirt bikes, and several little produce stands scattered about. The latter was our reason for passing that way, looking for just the right watermelon to take out to the country with us. We all plunked and poked, finally agreeing on just the right specimen before we headed out Route 7, toward Winchester.

In those days, it was not uncommon to see roadside picnic tables along the highway, or to see a traveling family pull over and spread a blanket on the edge of a farmer's field, to enjoy lunch packed in a big picnic hamper. We, too, were looking for just the right spot to get out and stretch our legs, and dive into that luscious melon.

Many other people seemed to feel as we did, piling into their cars and heading west to leave the city heat behind. After driving about ten miles, we passed through the little intersection called Sterling, and were immediately attracted to an exhibit to the right of the roadway. Strings of colored flags were strung up like those used at car lots, and a sign read: Own your Own Pool! Turn Right Here!

"Hey, wanna have a look, Gil?" I kidded.

"Sure, why not? One of us is bound to have a pool someday!" he laughed, pulling off to the side of the road. We piled out of the car, and clamored up a slight embankment leading up from Route 7. I was the last one to make the climb, and as I reached the crest, I felt light-headed and faint. I glanced at the slight incline, then looked at my family ahead of me, moving as a group to look at the pools. My heart was racing and my stomach was fluttering. I wondered fleetingly if I were having a heart attack. Except I felt no pain. It was a delightful euphoria, as though I were floating or flying. My feet no longer touched the ground, my eyes no longer focused on the pool display. It was as though I had been utterly transported for a few moments, and when the feeling left me, I was disappointed to be standing on the side of the road in the blistering heat, struggling to hold onto the memory of the experience. My hand was still over my heart, which had restored itself to normal, and I felt that I was smiling from ear to ear. I could just imagine trying to explain it all to Gilven and Nila. But somehow, I knew Betty would understand.

That evening, as we prepared for bed, I told Betty what had happened. The great thing was that I didn't have to start with "You'll never believe this" or, "You'll probably think I'm nuts." I just told her how I had felt, and she nodded her head.

"Betty, I think it might mean something. About those pools—or something. Maybe we're going to get one? Or maybe we're going to be selling them in the future. Something good is going to happen."

She smiled at me and nodded again. "You're probably right. We'll just have to wait and see." Years passed before that day was brought to mind again, but when it happened, I remembered.

Nearly Perfect

Meanwhile, our first summer was drawing to a close, and we would soon be returning to our lives of academia. It had been a leisurely two and a half months, during which time I fished several times a week, either with my brother or my closest friend, Don Eckelhofer. Betty read books, just as she had when we were children, utterly content, whether in an easy chair or a lawn chair, or stretched out in the shade near the water I was fishing. Idyllic as those days had been for us, I had a sense that reading and fishing were not going to be enough for us our second year.

I guess the bottom line was that I almost felt a little guilty about taking it easy during the long summer vacation. It was as if I were bored and maybe a little lazy. I began asking my colleagues for ideas about what to do for summer employment. I was directed to Larry Fones, head of the Fairfax County Summer Recreation Program. Larry informed me that he would indeed have a place for me the following summer as director of the Recreation Department Program at one of the schools.

So, when school ended in the spring of 1960, I was as eager to start my new job as I had been when I first started teaching. I seemed to have a great rapport with young children. Developing the summer program seemed to allow a little more creativity than my regular teaching position. Each day, we had around one hundred children come to the program, where my aides and I worked with them on games, coordination, sportsmanship, crafts, and so on. I enjoyed it thoroughly, and was immensely pleased when Mr. Fones came in one afternoon and asked for a word with me.

"Bill," he said, "I like what you've done here. Your program is the best in the county."

"Thanks, Larry," I said with a smile. "I'm really enjoying it. The children are great."

"The kids are great because the program's great," he responded. "I'd like to bring some visitors in to observe, if you have no objections."

"Sure! Any time, Larry. I'm glad you're happy with my work."

And so, from time to time, Larry would bring in people from other schools, and sometimes even other counties, to show how my recreation center, one of fifty in the county, was run. I was very proud and excited, and found that though I enjoyed the extra money that was generated, I was more motivated by what I had accomplished.

Early in the next school year, Larry approached me about another position for the summer of 1961. "Next summer, I want you to oversee the program structure in one of the districts. You know, train the teachers, visit them, make suggestions, review and critique their weekly plans ... it's perfect for you, and we have the money in the budget. I'll still be here, doing the paperwork, budget stuff, and all. All you'll need to do is what you're already good at!"

I was flattered by his offer, and couldn't wait to share the news with Betty. She smiled proudly, but couldn't resist a word of admonition.

"Just remember, the higher you go in administration, the less contact you will have with the things you actually love—the kids, the ideas, the creativity."

I nodded pensively. I knew Betty was right, but it was not some lofty office job. Larry would do the pencil-pushing, and I would still be doing the things I loved. I accepted the job without reservation.

Larry came to me in April, explaining that we would need to get together soon to work out some of the details for the summer program. He asked me to give some thought to a "curriculum" and be ready to present it to him at a meeting in two weeks. I began working on the details immediately, excited with my ideas and eager to talk them over with Larry.

Our meeting went well as we hashed out ideas, and came up with a plan that gave each program a backbone of structure while leaving plenty of room for individual creativity for those who needed that kind of freedom.

As we concluded our meeting, Larry said, "Bill, I'm shooting for a Saturday training seminar on May 22nd. We'll get all the instructors together, maybe do a box lunch, and go over the program, give out manuals, take questions, and so on. That will still give the teachers three weeks to get set up before we get started. You and I will split up the meeting agenda. Here, I've jotted down my thoughts—we'll talk next week."

I left feeling invigorated and excited, and went home to start right in on preparing my meeting presentation. My audience would be one hundred fifty of my peers, some of which were seasoned veteran teachers, taking instruction from a newcomer like me. I knew it better be good.

Looking down at Larry's agenda, I learned he had me set to speak from 10:00 am 'til noon, about various aspects of the sports program. That was my forte! I would be right in my element. I grabbed a yellow pad and began to jot down ideas in response to each of the topics Larry had listed. The fifth item on the list was tournaments, and underneath it was written, "elimination rounds, play-offs, round robins, ceding, etc."

I grimaced, and fought back a sour taste in my mouth. Like the high school graduate who manages to hide the fact that he cannot read, I was the only person who knew I could not explain these concepts to a group of teachers—because I did not understand them myself.

As a physical education major, I had learned the major muscle groups, gross anatomy and bone structure, the rules and strategies of every major sport, as well as the ones like rugby and soccer, which had not yet gained popularity. I taught health and driver's education, and was able to explain the physical and chemical changes that changed adolescents into men and women, as well as recite every speed limit and following distance in the driving manual. But I could not understand the logistics of tournaments.

I became very quiet and moody for several days, until Betty finally coaxed me into telling her my dilemma. Ever the optimist, she suggested bringing home some library books so we could try to figure it out together. We studied the information we could find, and Betty asked me if I thought it was helpful. I didn't want to disappoint her, so I told her I felt much better. But as I read and re-read pages, the words blurred and I simply took in none of it.

With a week and a half to go, I fine-tuned my presentation on all the other topics. I considered using up all my time, then glancing at my watch and announcing we had run out of time and wouldn't be able to cover the tournament section. Twice, I dreamed about the actual seminar. In the first dream, every time I said anything, someone would stand up and say I was wrong, or even "I object!" In the second, everything went well, but the audience laughed uproariously from start to finish, and when I left the stage, I caught a glimpse of myself in the mirror—I was buck naked! A throw back, no doubt, from my time as basketball team manager, when the leaking battery acid nearly did strip me to the buff.

As that week flew past, I lost my appetite, and began to lose sleep over the whole thing. Occasionally, I would open the notes I had made, but my mental block had grown insurmountable by then. When May 22 arrived, I knew I was going to made a complete fool of myself.

The program started as scheduled, at 8:00 a.m., with a break set up before my presentation at 10:00 a.m. My stomach felt as though lava were flowing through it and when that break came, I walked straight down the hall and let myself out the side door of the school. And I kept right on walking.

I found myself at a nearby McDonalds, and ordered a hamburger, French fries, and Coke, without any realization of what I was doing. I sat by the window and ate slowly and deliberately, watching the morning traffic move by. When I had finished, I returned to the counter, and placed the same order again, as though in a hypnotic trance. I returned to the counter several more times over those two hours, sometimes getting only a Coke, sometimes only French fries. My mind was a complete blank.

When the nearby firehouse blew its noon whistle, I seemed to come to and realized where I was and what I had done. The gravity of the situation caused my heart to lurch. I had left one hundred and fifty colleagues hanging. I had made Larry Fones look ridiculous for the confidence he had placed in me. I had ruined my standing as a teacher or summer recreation director. I had eaten four hamburgers, five orders of fries, and swilled down who knows how many Cokes, in an effort to relieve the horrible burden I had been running from. Why hadn't I told Larry in the first place that I couldn't do that part of the talk? It would have been so much better to just face the music than have to face the consequences of my odd behavior.

But I knew what I had to do. I made my way back to school, with face composed, and head held high. On the way in, I joined those returning from the hour lunch break, nodding and greeting like I was any other attendee. In other words, I acted as though nothing had happened, and took my place in the audience as the 1:00 session began.

When the seminar ended at 3:00, I went up to the stage and began to help disassemble the equipment with Larry, not having any idea what I could say. Larry looked at me, his expression one of confusion.

He shook his head slowly, and said, "I don't understand what happened, Bill. Tell me what happened." His voice was not angry or harsh, which is what I had expected and deserved. For a moment, I didn't trust myself to speak.

"Larry, I don't know what happened. I was ready to do my talk, but I couldn't nail down the part on tournaments, and rather than tell you that, I kept working at it, trying to get it. But I got so discouraged that when it was time for me to speak, I just walked out. I can't believe I did this."

"Neither can I," Larry said evenly. "I had no idea what to tell the audience."

"I just blew it," I said. "I am so sorry. There is absolutely no reason why you should give me another chance. I realize that. Losing the position would be a reasonable outcome for my actions. But I want that job. I know I can do a bang up job. I won't let you down, Larry. I promise, you will never regret it if you let me do this, even after what happened today."

Larry looked at me, and nodded somberly. "OK, Bill. I know you're the right man for the job. We'll put today behind us, and move on. Deal?" He extended his right hand, as did I. We never mentioned it again, but from that day on, I always gave Larry Fones one hundred and *ten* percent. He was a worthy man.

Larry supervised over one hundred people, yet, even in the face of that disastrous presentation, he was able to see me as an individual and recognize my strengths. His reaction to my shortfall that day taught me a lesson I have always remembered. These days, I try to imitate his willingness to accept and work along with people's weaknesses when handling my six to seven hundred employees. I try to integrate compassion, patience, understanding, and forgiveness in my management style as Larry Fones did then.

There are always consequences for our actions, but I am grateful that there is also forgiveness.

That summer went terrific, as I had hoped, and I was invited to do it again. But that was something I had to give some thought to.

Betty holding Cindy, Jay, and Farmer

Farmer and Jay, 1962

The boy who would be president sets up

Chapter Twenty-One

The Boy Who Would Be President

Betty and I had exchanged some ideas about expanding the Meadows family. One spring day, as we walked in the neighborhood, some beautiful babies caught Betty's eye.

* * *

"Oh, look, Bill! Twins!" I looked happily into the baby carriage we passed, as the mother stood aside, beaming.

"Well aren't they adorable!" my husband agreed, while gently leading me back to our original path.

We walked on in a comfortable silence, but I wanted to talk to Bill about starting a family. It was not a new topic, nor were we at odds over it. Starting a family played an important part in our master plan. But first we had dealt with the Army, then college, and next the beginning of our teaching careers. But after that, in 1960, I felt that the time was right.

"I can't wait to have a baby!" I began with great enthusiasm, utterly prepared for my husband to tether me back to reality with the plan. His response surprised me.

"You and me both, honey. The sooner the better!"

"You mean it, Bill? No more waiting?"

"I do mean it! We're as ready as we'll ever be, and we better get busy if we want to have more than one. We don't want to be raising babies when we're in our thirties!"

From that point on, we spoke often of our family and "the baby," but for all our good intentions, and a darn good idea of where babies come from, we weren't able to think or speak our baby into existence. It just wasn't happening. Discouraged, I had a checkup, and was given the optimistic pronouncement that there was no reason I could not conceive.

"Maybe it's me," Bill suggested somberly when I relayed the doctor's findings. "I guess I better be checked out, too."

"Give it time," his doctor advised. "And lay off the hot showers and the jockey shorts. Your count for live sperm is a little on the low side, but nothing to be concerned over."

I read about something called artificial insemination, which was being tried in England. "Hey, how about this?" I ventured. "Can you imagine getting a baby that way?"

Bill shook his head in wonder. "No, I definitely cannot imagine that! What a concept!"

Weeks turned into months, and finally more than a year had passed with no pregnancy. Then, one morning in January, I felt a little not right; I wasn't really nauseous, and not exactly dizzy, but something was different. I sat down for a moment, willing myself not to think that thought. Nevertheless, I couldn't resist going to the kitchen calendar and doing some fast figuring. It might just be possible, I thought warily. But time would tell.

My suspicions proved right. Bill and I rejoiced at the thought of impending parenthood. It was a truly happy time for both of us. Though we both loved our careers, I was just as glad not to renew my contract with the county, and try my hand at mothering. The end of the school year in June could not come quickly enough! I began to plan in earnest for the birth of our child.

Bill and I talked about names and philosophies, colleges and anything else that might play a part in the life of our little one currently in production.

When I was alone, I basked, savoring the little butterfly like ripples that the baby gave me from time to time. I relished time spent reading books and eating popsicles—and daydreaming. I couldn't remember a happier time in my life. It was even better than those blissful times studying and talking with friends on the banks of the Ohio. Life was nearly perfect.

We had moved to a little apartment upstairs in the home of a retired couple. We knew that there would be no problem at first, but figured we would *eventually need to find a little bit more space.*

"There'll be a lot of adjustments," I forewarned the father-to-be.

"There'll be some adjustments," Bill said, "but the baby will have to fit into our lifestyle, not the other way around."

I laughed, picturing our child riding off to work to teach physical education along with Bill, or sorting materials in the libraries with me.

"I'm serious, Betty. We have a wonderful life, and I want our baby to be part of it—our families, our business, our trips … If I give up all that great stuff for the baby, what will I have to offer him? And I still want you and me to have our Friday night dates. Alone! That is definitely not going to change!"

I hugged my husband, glad that he felt the same way I did about our upcoming parenthood. I knew we were going to have a great time.

As the summer wore on, I watched my bulging mid-section with great interest. I felt heavy and slow, and sometimes fretful that I seemed to tire easily.

"Now, baby, you just relax, and keep your feet up and try to stay cool," Bill would comfort me. "It's just going to get hotter."

"Oh, by the way, Betty, do you want to go on a picnic with Gilven and Nila on Labor Day? He called while you were out."

"I don't know. I'm not sure."

"It was a pretty open invitation. Either way is fine with me."

"It's not that. I just want to stay kind of close to home. The baby's due right after Labor Day, and it could come early—you just never know!"

"OK, that's fine with me. I'll get a watermelon and we can cook a couple of burgers on the grill—just the two of us."

"Thanks for being so understanding, Bill," I said, truly grateful.

"That's my job!" Bill said cheerfully.

Well, we never had our cozy little cookout. Instead, we welcomed our beautiful baby boy into the world that weekend. Baby William Jay Meadows was perfect in every way, as far as we could see. But what we could not see was a tiny heart that wasn't put together quite right.

"We'll care for him like he was our own," the head nurse assured me as we left. These days, the surgery would have been performed immediately. But in 1960, the preferred approach was to let the baby gain a little weight and get stronger. He was to be kept in special care at the hospital until his surgery.

But within only a week of his birth, he lost his struggle for life, and our little one was gone. We were thoroughly devastated. It had taken us two years to conceive. Then, after carrying the baby for nine months, it was an indescribable feeling of near despair to suddenly have no little one to care for and give love to. We wondered, in fact, if we were destined to become parents.

"We'll adopt a baby," Bill suggested optimistically. "We'll still have our family—you'll see!"

"Maybe," I responded morosely. I felt fat and empty and despondent, and wasn't quite sure where to go from there.

My mother suggested I go back to work. "Betty, you're used to being a working girl, and you'll feel better when you get back into it."

"But I quit my job, Mother. What can I do now?"

She was quick to remind me that I had plenty of work experience, not to mention a full course at secretarial school, topped off with a college degree. "What can't you do now?"

Though my heart was leaden in my chest, I made a quick job search and took a position as a typist for a construction company. To the untrained eye, things had returned to normal, but I still glanced wistfully at every passing baby carriage.

I wanted to be a mother, and sometimes thought about that tickly flutter in my belly that had brought me so many smiles the summer before. I longed for that sensation, even to the point of imagining I could feel it again. I placed my hand lightly on my abdomen, then sat forward with a start. I felt that flutter again, I was certain!

Once again, I went to the calendar, thinking, figuring—wondering how much time had slipped by since our baby, whom we had named William, had been born. There we were at the end of June and I had not marked my period or made any other notations for that matter. It was as though I had been in a state of suspended animation since September. I began to speculate whether or not I could actually be pregnant again.

"Wouldn't that be something?" Bill laughed, when I told him what I was thinking. "I hardly think you could try to make a baby for as long as we did, then get pregnant twice in two years!"

"But it's impossible," I insisted.

"Well, go and find out. Maybe you are!"

Two weeks later, I waited for Bill to get home, hardly able to contain myself. "I'm pregnant," I gushed, "It's official! Three months!"

"Oh my heart, Betty! Only six months to go!" And once again, we went on baby-watch, expecting our new one around New Year's.

On January 9, 1961, we became parents once again. Bill and I looked at our little boy, then looked at each other in disbelief. "It's him!" I whispered. I had always remembered how baby William had looked when I first held him in my arms. He looked just like the soft, little bundle that I held close just then.

"He looks just like William!" Bill agreed. *"He's beautiful!"*
"But he's not William," I reminded myself.
"I know that, too, Betty, but I always wanted my son to carry my name."
We took turns passing our little boy back and forth, and eventually came up with the name Jay William.
"Perfect!" I whispered in my little boy's ear.
"Perfect," my husband agreed, wrapping his strong arms around us both.

* * *

That little fellow looked just like me! Betty seemed to think he resembled her somewhat, and I would go along, but in reality, I knew he was my spittin' image. It was a wonderful thing, the fatherhood adventure. I remember bringing little Jay home from the hospital, and not being exactly sure what to do next, but somehow, miraculously, Betty seemed to know, although she had had no more experience than I had.

"We're going to have to move," Betty announced with authority one day. "This apartment is not going to work for three of us."

I appraised my bride carefully. It was the very same woman who, a few short years before, had been content to set up housekeeping in a bungalow without heat or running water. My, how things had changed!

"You're absolutely right, baby," I quickly agreed. "I'll pick up a paper and we can start looking for another place. I'll put the word out at school, too."

Betty spent the next several days circling ads in the paper and making phone calls, and by Saturday, she had lined up several places for us to look at. One looked especially interesting to us. Dr. Julius Parmelee, a local widower of some prominence, was looking for some companionship in his big empty house. Years before he had founded the Arlington Savings & Loan, and had always lived in style. At that point in his life, he was a lonely old gentleman, short and round, with a pleasant twinkle in his eye. He had a housekeeper, and a gardener who doubled as a chauffeur, but he ate his dinners alone.

When we arrived at Dr. Parmelee's house, there were six other couples ahead of us. We were the only ones with a baby.

"He's never going to go for the baby," Betty predicted.

"Probably not. On the other hand, he may enjoy it. All we can do is try."

No one was more amazed than we were when we were offered the position. It seemed that Dr. Parmelee had always wanted children of his own, and was delighted to have our whole family move in. In return for our almost luxurious

Meadows

lodging in a private apartment there in his house, Betty would cook a nice family dinner each evening and we would all sit down to eat together. Dr. Parmelee gave Betty one of his cars so she was able to go grocery shopping or run errands. It was the first time we had ever had two cars. We were paid a modest income, as well, of about two hundred dollars a month, which suited us just fine, as Dr. Parmelee paid for all groceries. We had very few expenses to contend with.

Suddenly, we were learning how the privileged few lived, enjoying things that had only been real in magazines and movies, such as fine china and silver, a luxury Lincoln Town Car, the best cuts of meat, and the services of a maid and a gardner.

"I could get used to this!" Betty grinned.

"You go right ahead and get used to it, Mrs. Meadows. Consider this a preview of our future together. We won't always be living in apartments or as caretakers in someone else's house. This is a pale shadow of what I intend to give you someday!" I meant it with all my heart. I dearly loved seeing my wife and young son in those nice surroundings. I was willing to work to provide that much and more. But for time being, Julius Parmelee's home served as an appetizer to our many rich courses to come.

It seemed like we had just gotten used to the soft deep carpeting, when it was symbolically pulled out from under us. Julius had a severe heart attack, and he struggled for his life for the following two weeks. We visited him often, and he almost begged for our assurance that we would be there for him when he was released.

Betty, visibly moved by the old man's affection, squeezed his hand with assurance. "Of course we'll be there! I would not dream of letting someone else look after you, Dr. Parmelee. And you'll be home before you know it!"

A few days later, the dear man was discharged. He returned to his home looking small and frail. "They say I have to lose a few pounds, Betty," he said. "No more of those great mashed potatoes of yours for me!"

Betty spent many hours each day with Dr. Parmelee, getting things for him, writing letters for him, and generally doing everything she could to make him comfortable and give him encouragement. Yet, several days later, when she returned after making some refreshments, she found that he had passed away. He had suffered another and final heart attack.

Dr. Parmelee left his entire estate to charity. He had also provided that his housekeeper and chauffeur continue living on the grounds for a period of one year after his death. Betty and I had contracted to be caretakers for one year, and the executor of his will granted us permission as well to continue living there for a year. However, before long, Betty began to feel a little antsy.

"When Dr. Parmelee was here, I was running around for him, visiting with him. But now, there's just not much to do."

"There's still the baby," I suggested.

Betty smiled. "You know I love being with Jay. He's such a good baby that he really doesn't demand much at all. I read to him, and take him for walks, play with him, but really that's about it. You know how quiet he is—acts like he's got a lot on his little mind!"

"Betty," I asked, "are you thinking of going back to work?"

Betty looked almost guilty. "Well, the thought had entered my mind, but of course, I couldn't leave Jay."

We left the idea alone for awhile, but my thoughts were churning. For years, my father had been office manager for Senator Byrd. My parents had spent many years in northern Virginia and were used to the demanding metropolitan pace kept by those in the Washington political circles. We had enjoyed their company while they were in our area, but they had returned to West Virginia before Jay was born. They swore they were ready to return to the quiet life they had once known, but I was willing to challenge that resolve.

During one of our regular Sunday afternoon phone calls, I said casually, "Mother, do you ever think of coming back up here?"

"Lands, no, Billy! That place is too crazy for me!"

"I know just what you mean, Mother. I was just asking. You know, Betty hasn't come right out and said it, but I think she wants to go back to work."

"Work? I would think taking care of a baby is work enough! And who would watch him if she went to work?"

"Oh, we'd find someone, I'm sure. Babysitters are a dime a dozen!"

"No, indeed, Bill Meadows! I'll take care of him myself before I let some stranger watch my grandson!"

"You will? You mean it?"

"Will I what?"

"Take care of the baby? That would solve everything."

There was a telling silence on the other end, then very softly, "I'll talk to your Daddy about it."

It wasn't long before Mother and Dad joined us in the six-bedroom Parmelee home. They looked after Jay while Betty returned to work for the county.

It was a wonderful year for us. Our little boy was strong and healthy, and by all standards, what they call a good baby, not given to wild, inconsolable fits like some of the babies we had seen. It was a joy to have my parents there, as well. My wife and my mother got along well, and Betty was always full of appreciation for what my mother did for us.

At the end of our year in Dr. Parmelee's home, we moved into a townhouse in a development called Tyler Gardens in Falls Church. My parents also moved there. It was at that time that Betty and I had more good news—we were expecting another baby!

It was a joyful day on August 6, 1962, just nineteen months after Jay had been born, to welcome our precious baby girl, Cindy. Betty and I shared the conviction then that we did, in fact, lead a charmed life. A son and a daughter, loving parents, good jobs, and a blossoming side business (which I'll tell you about next), gave us a life bounteously full of joy and blessings—nearly perfect.

Betty would look down at the babies sleeping, and then give me a big kiss. That had to be one of the finest things about being parents; the way we felt about each other had only gotten better. We had not suffered some of the stress and strain that we had seen others undergo when entering parenthood, probably due to a number of factors working to our benefit. Though we were working our regular jobs as well as starting our own business, we had my parents and other family members in close proximity. Their help was immeasurable.

We had also taken the time to create our own philosophy of child rearing before we had the babies. That eliminated a lot of the squabbling that new parents inevitably experience as they feel their way along in the dark. And, above all, the babies were so good! Jay was an especially tough little guy who slept well, didn't cry much, and was never sick. We could set him down on the beach with a bucket and shovel, and two hours later, he would still be there, filling the bucket or happily digging in the sand.

One of our young sisters-in-law asked Betty one day if he was all right. "He's just so quiet, Betty," she explained quickly.

"Can you believe that?" Betty asked me, brimming with indignation. "I told her he was quiet because he was thinking!"

I laughed at the lovely, protective streak in my wife. It was a wonderful quality, and I didn't want to tell her that it probably would not be needed much in Jay's life. I had a feeling that that boy was very much able to take care of himself.

Later, at family get-togethers, my brother, Gilven, would tease Jay, calling him, "The Judge," because of his serious, thoughtful nature. That delighted the older cousins BJ and Pam, who would sing out "Here come da judge, Here come da judge!" mimicking the Laugh-In catch phrase of the time. Jay, of course, took it in stride, either ignoring the razzing altogether, or offering up one of his serene grins, which somehow spoke of dignity and class, even in a small boy.

The arrivals of Jay and Cindy marked a measure of happiness greater and deeper than either Betty or I had ever known. And it was right around then that other doors were opening for us—this time in the business world.

A typical Meadow's family roadside stand, 1962

Chapter Twenty-Two

A Little Idea Starts Growing

"Hey, Bill," my teacher friend, Ron Matalavage, said to me one day, "are you planning to do the recreation center program again this summer?"

"Yep, I'm planning on it. It's worked out pretty good for us."

"Yeah, but don't you ever want to do something different? Work as a carpenter maybe? A mechanic? You know, something different than just the same old thing."

"Those are different all right!" I laughed. "But none of them really grab me."

Ron and I commonly bounced ideas off each other at lunch. We had developed notions of independent business ventures and enjoyed pooling our thoughts. Ron's incentive was a little more money. It was really just that simple.

"You know, Bill, teachers make only so much. That's how it's set up. There will never be that much of a pay differential between the best teacher and the lousiest teacher. Heck, even if you became a principal, there's a cap as to how much they'll ever pay you. Where's the incentive?"

Ron's words hit home. I would always make less than old Mr. Parker, who allegedly taught the most boring algebra class in the history of the county. But he had been there forever, so he would always be ahead of me, making more than me. No matter how hard I worked at making my classes interesting and valuable to my students--that was the dictate of the system.

I thought of becoming a principal, working on my masters degree at night through American University so that I would have the proper credentials when the time was right. It would mean considerably more income, but I would still be mired in the public school bureaucracy. That meant following someone else's plans and guidelines, and for all their value, also having to suppress my own natural instincts and creativity.

"I've been thinking," Ron went on, "these public pools are getting popular. One of my student's parents is on the board of that new one down Lee Highway and Graham Road. He says it's a real pain lining up lifeguards, doing the maintenance, getting the chemicals, all that stuff. I could maybe manage the pool for them this summer and handle all that."

"What do you know about managing public pools?"

"I can learn. But more important, what do *they* know? I can offer a valuable service!"

I thought about Ron's idea. A little summer business would be a lot of fun. It would give us something to do, possibly offer a service to the community and create a little income. I loved the summer recreation program, but I felt I was pretty tapped out for new ways to do the same old things.

I thought back to our family's little Central Grocery in the early 1950s. I had always enjoyed working the counter with my brothers on Saturdays and didn't mind the grunt work, like sweeping and mopping and hauling garbage. At the end of a busy day, my dad would carry the till into the back room and count out his money, stuffing it into a worn leather pouch. Then he may say, "It was a good day, boys. Look at the shelves. We sold right much today, and Monday we'll have to restock. If we have what the people need, there's no limit to what we can sell here!"

Then he would reach into the sack of money and hand each of us a bit of cash for our efforts. "Now, mind what you do with that money, fellas. The first portion is always for the Lord." He would reach into the bag again and pull out a fistful of bills, fold them neatly into his shirt pocket, pat it with a smile and say, "This here is for the offering plate tomorrow. The Lord has blessed us again. And this," he would say, flourishing another fistful of bills, "is what your mother and me are saving up. That's called *paying yourself.*"

Then, holding up the pouch, he would grin and say, "and this here will pay our bills and restock our shelves. This business is our investment."

We listened solemnly to his economic lessons, each of us separating out part of our pay to drop in the plate when it passed us on Sunday.

Working at the store was a "people" job. My dad had a knack for that and we did our best to emulate the desirable quality. As I considered the idea of starting my own little business, I thought of the many things my dad had taught me. I also wondered what kind of business I could start.

Maybe I could sell something. But what? I had often worked with the produce back at the store, and knew a fair amount about quality and what people liked. But that was back in the country. There, in the more urban northern Virginia, did people long for tomato sandwiches all winter and spring the way we had back home?

I thought of the pinkish-orange tomatoes at the local Kroger, and how Betty would shake her head disdainfully, saying, "Hot house tomatoes! Forget it," before moving on. Our landlady had been delighted when we offered to make a little tomato patch behind the garage where we lived, and when our crop ripened, she passed them out up and down the street. It seemed that city folks *did* enjoy good tomatoes.

"Betty," I asked one day, "what would you think about a little tomato business in summer?"

"A produce stand?"

"Not exactly. I'm thinking more about selling tomatoes door-to-door."

Betty flinched a little. "You mean like the Kirby vacuum man?"

"Sort of. But not everyone can buy a Kirby vacuum cleaner. But who could resist a basket of freshly picked tomatoes?"

"Hmmm," she replied.

The next morning, I sat down at the breakfast table, and Betty poured me a steaming cup of hot coffee. "Have you talked to Larry yet?"

"About what?"

"About not doing the summer recreation program. It's only right that you give him as much notice as possible."

I grinned up at my bride, and she smiled back. I could not think of a single time when she hadn't given me her support and confidence, no matter what my idea might be. Always the voice of moderation and reason, she somehow managed to channel even the wildest notions into reality, without ever putting a damper on my enthusiasm. We started planning right away.

By the end of May, everything was in place. I had recruited my five best students to help me with the project, all of whom had the clean-cut look and enthusiastic personality to make this thing fly. Most of the local produce stands didn't really get going 'til the middle of July when local crops began being harvested. But I wanted to get going right away, so I asked around and found a place where I could buy vine-ripened tomatoes from the south, right at the beginning of June. I had purchased a fleet of red Radio Flyer wagons, paper bags, one-quart sized baskets, which held about two pounds of tomatoes, and a local map. Betty made copies of various sections of the map, highlighting little paths through the nicest subdivisions, so that each student would have a route to follow.

I loaded up our station wagon with twenty, forty-pound boxes of tomatoes, which cost three dollars apiece, and we were ready to roll. I would drop a boy off with his map, and wagon full of tomatoes and bags, and tell him where and when to meet me, then race back to get the next boy. Once I had all the boys in the field, I would drive around checking on them, re-stocking them with tomatoes or supplies, and offering a quick drink of water from my thermos jug—with separate paper cups, of course! The boys pressed on doggedly, each to make their one-dollar-an-hour wage.

People were very receptive to what we offered. For fifty cents, they had fresh tomatoes delivered to their doors, while helping a teenager earn summer money and stay off the streets. It was a win-win endeavor, and we knew right away we had a winner.

We peddled tomatoes six days a week, resting on Sundays as we had always done. We averaged about one hundred dollars net each day—a far cry from the net twenty-five dollars a day we were paid as teachers. There was definitely potential in my idea!

My confidence soaring, I purchased five more wagons, recruited a few more students, and eventually purchased a used stepvan. By the end of that summer, we had cleared close to eight thousand dollars! It was an *exorbitant* amount of money for three months of work.

During that summer, as delighted as I was with the outcome of my idea, I realized that the door-to-door method of selling was not as satisfying as I had hoped it would be. Despite a few snags here and there, it had all gone smoothly—which was the problem. I had made the thing work so well, I felt I needed a greater challenge. Also, although my idea had been a good one, I was not able to visualize any way to further expound on it.

"Let's see what other produce people are doing," Betty suggested one Saturday night. "We could drive out toward the beach tomorrow and look at some of the stands out that way. It might get us thinking."

Early the next morning, we headed out Route 50 East toward the shore,

Nearly Perfect

figuring on a leisurely day with time to think and talk. We headed down Route 404 toward Delaware, stopping at both Adam's and Elmer's produce stands, two of the most well-known at the time. Both were a hive of activity, with the registers constantly jangling, people re-stocking and customers filling their trunks to capacity with fresh produce to take back home with them.

"This place is a real happening," I said. The atmosphere was electric, and I knew it was something I could enjoy putting my efforts into.

I spotted an older man in overalls, picking through the bins, neatening things up and answering questions. "You wouldn't be Elmer, would you?" I ventured.

"I would," he answered and continued on his way.

Following close behind, I asked, "Would you mind if my wife and I just hang around for awhile and observe? We're very interested in how the produce business operates."

"Suit yourself," Elmer replied. He was neither friendly nor rude. Just a busy man, going about his business. Betty and I shrugged and positioned ourselves on the hood of our car where we could observe the weighing, stocking, checkout, and so on of the business. It was very educational for both of us.

We made several trips over the remainder of our summer, then, once school restarted in the fall, we put our wagons away for the season, and began checking out the fall produce markets.

"Betty," I said, "I *know* we can do this! We've just barely scratched the surface of the tomato market in our area. Everybody loves tomatoes."

Betty smiled. "Well, I don't know about everybody," she said, "but there's sure a lot of potential out there. But how could we ever afford a produce stand?"

It was something to think about. But I'd done a little research.

Driving out Route 50, toward Chantilly one day, I saw a beat-up old pickup truck along the side of the road. A four-by-four piece of plywood was crudely lettered, "Lopes/Corn/Maters FRESH!" The sign had been leaned up against a stake in the ground. A rotund man in bib overalls and a white undershirt worked on his display on the tailgate, as people pulled over. Periodically, he would take off his straw hat and use it to fan himself, though it was still early in the day. There was no doubt in my mind that he had grown the produce himself. I pulled over.

There on his tailgate sat a cantaloupe, cut open to show the juicy orange flesh. Catching me observing him, he urged, "Taste it! I just picked 'er this mornin'!"

The melon was exquisite, and my experience was heightened by my knowledge of the fact that a few short hours before, that melon had been laying in a field somewhere. Farm Fresh. That's what it was. "I'll take three," I said.

That was the way a lot of farmers did it. Why waste money on fancy accommodations when a tailgate worked so well? I couldn't wait to hash the idea out with Betty.

"Honey, we already have the stepvan. We have a tremendous labor pool to tap into. Look how well the students have done so far. We rent a little corner somewhere and open the back of the van, and *voila*—instant produce stand! Can you see it?"

"I can see it, Bill," Betty said. "I can definitely see it. But I don't know that a produce truck on some corner will actually do better for us than those students working the neighborhoods."

"Not *a* produce truck, baby. Three or four trucks, with each one selling a ton of tomatoes a day. I'll be the tomato king! We could even call the business Tomato King, and I could have a crown ... "

"Slow down, Tomato King!" Betty laughed. "I think we need to put a pencil to this project, and see if it really makes sense. OK, Your Majesty?"

"OK, you're right. But I know we can do this."

I grabbed my yellow pad and began sketching, jotting down figures, and making notes off to the side, the whole time thinking out loud so that Betty could see the same vision. An hour or so later, Betty was nodding.

"I think it *will* work, Bill. And you won't be happy unless you try anyway," she said patting my shoulder.

We had about twenty thousand dollars at that time. We moved forward cautiously, but surely. First, I began to look for exactly the right vehicles. I liked the idea of the stepvan, which could be left in place and locked up at night like a shed or store, then easily opened back up in the morning. The sixteen-by-seven bed area was just the right size, and allowed us to use an eight-foot piece of plywood as a sort of counter if we needed to. I figured that even a truck with no motor would work—we would have it towed to the right spot, and just leave it there all summer.

Several weeks after I began looking, I passed the Sunshine Bread Company in Arlington. A whole fleet of bread trucks was lined up out front. A big banner overhead said, "Total Liquidation—Everything Must Go!" Pulling over to the parking lot, I got out to survey the trucks. They were the perfect size, and there were quite a few to choose from. Several of them looked nearly new, and several were in bad shape.

Before long, a man approached me to see if he could be of assistance.

"I'm looking for three trucks, like these. How much are you asking?"

"Depends on which ones," he told me. "These here are almost new, run great, they're thirty-five hundred each. These next couple are older and run OK. They're eighteen hundred. These last few don't run at all, and they're four hundred apiece."

I eyed the trucks dubiously. They were rusting and a little battered and dinged. But I had a vision, and these trucks were part of it. "I'll take these three," I said, reaching for my checkbook. I'll be back early in the week to have 'em towed."

Early the next week, I had the trucks painted a brilliant red, as befitting a tomato stand, while I found just the right spots to set them up. It had to be a busy place, with thousands of cars passing each day, close enough to the road for people to see what we were selling, yet with enough space for cars to park. It also had to be a piece of land that no one was using so that the owner would be glad to lease it for just three months. It had to be… the American Station at the corner of Backlick and Braddock Roads in Annandale. I passed it all the time—it was perfect! I approached the owner that same week, introducing myself, and explaining how the arrangement might benefit both of us. I explained that I could afford to pay him twenty-five dollars a week—cash—which would net him an extra three hundred bucks for his doing absolutely nothing. He understood perfectly, and we struck a deal.

I was able to arrange two other similar spots in the area, and became more and more excited as the school year drew to a close. I had already drafted my team of employees, and worked out a plan for stocking the vans.

By that time, Betty and I had purchased a twenty-acre farm in Chantilly, and I suggested planting it in tomatoes.

"Bill, we'll never be able to work a farm and run the produce stands, too," Betty said. "Besides, we wouldn't be able to grow enough to even stock *one* stand."

"I know that," I reasoned, "but listen … people appreciate farm fresh produce. Remember those cantaloupes I bought off the farmer's pickup out Route 50? Even if we had gotten the exact same melon at the Kroger, it wouldn't have tasted as good!"

"But how does that … ?"

"If people ask us if we grow our own tomatoes, we could answer, 'We grow some of them, but not all of them.' See what I mean? It would be the truth, and it would make people feel good about what they buy."

Betty agreed to plant the farm in tomatoes, and we then had a real farm. *The Meadows Farm.*

Meadows

Meanwhile, as summer grew closer, and I proudly looked at my bright red fleet day after day, I felt that something was missing. I wanted people to instantly recognize my produce stands, even from a distance. If I put up more, I wanted them to look the same, so that people could say, "Look! There's another one!"

My trucks needed a name, though. Something big and bold. Huge eighteen-inch white letters—Tomato King! I could just picture it. Betty laughed at first.

"I agree you need a name," she said. "But Tomato King? I thought that was just a joke. We need something with more dignity. Something with our name in it. Tomatoes by Meadows, something like that."

"How about Meadows Farm's Fresh Tomatoes? I think that has a nice sound to it."

"How about Meadows Farms? It tells our name. It tells what we do. And it sounds like we have more than one location."

"I like it. I can't wait to see how it looks on the trucks!"

Betty turned suddenly, wrapped her arms around my neck, and met my lips with a deep, heartwarming kiss. "You'll always be my Tomato King!" she said.

That moment crystallized the beginning of our new venture. All that needed doing was for us to get started. And that was a real adventure!

The Farmer, 1967

Chapter Twenty-Three

Farm Life & Growing Pains

When we started that summer of 1963, our savings account balance consisted of twenty thousand dollars. Over the following ten years, we would increase that net worth beyond our wildest dreams—or at least Betty's. I had financial intentions at that point that I aimed to satisfy.

Those next few years were exciting ones. During the school year, we continued our employment with the county, while we continued night classes, and Betty taught Library Science one night a week at the local University of Virginia campus. In December, we would sell Christmas trees at our truck sites, leasing them for the month, and then we'd start up in spring with our regular summer produce.

During the summer months, each morning I would get up at 3:30 a.m. and head to Washington, D.C. to buy tomatoes at the Farmer's Market. Several hours later, I would return and pick up Betty, dropping her off at one of the stands, which she ran alone. Then I would make my rounds of the other stands, filling shelves with boxes of tomatoes, checking supplies, and locking up a bag of money to start the day, as my dad had done at Central Grocery so many years before. Throughout the day, I would make my rounds, observing business, helping out for twenty or thirty minutes where I was needed,

Meadows

restocking, relieving someone who might need a break, carrying away the rotten tomatoes, and so on. My staff was the cream of the crop, hand selected as young men of character and integrity, reputed to be honest boys, many of whose parents I had become acquainted with in my years of teaching and coaching.

We kept up our frenetic pace until we closed the stands at 9:00 p.m., when I picked up Betty and our sleepy babies, and we all fell into bed, thoroughly exhausted; only to awake a few short hours later to begin again. That was our routine, seven days a week, throughout the summer. It was a heavy schedule, but I can scarcely remember a time when I felt more alive—and in love with life!

By the time we had six produce stands, I began to give some consideration to the money I was making, and the number of hands it passed through before it reached mine. It was an odd thing to think about. Perhaps it never would have come to mind if not for a few unrelated incidents that summer.

The first occurred when one of my boys had to go away for two weeks for a family vacation. My little brother, Vic, was old enough to work, and eagerly agreed to take the boy's place for two weeks. When I counted the first day's till, I was baffled. That particular stand always seemed to come in fifth in sales, out of the six stands, yet on that day, it came in second. That had simply never happened before. All I could say was, "Good job, Vic!" The next day, Vic's stand came in third, and first the following day.

That night I lay in bed staring at the ceiling. Betty's soft even breathing told me she was already asleep, but I needed to talk to her. I pushed gently against her shoulder, and whispered her name. I knew she was exhausted, but this couldn't wait.

"Betty, Kenny Watts has been stealing from us."

"What? What do you mean, stealing?"

"Stealing. Look here," I said, flicking the light on to show a pad of figures I'd been working on. "Everyday this summer, Kenny's stand has ranked fifth. That means for the past three days, it should have brought in something between forth and sixth, see?"

Betty nodded groggily.

"But Kenny isn't here. Vic has run the stand for three days, and look what he brought in! Do you see how much I would have lost if Kenny were here? Do you see how much I've lost so far this summer?" By now, I had Betty's full attention as she stared at the numbers, then murmured, "Not Kenny of all people! He *loves* you!"

Nearly Perfect

The very thought of it made me sick. I had stolen once myself. A dime. And the shame of such a despicable act caused me to confess my crime and all but beg to be suitably disciplined. Was it possible for a fine young man like Kenny Watts to smile, shake my hand, and call me "Sir," while helping himself rather generously to *my* profits? I had no choice but to believe it was so, as the rest of his two-week vacation played out and his stand consistently ranked number one or number two in sales everyday. I was heartsick.

During the same period of time, something else happened that made me second guess my own ability to read people and judge character. On a busy Saturday, I had several young men working at the stand, and I was observing them carefully, thinking about ways that a businessman might reduce internal theft. While I stood there watching, two Fairfax County Police cars pulled onto the lot and the officers approached me.

"We're looking for some young men whom we believe are working for you," one officer stated. He then read a list of five names—all of them my special students.

"What's the problem, Officer?" I asked with a slight tinge of apprehension. Three of the boys were waiting on customers at that very moment.

"Well, they're wanted on suspicion of grand theft auto." He held up a photo of a barely recognizable Volkswagen. "We've pulled quite a few of these out of the woods down by Lake Barcroft. They steal 'em, drive 'em, and then trash 'em. Do you know the boys?"

I felt as if my heart were in a vice grip. I pointed, my hand shaking, toward the stand. "The one in the striped shirt, the real tall one, and the one with the buzz cut. The other two are not working today." I watched the police approach the boys, then turned away for a moment as they were read their rights and taken away. I stepped quickly behind the counter. "Who's next, please?"

Later that evening, I told Betty all that had happened.

"It really makes you wonder," she said, shaking her head sadly.

"I know. I couldn't help but remember my first year of teaching. Remember how Mr. Lloyd told me I had to do something about the stealing in the locker room and I refused to even believe him?"

"I remember. You ended up having to hide in the closet to catch the thieves, and you were so shocked."

"Yep, my own students. Just like now. Is it really possible that even good people will steal if they have the opportunity?" What in the world was I going to do? "Well, I guess we may as well check out Denny Morgan, too," I said. Denny's stand was usually number two in performance, so I really doubted

Meadows

that I had anything to worry about there. Nevertheless, the stand was located right across Columbia Pike from the Gifford's Ice Cream Parlor, where Betty and I liked to treat ourselves on payday.

That time, we took a pair of binoculars with us, and I braced myself for what I hoped I would not see. I felt sneaky and low, spying on my own employees, just as I had felt hiding in a janitor's closet in the boys' gym that day. And same as then, I saw what I hoped was a terrible mistake. I saw Denny take something from the moneybox and slide it into his pocket. "Come on, Betty," I said, as we crossed the pike together.

"Hey, Mr. Meadows! Mrs. Meadows," Denny said, looking at us with his guileless smile.

We smiled back. "Denny, do you have any money?" I asked, not sure where to go with my line of questioning.

"No, sir, I had some soda money, but I bought a Pepsi over at the Esso Station."

"That's all the money you brought with you today?"

"Yes, sir. Why do you ask?"

"Denny, Mrs. Meadows and I have been watching you from Gifford's, across the way. I saw you slip something into your pocket. What did you put in your pocket, young man?"

"Nothing. I didn't put anything in my pocket, Mr. Meadows." Denny's voice had acquired a slight quiver, and he had a problem maintaining eye contact.

"Would you mind emptying your pockets? Just for my peace of mind?" Denny reached into both pockets, keeping his hands as flat as possible, but his right hand still managed to pull a twenty dollar bill out, and the three of us watched as it fluttered to the ground. "That yours, Denny?"

"No, sir, it's yours."

"Denny, I have to think of what is the right thing to do here, you understand. Now I have a son who will someday have a job, and I have to wonder if he were to ever steal, wouldn't I want to know about it? Wouldn't that be the right thing?"

Denny nodded, slowly, silently.

"Denny, we're going to drive you home now, and we're going to tell your dad what you did. Then I'm going to leave it to you and your dad to work out the details of this thing, understand?"

He nodded, his eyes downcast.

The ride to Danny's house seemed eternal. He lived in a lovely neighborhood with well-manicured lawns and nice cars in every driveway. I was sure Denny's father would be devastated.

He opened the door with a friendly smile, then a look of bewilderment.

Nearly Perfect

"Mr. Meadows? Danny? What's going on? Why aren't you at work, son? Is something wrong?"

Denny kept his eyes lowered as I spoke up. "Mr. Morgan, it pains me to tell you this, but this evening we caught Denny stealing from the produce stand."

Mr. Morgan's face crumpled in disbelief.

"Denny! My God, son! How could you do this after Mr. Meadows was good enough to offer you a job?"

At that point, Denny looked at his dad with clear blue eyes and said earnestly, "I didn't, Dad. It was all a big mistake, but *he* doesn't believe me! Why would *I* need to steal anyway?"

Morgan looked from his son to me, and back several times. I saw the tide change before my eyes. He turned his rage on me. "Well, of all the nerve!" he began, "you think just because we have money you can come in here and accuse my son of stealing? Did you think I would pay you to keep this quiet or what? Get off my property before I throw you off!" His anger continued to mount. "And get that jalopy out of my driveway before I call the police!" He took several steps toward me as I turned and hustled out to the car, where Betty was waiting for me. The look of alarm on her face told me that the man was close on my heels. But I made it to the car and out of the driveway with a squeal.

Betty and I rode in silence for several minutes, each of us lost in our own thoughts about all that had happened. Part of me was thinking of the lost money—how much I might have brought in over the previous several seasons if a healthy chunk hadn't made its way into other people's pockets. Another part of me was feeling disheartened over the broken trust. Was everyone a thief deep down inside? I had to wonder.

"Betty," I said at last, "something's got to change."

She reached over and squeezed my hand as she so often did when we were driving. "Let's go home, Bill. We'll get this thing sorted out in the morning." Then, a few quiet minutes later, she said, "I know what you're probably thinking, but I still don't think *everybody* is a thief. It's just that there's no way to tell."

The easy part was devising an inventory control system that would work for our business, without its being too cumbersome to manage. The most obvious way was for me to count the cases of tomatoes I stocked in a given stand, and leave a note telling the employee how much money needed to be brought in. At the end of a shift, there would either be money or tomatoes—it was that simple.

The hard part was telling my students that from then on, I would be checking on them. I remembered the feeling of watching Denny through the binoculars, and of hiding in the broom closet in the gym. There would be no more

Meadows

sneaking around for me. I just couldn't do it and hold my head up. I called everyone together early one Saturday morning and laid my cards on the table.

"I don't know who among you would steal, and who would resist that temptation. A couple of weeks ago, I would have said I knew you all like the back of my hand, but it turns out that's not the case. It turns out that some people will steal, and because of those people, everyone is under suspicion. Everyone's honesty has to be checked, and because of that, I am, in essence, treating every one of you like a thief."

A slight murmur of surprise rippled through them.

"If you have never stolen," I went on, "you probably resent that. You should! Some of you will probably say you can't work under those conditions. I understand. I want you to talk this over with your parents. Some of them may object, even if you don't. Let me know if that's the case. If you want to give your notice, I'll understand."

Several of the students looked around at each other, but no one moved.

"As you make your decision, please keep a couple of things in mind. My objective will be to continue treating you with dignity and respect. I like you all. I really do. And I aim to treat you right. Now, that's not the same as being treated fairly. If I were fair, I would assume you aren't stealing unless I catch you. But I can't do that anymore. So the *right thing* for me to do is to let you know that I'm checking on your honesty, and not to sneak around behind your back, pretending I'm not."

I dismissed the meeting, only to find a line of young people standing in front of me. "I'm still on board, coach." "You can count on me, Mr. Great!" and so on. I was relieved as I left that day, that not a single person had come forward to give notice.

Lying in bed that night, I thought of all that had happened in our fledgling business. "Betty, it's hard to imagine we came this far with so little attention to the money!"

"Well, honey, I guess we were too busy having fun!"

"Fun, yes, but out-and-out ignorance? I'd say *keeping up with the money* is a pretty basic principle. We'll be out of business in a hurry if we ever let that one fall to the wayside again!"

"What about how we treat people? Don't you think that's just as important?"

"It's a close second. I'd say *treating employees right* is the second most important principle."

"And don't forget what you're actually selling—if the produce is spoiled or not fresh, or too expensive, you won't be in business long, either!"

Nearly Perfect

"Right—a quality product at a good price. That's it."

My three basic principles of business. I think I'm going to write them down."

"Can it wait 'til morning?" Betty asked with a twinkle.

"OK, I guess it can wait. But don't let me forget, all right Betty? ... Betty?"

I actually did write them down and have kept them in force ever since.

Farmer's Key Business Principles:

1. Keep up with the Money!
2. Always treat all employees right and with respect.
3. Always sell the best products at the lowest possible prices.

A few weeks later, we happened to be approached by a neatly dressed business man, who looked over our produce stand thoughtfully, clearly without interest in our wares. "Are you the proprietor?" he asked me.

"Yes," I answered, extending my hand. "William Meadows. And you are?"

"David Riley. Zoning. This business is in violation of Code 391-04. You don't have a permit on display."

"Permit? What sort of permit?"

"Well, in this case, I presume a temporary occupancy permit would do the trick. You'll need to go to the county courthouse. I'll give you seven days to get your permit displayed. No citation this time."

Betty looked anxious. "The courthouse, Bill! That sounds pretty bad for us. And 'no citation at this time' sounds like next time ... "

I held up my hand. "It's no big deal, Betty. Just a formality. It means somebody's noticed us. We should be flattered!"

The very next morning, we made our way through the labyrinth of hallways and offices, 'til we finally located the zoning office. Stepping up to the counter, I cleared my throat ever so slightly, causing the woman on the other side to look up irritably. "Uh, I'm here about a temporary occupancy permit," I said.

"Yes?"

"I'd like to get permits for my produce stands. Six of them. Stepvans, really. I run them June through August. Three months ... "

It takes a special person to run these offices. She didn't let us down. After a long hesitation, she said, "I'm afraid not. That sort of thing would not qualify for a permit in the county." At that point she returned her attention to the sandwich she'd been navigating when we arrived. We were tacitly dismissed.

We walked down the long corridor, nearly shell-shocked. Finally we took a seat on a bench. Betty touched my arm. I looked over at her, surprised to see tears in her eyes.

"We can't just give up, Bill," she said. "This is our dream. Let's go back."

"Now Betty, these government folks have ways of getting real annoyed if you pester them. Let's go on home and maybe try to write a letter to someone."

We started to leave, but then I began to feel Betty's sentiments. "What if we go back? And that woman ignores us? It's still worth a try."

I had to clear my throat again, and the woman turned to me as if I were a naughty boy and said, "What is it?"

"We'd like to see whoever's in charge," I said as evenly as I dared.

"Why, I'm afraid that's impossible," she said. "Mr. Covington is a very busy man. He is booked solid today."

"We'll wait," I assured her.

"Well, I'm afraid it will be a long and disappointing wait. He simply cannot see you."

"If he doesn't see us today, we'll be back first thing in the morning. Eventually, he will have to see us."

The woman arched her eyebrows, apparently in an effort to challenge our tenacity. Several minutes later, she managed to raise herself from her chair and waddle around behind a paneled room divider.

Betty and I exchanged glances, wondering what her next move would be.

After another fifteen minutes, a door to the right swung open, and a well-groomed man stepped out, hand extended. "Wally Covington. Won't you come in?"

Betty and I gaped in amazement, following him into his well-appointed office.

Cheerful stood back as we entered his office, and then returned to her lunch.

"So how can we help you today?" asked Mr. Covington, motioning for us to sit.

I began to explain our business to the head of zoning. He nodded as I spoke. Then said, "I'll need a little time to work on it, but I think we can get those permits for you. Can you come back in the morning?"

The next morning, the woman greeted me before I had to clear my throat. "Your permits will be done in about half an hour. I'm working on them now."

It was that occurrence that proved to be a very pivotal time for us. If Wally Covington had been the kind of County Zoning Administrator who sought to find ways to *prevent* people from doing what they wanted to move ahead, things would have turned out very differently for us. But, instead, he was a person who tried to *help* others if at all possible. It is due to people like Wally Covington—and *not* luck—that helped make me successful.

Betty and I exchanged glances again—this time happy ones. Life was nearly perfect.

It was around that time that I first began to be called *Farmer*. Each morning, I would wear a plaid shirt and bib overalls, and a wide-brimmed straw hat. When I pulled up to one of my stands, the employees would call out, "Here comes the Farmer!" The customers would turn and sometimes say, "Oh, so you're the Farmer? We love your tomatoes. Where's your farm?" And of course I could truthfully answer, "I have a little place in Chantilly." I liked the feeling. I had grown up in rural areas, and my father had taught us to be respectful of the food we ate, the hands that prepared it, and the farmers who had grown it. I was proud to be called *Farmer*, though I began to realize that many people did not respect farmers.

I remember waiting on a well-dressed woman who pulled up in a fancy car, sporting an expensive fur jacket. I immediately sensed that she looked down on me as a farmer, and enjoyed asking me to pick out her produce and carry her things to the car. I felt a resentment rising in me as I knelt at her feet to pick the exact items she wanted. Looking up, I felt she was smirking at me, and I was tempted to tell her off in no uncertain terms. But I reminded myself that there were those who weren't taught to respect others. This woman just didn't respect farmers in general, and it had nothing to do with me. I thanked her for her business and sent her on her way, still proud to be a farmer.

Of course, my kind of farming had its down side. When you are dealing with a perishable product like tomatoes, there will always be a few that spoil before you can sell them. No matter how delicately they are handled, there will be a bruise here, a puncture there, and rotten tomatoes have to be removed quickly. Each of my produce stands had a thirty-gallon trashcan, into which all rotten tomatoes were unceremoniously tossed. As the containers filled, the tomatoes quickly decomposed into a rotten, fermented juice that smelled and attracted flies. There was also the problem of disposal.

At times, I longed for the little pig pen on our West Virginia homestead, where our hogs would have been delighted with the luscious rotten tomatoes. But here in the city, no one kept pigs. And I had to collect the spoils and get rid of them somehow. I had figured out a way to tie three of the big containers on the back of my station wagon at one time, and from there, I planned to drive around 'til I found a suitable dumping spot.

I was at my stand at the intersection of Annandale Road and Route 50, a very lucrative spot for us, as Route 50 was the main artery into the nation's capital, only eight miles away. I saw a break in the traffic, and pulled out a little too suddenly, causing those three thirty-gallon vats of slime and stink to break the cord that held them to my car, spewing ninety gallons of rotten tomatoes all over the highway.

My first instinct was to hit the gas and keep on rolling, but I was too well-known in that area to get very far. I pulled onto the shoulder, and got out to survey the damage. The stench was horrendous, as was the sight of cars splashing through the mess. I looked around, wondering about my options, when I was suddenly confronted by one of Fairfax County's finest.

"Are you *crazy* or something?" he demanded. "What in the world were you thinking? You've got to get this mess cleaned up, now! I don't care how you do it, just do it!" I could feel my face reddening under the assault. I was embarrassed enough about the incident itself, but going about cleaning it up in my overalls and straw hat intensified the sentiment.

I ran to the corner Esso Station. "Hey, Dave, do you have a pushbroom and a shovel I could borrow?"

"Sure," he said, "What's up, Farmer?"

I pointed to what appeared to be the most gory of all highway calamities in Fairfax history.

Dave was supportive. He burst out laughing. "You did that?"

I thanked him with a look that could have committed murder and headed back out to the highway, my hat flapping in the wind. Once I had retrieved enough of the awful stuff to allow the reentry of traffic, Dave assisted me in getting the containers back up onto the truck. I realized at that moment, that I was not always in favor of my role as Farmer.

Eventually, I found a solution to my disposal problem. I found a wooded area near Tyson's Corner where I was able to dump my slop three times a week, and no one was the wiser. But once again, I came face to face with the law, who accused me of trespassing, causing a health hazard, and something regarding a public nuisance. I explained to the officer that I was very sorry, hadn't meant to break the law, and that in West Virginia, where I was from, such a thing was commonplace.

He eyed my old car, my straw hat and overalls and nodded. "Well, consider yourself warned, Mr. Meadows. You have seven days to get this mess cleaned up, or I'll be knocking on your door with a warrant."

It took the better part of those seven days to get the job done, even with one of my hardest working students, Big Al Plummer (my very first employee), but we were able to avoid any further brushes with the law over my rotten tomato potion.

After we had been running our stands for four years or so, and had established ten or twelve profitable locations, a disturbing trend began to develop. We would go to our spot in May to touch base with the owner, only to find that he had decided to try his own hand at selling produce, perhaps setting up a son or nephew with a little business. It was very disheartening.

"Why can't we just buy our own place?" Betty finally suggested. "We've got the money. We've been saving all this time for our future. And this *is* our future."

"You're right, Betty. We need our own place, where no one can kick us off. Let's look around and see what we see."

It had taken a long time to save two hundred thousand dollars. We had watched our friends turn every raise into a new car, or a new pool, or some kind of new debt. We still lived in an apartment, had old furniture and saved as much as we could. We had done without many of the finer things. Maybe it was the time to make our move.

Our search for property in the area where we had our stands proved to be discouraging. It was a time when lots were being sold by the square foot, rather than the acre, and it didn't look like we would be able to afford anything close in. We returned to our old habit of driving out towards the more rural areas, looking for sale signs rather than picnic tables. On one such drive, we headed west on Route 7, and came to the town of Sterling, ten miles out of Tysons Corner. There on the right was a lot for sale, and two cars were already pulled over, prospective buyers walking to the site. I pulled over to the shoulder and said, "Let's take a look."

Betty walked a few steps ahead of me, up the embankment from the side of the highway. I followed behind her, my heart beating wildly. My head began to feel as if it were spinning off my shoulders, and my feet no longer touched the ground. I remembered the string of colored flags, but instead of the display of pools, I saw the grand opening of my produce stand! I felt exhilarated beyond description. Betty turned and saw me holding my hand to my chest.

"You OK, Bill?" she asked curiously.

At the same time the salesman was showing the property to another man, he made his way toward us. "You folks interested in the land?" he asked.

"I'm interested in knowing the price," I blurted out.

"It's eighty thousand dollars."

"How is it zoned?"

"It's zoned commercial," he answered.

"I want it. But I'd have to get it for seventy-five thousand. That's my offer."

"I think we can do business, sir. Can you come to my office and we'll draw up a formal contract?"

Betty and I returned to the car and she turned to me, a little confused. "Bill, we never make that kind of decision without talking first. You didn't even think about it—let alone discuss it between us. One minute we're standing there looking, the next we're buying."

"Betty," I said, looking her in the eye, "don't you remember? It's the same lot!"

"Same as what?"

"Remember? We bought the watermelon with Gilven and Nila—and we drove out here and pulled over to look at the swimming pools?"

Betty looked out the car window. Her eyes showed a glimmer of recognition. As her eyes widened, I could see she did remember. "You told me that later something good was going to happen in connection with those pools," she said, smiling. "How did you know?"

"It's the property, Betty! It's ours. We're supposed to have it," I said. "It's a new beginning for us. We'll build a permanent produce stand here, and never have to worry about someone else taking over, ever again."

We paid for our little lot in cash, and so it belonged to us right from the first day. I could barely stand the excitement of watching as the bulldozer cleared and leveled our site. I wanted to be there every minute as my eighty-by-forty-foot building went up. When my twenty-four-foot Meadows Farms sign was erected, I was glad it didn't say Tomato King.

With the purchase of our new land, in 1968, we were readying to start an exciting and wildly successful chapter in our lives. And we could hardly wait!

The farmer and the farmer's wife, 1970

Farmer and Betty with first load of nursery plants

Chapter Twenty-Four

The Last Stand

*B*y the beginning of 1969, my family had joined in and helped us put up our building. It was a frantic pace.

"Are you sure we're going to be finished with this thing by Easter?" Bill's younger brother, Dave, seemed a little skeptical, but his father smiled and clapped him on the back.

"We'll finish if you and Vic get a move on! Bring over another sheet of plywood, will you?"

Dave and Vic were our unofficial gofers, but the whole family had a hand in getting the produce stand up and going. They were a handy group, each having gleaned bits and pieces of knowledge wherever they went, and bringing a full range of skills and talents to our construction project.

"We have to be open for Easter, Dave!" I said. "We're going to have Easter flowers and we'll be the very first place anywhere around here to have vine-ripened tomatoes!" I poured everyone a cup of coffee from the big thermos jug, and stood back to admire the project.

That time, we'd managed to get permit information ahead of time—neither of us wanted to go through the trauma we'd experienced with the stepvan outlets.

Meadows

Before long, I felt Bill's arms slide around me from behind, and heard him whisper, "What do you think?"

"It's beautiful, Bill! It's really the start of something big for us. I can feel it!"

It was February, but we had been blessed with some reasonably warm weekends for working on the produce stand. Still, periodically I consulted the calendar and thought about the amount of work that still needed to be accomplished before we opened. It would be close, but I knew we could do it.

Easter, that most unpredictable of holidays, arrived amid white puffy clouds and temperatures in the seventies. It was a perfect weekend for us to christen our new enterprise, and we took the fine weather as an omen of good things to come.

At the end of the weekend, we fell into bed exhausted. Our babies had long since fallen asleep, even as Bill and I talked excitedly all the way home. The family had pitched in, as usual, to finish the job on time, and then spent the weekend helping out wherever they were needed.

Monday morning came painfully early as we slipped back into our professional clothes and headed for our professional jobs. Our hectic pace served only to energize us rather than enervate us. Bill's mother watched the babies and did a wonderful job of it, while we worked our day jobs. Then, on Friday mornings, Bill would leave for the D.C. Farmer's Market at 2:00 a.m. to stock up, and be back in time to get to work by 8:00 a.m. After school, on Friday, we would head to the produce stand for the evening, then return the next morning for another twelve-hour day. Jay and Cindy learned to fall asleep wherever we put them down for their naps, while somehow maintaining their pleasant dispositions. By the time we finished up another weekend, drove the twenty miles back to Falls Church, bathed the children, and put them to bed, we would be running on fumes. Yet a hot shower and a cold soft drink always brought me back to life, and I would be eager to join my husband in bed for a weekend recap, and hopefully some quality time. It was a period in our lives when we were pushing ourselves beyond reasonable limits, yet we were wonderfully happy and alive.

Our little business seemed to pick up momentum at an astonishing speed, and we soon became dependent on Bill's mother to wait on customers and help with the money. Bill's brothers and sisters-in-law rallied around us whenever they could, their assistance providing us with the much needed extra hands during that frenetic time.

It was on one of those crazy, successful Saturdays that our neighbor, Chip Canty, came by the stand. He watched us with interest as we bagged, toted, sorted, and boxed. As Bill lugged two huge boxes of tomatoes over to the counter, Chip stepped toward him.

"Do you need some help, Mr. Meadows?"

"Oh, thanks, Chip. I think I've got it, though."

"No, I mean, do you need some help here? At the stand? I could work for you on weekends."

Bill and I exchanged glances, wheels turning in both our heads, followed by little grins.

"Why, Chip, I believe we could use some help. I tell you what—I'll pay you a dollar an hour, and I'll buy your lunch. How would that be?"

Chip thrust his hand out to Bill. "That'd be swell, Mr. Meadows. I'll be back after I go tell my mom." We watched, amused, as the tall, gangly teenager literally skipped across the parking lot toward his home.

Well, Chip proved to be a real godsend. He was possibly the brightest boy I had ever met, and he would astound the customers as he added up their orders in his head, rather than on the adding machine. Some customers seemed to feel they needed to see the addition on paper, and it seemed ludicrous to actually have to call him aside one day and tell him, "I know it'll slow you down, Chip, but use the adding machine. Some folks get suspicious when they don't see any actual ciphering going on."

Over the years, the Canty family contributed a lot to our work force. Chip's participation was followed by sisters Debby, Eileen, Carla, his brother Greg, and probably most indispensably, his mother, Carol. She was a people person, and her easy way with customers was a real asset to what we were attempting to do.

As so often happens, our successful produce stand became too much of a good thing. My husband was working seven days a week, sometimes eighteen hours at a shot. But I became truly concerned one summer day when Bill actually seemed a little disoriented. He was preparing to go to work, but was talking as though he had just come home from work. The days were running together, and I knew he was suffering from exhaustion. Over a quick cup of coffee, I tried to get Bill to remember when he had last had a day off.

"I'm fine, Betty," he assured me. "I appreciate your concern, and I know I sounded a little mixed up for a minute there, but I am really OK." Unconvinced, I took the calendar from the wall and laid it on the table in front of him.

"Look here. Your last day off was the week before Memorial Day. You've worked every single day since then." Bill nodded thoughtfully, as I counted back. "That's forty-nine days in a row. That's ridiculous. No one can keep up that pace."

Bill squeezed my hand. "I'll take a day off soon, honey. But I'm fine, I promise."

I sat at the table fretting a bit longer, then got busy making some phone calls. Bill's parents readily agreed that he needed some R&R, and we hatched a plan for taking care of the children and running the produce stand so I could take him away for a little rest.

Meadows

I was surprised at how little it took to convince Bill that he needed to get away. Once he knew the bases were covered, he fell into the passenger side of the car and I headed for Ocean City, Maryland. His heavy, even labored, breathing in the seat next to me convinced me that I had done the right thing.

We ended up getting a room by the Chesapeake Bay Bridge, and were both fast asleep moments after entering the room. The next twenty-four hours passed in a deep, dreamless sleep, interrupted only by occasional trips to the bathroom or to get a drink of water. It was the greedy sleep of people who had been deprived for too long. We stayed for four days, indifferent to our surroundings, and virtually unaware of anything other than the bed. I would read a magazine from time to time, but realized that it wasn't only Bill who had come close to collapse. As a working mom, whose husband had not been around much lately, I also needed a rest. In one of my more lucid moments, I assessed the situation, and vowed things would change.

Bill's awake time gradually lengthened to the point where we could have a bit of conversation, or get a bit to eat. "I know I haven't been very good company," he said, apologizing.

"Don't be silly, Bill. I didn't take you away from it all only to have to sit here and entertain me. But I do think we need to talk."

Bill nodded.

"It's too much for anyone! You can only work two full time jobs for so long."

We talked and reasoned, as we had so many times before, always finding ourselves caught in the same old conundrum.

"I want to teach school," he said. At that point, Bill had been a successful and very popular teacher and football coach for ten years. Obviously, at that point, it wasn't the money that kept his interest. He not only loved the boys he taught and coached, but he was loved by them. The teams he coached were consistently victorious, losing only four games throughout his coaching career, which made students, faculty, and parents happy. Despite the troubles we had had with some of our helpers, he remained the most popular and sought after teacher in the school. As he had when we were in school, he drew a crowd easily and kept everyone's spirits up and interested in whatever was going on. It wasn't only the students that were drawn to him; he was awarded Outstanding Teacher of the Year in Fairfax County. The idea of leaving all of that was probably like entertaining the notion of cutting out a piece of his heart.

"You can't be in two places at one time," I said gently, but firmly.

"I can't give up the produce stand," he said evenly. "I make sixteen thousand, five hundred dollars as a coach and a teacher with a master's degree, and I make eighty-seven thousand dollars at the produce stand in three months."

"Can you give up teaching—and coaching?" That was the one million dollar question.

There was silence for a while, after which Bill said, *"I'll think about it."*

I knew it would be a painful decision. Ultimately, it was his decision to make, but I hoped deep down in my heart that he would be happy with his determination. In time, he concluded, *"I'll finish out the year, Betty, and then I guess I'll resign. That'll have to be it."*

We talked of it often, as he got used to the idea. Yet, it wasn't going to be as cut-and-dried as we had first imagined. As the business grew, we found ourselves surrounded by teenagers—and Bill remained a great teacher, even outside the classroom.

For me, it was all good. I got to see more of my husband, at work, at meals, and in our bedroom. And our children saw more of him, too. We reinstated Bill's pronouncement years before regarding those Friday night dates. The change took some of the frantic quality out of life without losing any of the excitement. We even took a few more trips on our own to the beach.

I longed to join Bill full time at work, but we had agreed that I would continue as librarian for the county for another year to provide a safety net in the event of a reversal of fortune.

"You know, Betty," Bill said as I rubbed his back after a hard weekend. *"I wouldn't mind if we lived about twenty miles closer to the produce stand. I get pretty stiff after that long ride home."*

I jumped on it. *"Wouldn't that be great? Getting the children to bed at a decent hour, running home to get dinner started ... Maybe we could put an addition on the stand!"*

"Seriously," Bill said, the wheels turning, *"wouldn't it be great to have a house right next to the produce stand?"*

A house of our own—how many times had I thought of that? Our friends were regularly buying new cars and furniture, taking trips, and had had their own homes for years. We were still renting a place to live in, and using old furniture and vehicles in order to stay out of debt for those things, despite our meteoric success.

"What about that empty lot next door?" I asked. We had never seen any activity on the adjacent lot, and had no idea who owned it.

"I think I'll look into that," Bill said with enthusiasm.

A few days later, Bill reported that the owners of the vacant lot lived in Florida.

"I'm going to call them and make an offer. All they're doing with it now is paying taxes." The owners were willing to part with the land for Bill's offer of seven thousand dollars.

Meadows

At that point, Jay was eight and Cindy was seven. I was ecstatic, imagining the joy of moving out of our cramped apartment into a home of our own. Because of our patience and self-discipline, we had amassed one hundred and fifty thousand dollars by then. We'd been married sixteen years, and it was time to move our family into a family home.

Well, we bought the property, but it took a little while longer before we actually had more than a nice view to boast about.

One of the many celebrations at Meadows Farms

Chapter Twenty-Five

Mr. Butler and the Truth about Tomatoes

Tomatoes had certainly been good to us. Their abundance and appeal had been the cornerstone of our produce profitability. But they did take time. They didn't come presorted and set up in bags. They had to be sorted, with the riper ones being set out for sale and the greener ones stored in our tomato house for ripening.

Sorting could be a long process, but time passed quickly with the right group of sorters, and just the right rock and roll playing on the radio.

My brother-in-law, Master Sergeant Bob Lewis was a career military man and worked hard to meet the needs of his wife and three little boys. I knew that at times he went without, and I wondered if he might like to earn a little extra money, helping me with the sorting of our tomatoes. I offered him twenty-five cents a box, and he readily accepted. Bob spent many long evenings sorting with us after eight hours of duty at the Pentagon. He was an excellent asset and great company right from the start.

On one of my many trips to the Farmer's Market, I noticed a sharply dressed older gentleman sipping a cup a coffee, eyes observing the bustling market. I figured him to be an administrator and wondered why he was there so early in the morning.

The next week I saw the same man, this time talking animatedly with some of the vendors. He was telling a long story, at the end of which there was much laughter amid cries of, "No way!" and, "I don't believe it!" The friendly laughter continued, as the man moved over to a tractor trailer, hoisted himself up in the cab, waved amiably and drove away. I was surprised the see the courtly gentleman in the position of truckdriver.

"Who was that guy?" I asked one of the vendors I knew.

"That's old Mr. Butler," he said. "He's the Tomato King. He brings tomatoes up from the south every week."

The Tomato King, huh? I thought I was the Tomato King, I thought ironically.

The following week, as soon as I spotted Butler, I approached him with my hand extended. He responded warmly.

"I'm Bill Meadows," I said. "That's Meadows Farms in Chantilly."

"Butler's the name. I haul tomatoes up here just about once a week!"

"So I understand. You been in the business very long?" He looked to me to be a retired professional, doing a little driving to supplement his income.

"Well, I reckon fifty years or so," he said. "I started with tomatoes when I was a teenager, and I'm sixty-six now. I'm the Tomato King, you know."

For a brief moment, I was grateful for Betty's veto of my first choice for our business name. Mr. Butler's fifty years clearly gave him more royal claim to the name.

As the weeks passed, I often found myself talking with Mr. Butler. He had a deep passion for the tomato business, and a healthy respect for the value of the little fruit. He would start his runs when the first tomatoes ripened in the deepest part of Florida and get them up to the northern markets early in the season. As the harvesting moved northward, so did Mr. Butler's destination until he was only going as far as North Carolina, to bring tomatoes up the coast. He spent most of his time in his truck, and so I was quite surprised to learn that he had a wife.

"How in the world can you be married?" I wondered aloud. Betty and I guarded our time together zealously—I couldn't imagine being gone most of every week!

"Well, I usually try to be home Friday night, or Saturday morning at the latest. I stay until Sunday night, then hit the road around 3:00 am Monday."

"I tried to imagine old Mrs. Butler, her white hair in a bun, wearing an apron, hugging her dear husband as he left, and passing him a sack lunch for the road. "You be careful, papa," she'd say. "How long have you been married?" I asked him.

"Let's see here. I've been married to Linda eleven years now. I think she just might be the one!"

"Oh, you were married before?"

"My stars, yes! Evie and I were together for close to fifteen years, and Lila and I for twelve. I truly enjoy being married. There's nothing like going home to a warm woman at the end of a hard week. A man can get might lonely on the road."

So maybe Mrs. Butler hadn't spent her whole life waiting for the crunch of her husband's tires on their gravel driveway. Maybe Mr. Butler had found a nice, attractive, newly widowed lady friend and proposed to save them both from being alone through their twilight years. It was sweet, really.

"What does Linda do while you're away?" I asked.

"Oh, she keeps busy. She's a dance instructor in town. She's always teaching or working on recitals, or something. She acts more like she's twenty-five than thirty-five."

I swallowed hard. "Did you say thirty-five? Thirty-five years old?" How did he manage that? It was a well-known fact that a woman in her thirties ... well, with a man his age—they just didn't get in the mood often enough to satisfy ... well, to be *compatible*, I thought. But I didn't dare ask.

Over the next several weeks, I looked around at women whom I figured to be around thirty-five years old and tried to imagine the old gentleman with such a young wife. It was a mystery to me. At last I gathered up enough nerve to ask him about his love life.

"Uh, Mr. Butler, I've sorta been wondering—that is, about you and your wife. My wife and I have been married a good few years, of course, and we're real young—well, I mean younger than, well uh ... "

As I ran out of right turns with my question, Mr. Butler raised his hand in understanding. But what he said was anything but explanatory. "Tomatoes, son. It's all in the tomatoes."

Obviously he had misunderstood the gist of my question, so I tried again. "Well, sir, actually I meant the ... the uh marriage *bed*, uh ... "

"Son, I know that's what you meant! And I'm telling you it's the tomatoes!" I stared dumbly as Mr. Butler laughed heartily. "Linda and I have the perfect relationship, believe me! When I come in off the road, we both want the exact same thing. It's terrific! I wouldn't be much of a husband if I couldn't meet my end of the obligation, would I?"

"OK," I said nodding, "but what's all that go to do with the tomatoes?"

"Farmer," he said seriously, "the tomatoes produce a special gas they give off as they're ripening. It's almost like a hormone for men. Why, if you're exposed to them over time, believe me, there are *no problems* in the bedroom."

Meadows

I was starting to feel as if I'd been had, but he went on.

"I swear to you, Farmer, it's a scientific fact. The night before I'm due home, I never sleep in my cab. I stretch out in the back, lay down in the trailer there with all those tomato crates. I breathe that crazy tomato gas all night long. Laugh if you want to, but I can assure you, Linda Butler is one happy woman!"

The next day, I told Betty what Mr. Butler had told me. We both laughed about it. "He sounds like quite a character, Bill! Imagine expecting you to believe a story like that!" Betty said.

"I know it sounds pretty crazy, but I guess at his age, you're willing to try anything!" I agreed.

As our business grew, and I sold more and more tomatoes, I eventually began to buy some of my stock directly from Mr. Butler. He would pull in with a delivery of twelve to eighteen tons of tomatoes and we would unload them for Bob Lewis to work on in the late afternoon.

On one particular day, we were missing a couple of our regular teenagers, who could usually help sort until 8:00 or 9:00 p.m., so Bob enlisted my help to get the job done a little faster. We would sort the tomatoes, one box at a time, by dumping them onto a plywood table, which had a kind of funnel at one end made of two-by-fours. We would pluck out the red ones and put them into boxes, then sort the pink ones into separate boxes. Finally, we would tilt the table on end, and funnel the remaining green tomatoes into boxes that went back on the shelves for a few days. Our last employee stayed until 10:00 p.m., but Bob and I still had several more hours of work ahead of us. We talked and listened to the radio as the hours ticked by, and by around 2:00 a.m., the last of the tomatoes were sorted. We'd been surrounded by tomatoes for over eight hours.

Bob and I cleaned up a little, locked the tomato house, and Bob headed across the street where he lived. I walked across the parking lot to our house, where I was sure I'd fall right to sleep, exhausted. Dropping my clothing on the floor, I pulled the covers down and slid in next to my wife. We have a wonderful habit of starting and ending each day with a kiss. As I moved toward her, she awoke enough to open her arms to me and return my kiss. Seconds later, she had cause to draw back in astonishment. "Oh my gosh, Bill! You've been in that tomato house, haven't you?"

It was quite a revealing moment. Later, as my dear wife and I snuggled close, she murmured, "I'm so glad we're married." I began to feel sleep overtake me at last, only to hear Betty's final, giggling remark.

"Next time you stay up until 2:00 a.m. in that tomato house and I have to work the next morning, you'll find me wrapped from head to toe in a blanket."

I smiled in the darkness as I thought of the amazing tomato gas.

The next morning at breakfast, I reminded Betty of my promise to be a millionaire someday. "You know, baby, we're doing quite well. But don't you imagine we could do even better if we could somehow bottle that tomato gas and sell it? No nightstand in America would be complete without it!"

Betty smiled. "You and your tomato gas," she said playfully.

As I crossed the lot to get to the produce stand, I ran into Shirley, Bob's wife. She looked a little cross that morning, and at that point, there was no way to avoid exchanging greetings.

"Good morning, Shirley," I said as cheerfully as I thought advisable.

"Good morning yourself," she said. "Next time you keep my husband in that tomato house for ten hours straight, you'd better have both doors open and fans blowing the air out in two directions!" She wore the distinct look of the sleep-deprived.

"What are you talking about?" I said, sounding as innocent as possible.

"Don't play innocent with me, Bill! You know perfectly well what I'm talking about. You and that infernal tomato gas. You think I can be up in the middle of the night like that and still make it to work intact the next morning? I'll lose my job!"

I nodded, trying hard not to laugh. "I'll keep that in mind, Shirley," I promised resolutely. "I really will."

Farmer looks over advertising flyer sent to the Washington Post

Chapter Twenty-Six

The Dream House

As we had agreed, Betty and I remembered to take time out for ourselves, and redeveloped our Friday night date routine. "Let's go to La Boheme this weekend," Betty suggested hopefully. "We haven't been there in ages."

Our favorite nightspot was tucked unobtrusively into the busy Bailey's Crossroads, and we loved the dark atmosphere with the deep red tablecloths and the soft circles of light in the middle. A nice little dance floor was situated at one end of the dining room, and we would always get up and dance after dinner. But this weekend didn't look so good.

"Aw, Betty, that sounds so nice, but I thought I'd work late Friday and Saturday, to finish up with the pumpkins … "

"Well," Betty mused, not very happy with my response. "We have something very important to discuss, Bill, and I'd rather not put it off any longer."

I assessed my flinty-willed woman. It seemed like a good idea to agree. "Sure, Betty," I said. "If it's important to you, it's important to me."

Betty looked especially pretty that evening. For the briefest moment, I wondered if I was going to be a father again, but quickly dismissed the idea.

When we arrived at the club, we were given a nice table near the dance

Meadows

floor, since we'd been regulars for a while and were quickly recognized.

"I'll have a White Zinfandel," Betty said quickly to the gentleman who seated us.

"Uh oh," I mumbled. My curiosity was suddenly peaked. "I can't wait to hear what's on your mind," I said out loud.

Betty smiled, but then turned serious. "It's about our house," she began tentatively.

"What house is that, honey?" I asked.

"Exactly," she said. "We don't have a house! Oh, I know we're fine, and we're saving for the future, and we're going to be millionaires some day. And I honestly haven't minded, Bill. Not the second-hand furniture, that same old car we've been driving forever, the dime store china and silverware … you know those things don't matter to me. But we've waited so long!"

She looked so beautiful to me, calm and reasonable, yet filled with hope for our future. I thought of the life we had had together and all that she had gone through gladly for love. I knew she would not be sulky if I told her I still wasn't ready for that house, but the fact is, I wanted what my wife wanted. I could not imagine going in a different direction. Her happiness mattered more to me than anything else.

She was still speaking pleasantly, making her case, " … and if we sold the twenty acres in Chantilly, we'd probably have close to three hundred and fifty thousand dollars. That's a lot of money, Bill. That would buy a lot of house."

I'm not sure what it was that Betty said, but as she spoke, I was overwhelmed by her beauty and my love for her. I remember nodding my head a few times, and squeezing her hand.

"Does that mean yes, Bill?" she said. "Are you saying yes?" Her voice cracked with emotion, and my eyes began to water for no apparent reason.

I took her hand and led her to the dance floor for the sole purpose of moving closer to her. As we melted together to the sweet strains of Al Martino, we whispered sweet nothings back and forth and were giddy with love.

When we finally returned to the table we were full of ideas, and the words couldn't flow quickly enough.

"I don't want a Colonial Style," Betty began, and together we let loose a flood of ideas between us over what we liked, loved, disliked and loathed. It was an exciting time, made all the more memorable by the romance and beauty of the night.

After that, we went on several trips around the area, looking at model homes and various developments. I could tell we shared reactions to what we'd seen when Betty said, "It seems like all these big houses have a whole lot of little rooms in them. It makes me feel closed in. It's like they want to be able to say they have a den and a library and a sewing room, but what's the point if they're not much bigger than closets?"

A slow drive through Great Falls took me to a unique looking house still under construction. It was not what we called a *cookie cutter* house—one that matched those around it—and it had dramatic lines and looked more contemporary. Most importantly, it was big! Since it was in its final stage of construction, I asked the foreman on duty if it would be all right if I took a look around.

"Be my guest," he said with a shrug.

With an almost reverent quiet, I let myself in the front door, and stood looking at the creation in awe. With mounting excitement, I moved from room to room, certain that I would find some disappointment around the next corner. But I never did. It was all outstandingly creative.

Scarcely able to contain myself, I dashed home to get Betty, and repeated the house tour with her. Her face told me what I had wanted to know—she could see us in a house like that.

Friends of ours had recommended their builder, a man name Joe Childers, explaining that he was easy to work with and had a lot of good suggestions. We met with Joe and took him to the house.

"We want this house … " I began.

"Well, more or less … " Betty continued

"Yes, with a few ideas of our own," I said. "But we're not sure how to turn our ideas into a house. So I guess the question is, can you build this house for us, only different?"

Joe laughed and folded his arms over his chest. "I believe I can, Mr. Meadows. Why, by the time we're finished it'll be completely different from this house—but still pretty much the same!"

We realized how we must have sounded to Joe, but knew, too, that most people contemplated building their first home were probably just like us—or worse. At least *we* knew what we wanted!

That summer was one of the most exciting times of our lives. We would work all day at the produce stand, and at the end of the day, we would cross the parking lot to our house in progress to see what changes had occurred that day. Jay would sit for long periods of time watching the big pieces of equipment as they moved a few trees and dug our basement. Cindy prattled on endlessly about her plans for her very own room.

Betty had determined pretty clearly that it was time to buy new furniture. So we had days of fun shopping for not only furniture and carpets, but new dishes, bedding, décor—we'd be leaving most everything behind. I was all for it. It was definitely time for that final plunge, and we could pay cash for the house and all the furnishings.

Although we were prepared by horror stories of long, unpredicted delays by construction companies, Joe seemed to have everything under control. He had given us a three-month projected completion date, and true to his word, he was finished in August of 1971.

The customizing Joe had done for us was perfect. Our bedroom had four sliding glass doors that opened on a large deck overlooking our backyard. A spiral staircase went from the third floor all the way to the first floor, where we had a bar and wine cellar at one end of a wonderful game room, which we outfitted with a pool table, pinball machine, jukebox, and little wrought iron ice cream parlor tables and chairs. A stage had also been built into the game room so that a full band could come in and set up. Just alongside the stage was one of the four fireplaces in the house. We had five bathrooms, and fourteen sliding glass doors to let in light.

More good news was that even after setting aside one hundred thousand dollars for commercial investments, and having denied ourselves nothing in the construction and design of our dream home, we still had money left over.

"Well, we don't *have* to spend it," I said.

"But we *can* spend it," Betty said with a smile. And that's how we ended up with the pool. I reminded Betty of the day we stopped to look at the swimming pool display next to the very property on which our house stood.

"Remember how Gilven said that one day one of us was bound to have a pool?"

"I know," Betty said, her eyes lit up, "and I thought it was just ridiculous!"

"You know, we really need some nice landscaping around the pool; the whole yard, really. It won't look finished until we have some trees and shrubs and flowers. And besides, all the really nice houses have … "

Betty interrupted. "You don't have to convince me, Bill! We have the money and you've always loved plants. You told me that our pool would have nice flowers around it as far back as my front porch in Crab Orchard!"

I hugged my wife. She remembered all of the good things.

"We'll have it done professionally," she said. "But you decide what we get."

I was surprised to find very few landscape architects in our area. The Yellow Pages listed only three, and I called a man named Byron Wates out of

Nearly Perfect

Fairfax. He turned out to be an older man, who had built his own local nursery business. I was fascinated by Mr. Wates' collection of unique plants—dwarf and rare specimen, and trees that had been manipulated to grow into odd shapes. I came to really enjoy Mr. Wates's company, and I was surprised when he deferred to his son for the landscaping of our home.

"Now Bill, I have all the confidence in the world in him. I just put him through college so he could do this exact thing. He's a registered landscape architect, you know. He'll do a bang-up job for you. And I'll keep my eye on him, don't you worry."

I learned quickly that Mr. Wates was correct. My relationship with his son, Byron, Jr., was to span the next thirty years as we became friends and professional colleagues. He was a talented designer with a real love for plants, and was a terrific salesman on top of everything else. It proved to be a winning combination and I not only loved my landscaping, but I learned a lot in the process.

Byron, Sr. had a hobby of making wine and would bring by a couple of bottles regularly. Byron, Jr. spent a month landscaping our new house and pool, and sold me new landscaping each week. We worked hard together, but when it got too dark, we'd drink some of that wine while shooting pool.

My relationship with the Wates was the reason I eventually went into the landscape business myself, and added fifteen million dollars to our annual sales. But that's another story that we'll talk about later.

That first fall after our house was completed, we were gearing up for the sale of cider, pumpkins, gourds, and apples, and looking forward to *walking* home after work, when a stranger stopped by the produce stand. He was neatly dressed and spoke with a southern accent. He sold plants for Grow Plant Nurseries in Florida. He had an idea.

"Now, Mr. Meadows, you are really bringing the folks in. It seems that half the cars on the highway out there are turning into your place. I think you could sell them more!"

He was right. People came from all over to "the country" where the ladies wore old-fashioned bonnets, and made apple butter, and passed out tastes of icy cider. It was an exciting atmosphere, and people would fill bags and boxes with produce, but most customers left having spent only about ten dollars or so. Even though we had the largest produce market in Virginia, selling four thousand gallons of cider and three thousand bushels of apples a week, I was into the idea of new ideas for products to sell.

"Have you given any thought to nursery stock?" the man asked. "Shrubs? Bushes?"

"I don't know that folks out here have that kind of money," I said.

"These plants would be cheap. That's the beauty of it. They'd be affordable, and they are big."

I knew that the two local nurseries had the business sewn up and charged high prices for their stock. It took me only a few minutes to decide to take the gamble. With virtually no real idea of what I was doing, I ordered a tractor-trailer load of plants, specifying only that they be as big as possible for the two-dollar cost we had agreed on. The salesman told me I would be really happy with what I got—in fact, he was sure the plants would sell. So on a Friday evening, we set about the task of unloading a thousand Hetzi and Andorra Junipers, Arborvitae, and Ligustrum, all about two to three feet tall.

We decided to sell the plants for two dollars and ninety-nine cents apiece, figuring we stood to make eight hundred dollars off the deal. It seemed well worth the risk.

Unloading eight hundred shrubs was harder than I had anticipated, and we plugged away at it into the dark to finish before closing up for the night. Betty sat up with a plant encyclopedia, making a sign for each group of plants, with a brief description and a price. Her eyes were dancing and I could tell she was excited about our new venture.

However, the real excitement came on the following day. Our customers gobbled up those two dollar and ninety-nine-cent shrubs and cried for more. By close of business on Saturday, all that remained were two junipers that had been backed over as a customer prepared to load his car.

My wife was rosy cheeked and enthusiastic, and I had to admit that the idea of *clearing* eight hundred dollars in one day, added to our normal two to three thousand a day, definitely had potential.

Monday morning found me eagerly calling the Florida salesman to order another truck for the coming weekend. "Hold it, better make that two trucks," I amended quickly. "I think we're on to something."

Farmer speaks to Northern Virginia nurserymen

Chapter Twenty-Seven

Birth of the Discount Nursery

*W*e loved our new home. My only regret was that my father had not lived to see it. I knew that he would finally have given Bill and me, as a couple, his stamp of approval if he had seen that at last, we had a home! He had struggled with cancer for several years and died before ever seeing how well things had worked out for us.

Because we lived so close to the produce stand, we could all sit down to dinner together every night. Bill would join us, even if it meant going back to work afterwards. Jay had started little league by then, and not having to drive twenty miles to work made it even more possible for Bill to go to the practices and games with him. They thrived on sharing that activity.

The business had grown considerably as the years passed, and it had gotten challenging for me to keep up with; the bookkeeping, payroll, tax reports, then work the produce stand on weekends, hold down my librarian job, and be the mother I wanted to be. So it was a tremendous relief when Tina Crawford, a local high school senior, came to work as our secretary, freeing up a little of my time to be with my children.

Our lovely game room was perfect for entertaining, and one of the first things we did after we moved in was to have a big party for all our friends and family. We had so much to celebrate!

That fall, we sold truckload after truckload of plants, and continued to be amazed at how high the demand was. Of course, nothing is ever as easy as it first appears. When Bill decided to run an expensive ad in our local newspaper, I thought it was a great idea. But it wasn't so great when the plant trucks never showed up and our customers left disappointed!

In addition to that, we didn't always sell out, so the plants had to be cared for and watered until they were sold. It seemed no one liked the mindless job of watering, and we were constantly having to remind someone to stay on task. Meanwhile, the seemingly endless supply of huge overgrown junipers seemed to evaporate. Our supplier was still sending shrubs, but each successive shipment seemed a little smaller, and the two-dollar cost didn't seem like such a bargain. And then one Monday, Bill was told there were no more plants ready for market, and for the remaining weeks of the year, we concentrated on selling Christmas trees, as we always had at that time of year anyway. But—Bill had gotten a taste of something he really liked!

* * *

It's true. I felt a truly renewed enthusiasm when we entered into the world of plants. And the life of a produce huckster was not an easy one. The hours were grueling, and those years of getting up at 2:00 or 3:00 a.m. to hit the market established a form of sleep interruption that would stay with me the rest of my life. Even after leaving my teaching career, and moving close to the produce stand, it was tough getting everything done. I loved it, though. I loved the people, and the fresh air, and the thrill of having so much control over my own destiny. I loved the idea that, unlike the county government bureaucracy from which I had emerged, private business allowed a man to move ahead by doing a good job. Being a businessman was definitely the life for me.

Of course I couldn't help but compare the two types of commodities I had dealt in. The plants were more expensive, but they brought in more money. They were perishable, but nothing like tomatoes. The work was hard, but the hours were better. I felt I was at an important crossroads in determining the direction our business would take.

Betty was to return to work after the Christmas vacation, and for the first time, I would have long days alone in our new house. The stand was closed during the month or so after Christmas.

"What do you think you'll do today?" Betty asked, as she got ready to leave.

Oh, did I feel decadent! I sat sipping coffee at the table, still in my pajamas.

"I'm going to work on the business. Try to come up with some good ideas. We have some pretty critical decisions to make, and soon!"

Betty leaned down and gave me a quick peck. "There's lunchmeat in the fridge for a sandwich later."

"Did you buy any Coke?" I asked.

Betty gave me a look. "What do *you* think?"

I had always loved Coca Cola. Of course we didn't have it at home, but my father carried it in his store, and when he paid us on Saturday evenings, I quickly gave up a nickel for the "pause that refreshes." Twenty-five years later, when everyone was singing, "I'd like to buy the world a Coke," I couldn't wait to crack open a cold one and get to work.

After a luxurious shower, I built myself a fire there in the game room, switched on the juke box, and grabbed my yellow pad. OK. I had everything I needed. Time to work. Just one problem. Nothing was coming to me. Maybe, I thought, I'd get a flow going if I shot a little pool.

I knew I would feel successful only if my business stood out in a crowd. Of course making money was important, but it wasn't the whole picture. We had plenty of money at the time. It was more important to me to be the *best*. I had enjoyed selling plants. I could see a future for us there, but we knew nothing about the nursery business. We had already determined that the garden centers in our area priced their goods and services for the higher income clientele, of which there were plenty in our area.

But there were also plenty of middle-income people, who liked nice things, worked hard to buy homes, and deserved opportunities to purchase landscaping at affordable prices. The need for reasonably priced nursery stock was clear. But my goal wasn't just to be cheap—I had to do it well.

I felt a gentle shaking of my shoulder, and came awake with a start. Betty was looking down at me, smiling.

"Wake up, my hard-working guy. Wow, you've been busy!"

The song, "Good Golly Miss Molly" was pouring from the jukebox. Empty Coke bottles lined the hearth where the fire had died down to smoke and embers. My stocking feet were propped up on an ottoman, and the pool table was clearly in lingering use. I pulled Betty onto my lap and nuzzled her affectionately. "Hey, baby, I know what it looks like. But this is how I do my best thinking." I showed her what I'd written on my yellow pad. "I can't wait to tell you what I'm thinking."

Meadows

During that following month, I did quite a lot of thinking. What would make us unique? Did produce have a place in our future? Was I crazy to think I could compete in the nursery business? What were people really looking for?

Each night, I would sit with Betty, bouncing ideas off her, listening to her thoughts and ideas. The yellow pads kept filling up, but I still didn't have a firm plan in place. I knew, however, that I wanted to concentrate on the nursery business, and slowly extricate myself from the world of produce.

Perusing the newspaper one morning, I came across an ad for a bus trip to the outlet stores in Reading, Pennsylvania. One of the lines said: Name brands at discount prices. For some reason, that sounded very enticing. I liked the idea of getting something just as good for a better price. Who wouldn't? The word *discount* implied that they could be selling it for a lot more—but they weren't.

The big junipers I had sold in the fall had been kind of like that. They were discounted from the price the nurseries would have charged, but they were nice big, plants, and the customers left happy. I came up with a marketing concept:

> Meadows Farms
> DISCOUNT NURSERY
> 40-60% OFF
> BELOW THE PRICES OF
> MOST LOCAL NURSERIES!

That night, I couldn't wait for Betty to come home. "This is it!" I said. "I can feel it! Look at this, Betty." I showed her my concept. "What do you think of this?"

I know some wives might have said, "Never mind that—did you defrost anything for dinner?" But the really terrific thing about Betty was how quickly she always caught the vision. Before she had even removed her coat and gloves, she was nodding in agreement, her eyes already full of light.

"Can we do that?" she wondered. "I mean, can we make money that way?"

"Well, that's my next step. I'll have to do a little shopping and see what the going price is on those things we were selling in the fall. I know we can sell them for less."

"OK, Bill, we can sell them for less, but it won't be the same as it was in the fall. If we're a nursery, we'll have to replace anything that dies. And we don't know enough about plants—we'll have to hire some of the Virginia Tech people, like Byron Wates, who know what we need to learn. And they're not going to work for two dollars an hour, you know."

"I see what you mean. Well, we'll take one step at a time, and see what we can do."

I visited every nursery I could find within one hundred miles of our site in Sterling. Everywhere I went, I took notes. After each visit, I made a list of what worked and what didn't. If it worked, could I improve on it?

I could see that there was a lot more to the business than unloading a tractor trailer on Friday night and selling out of plants by Sunday.

I had said many times that every customer deserves the best possible price, the best possible product, and the best possible service. I decided I could really do only two of these things and still make a profit—not all three.

Thinking like an average shopper, I knew price would remain a major consideration for most people. Of course, they weren't going to be happy with low prices if they didn't get a good product. Obviously, quality and price went hand-in-hand, and the right combination of the two equaled value.

I also knew that a lot of people were looking for service. I recalled some of my produce customers who wanted each tomato hand-selected for them and the little bag carried to their car. That was extreme, of course. But in the nurseries I visited, I did note the service I received—a greeting, an offer to help, someone to answer questions, a carefully worded guarantee, and someone to load the cars. Certainly, we could do a few things—saying Hello and Thank You didn't cost a thing, and we could surely help someone load their own car if needed. But we could compromise on providing some service along with the best possible price and product. That turned out to be the right choice.

The other things required additional discussion.

"The guarantee might cost us too much, Bill," Betty said.

"If we sell good plants, we won't have a problem," I said.

"What if someone leaves their plants in the car, or goes away on vacation and doesn't water them? Are you willing to replace them?"

"OK, maybe we don't have a fancy guarantee—maybe no guarantee. But what about some professional plant person on staff? Otherwise, we'll look like we don't know anything!"

"We can learn as we go, Bill. We'll become the experts. But we need to start out slowly, until we see what all we can afford to do."

We continued refining our plans over the next few weeks, having set our sites on March first as opening day. We figured we could use virtually the same work force—my family, the Canty family, the high school students we had picked up along the way—all would be able to work with the plants as easily as the produce.

We replaced the sign on top of the stand with huge four-foot letters saying: Discount Nursery. We knew that would get some attention! Of course, not all our produce customers commuted via the busy Route 7 corridor. I began to toy with the idea of a newspaper ad.

Betty was in agreement. "I think that ad we took out in the fall was less than a hundred dollars," she said. "We can do that. I think it'll be worth it."

"Well, I don't mean in the local newspaper," I said. "I was talking about the *Washington Post*, where everyone will see it." My research had shown me that a Friday morning *Washington Post* ad would cost close to four hundred dollars, but I wanted to start this thing off with a bang and Betty quickly assented. Almost everything was in place. We just needed the plants.

Grow-Plant, the vendor we had used in the fall, was eager to start shipping again, but I thought I would like to go to their nursery and see for myself what was available. Betty went to the library and found some nursery magazines, which listed some of the growers in the back. Armed with a little knowledge and a burning desire to succeed, I made my very first buying trip, heading into the rural growing areas of Tennessee and North Carolina, placing orders for trees and shrubs to begin arriving in just a few weeks.

One of my contacts, Hy Johnson of Wight's Nursery, was skeptical of our plans. "I've spent time up in your area, Farmer. Those people have money, and they're going to want service. It's that simple!"

I had a great deal of respect for Mr. Johnson, and appreciated his advice and his wealth of knowledge. But I had already made the decision to go ahead with the Discount Nursery. Several other people stated similar objections, and I merely dug my heels in deeper and prepared for the long haul.

Betty headed up a vast sign-making project for the business. "We don't have much choice," she explained. "People will want to know the names of the plants, how they grow, how much they cost, what they need to plant it, and where to go to check out."

We had decided on a broadly worded disclaimer in lieu of the guarantee: Only God can guarantee the lives of people and plants. But this statement needed to appear on signs as well.

"There are only you, me, Mother and Dad, and Carol Canty other than the teenagers," Betty went on. "We'll need some back up on these little signs."

The pieces seemed to fall neatly into place, and we really were ready to go on that first Friday morning. When I sat down for my cup of coffee, Betty had the paper open to our first ad. A smile came across her face.

"Don't you love this?" she said, "That's us! We are The Discount Nursery!"

At 7:00 a.m., I walked eagerly over to the nursery to make sure everything was in place. Betty had done a great job installing the signs everywhere, and the plants looked so fresh in the morning dew. A little before 8:00, I heard the crunch of gravel, and watched as a car pulled onto the lot, and proceeded to park, rather than turn around and pull off. I thought it peculiar, but continued walking through the nursery, only to hear several more cars pull in. Curious, I approached the first car.

"Good morning!" I said cheerfully. "Can I help you with something?"

The gentleman in the car held up a copy of my newspaper ad. "That's all right, son. I'm waiting for the Discount Nursery to open at 9:00."

"Oh—well, that's great! It's about quarter to right now."

"You work here?" he asked.

"Yes, I do," I said. "Actually, I own it." The words rolled sweetly off my tongue.

"Well, good luck to you, son! Boy, do we need this."

By 9:00 there were fifty cars on the parking lot. I gulped nervously as I convened a quick employee meeting to get the day off to a good start. Then, I headed for the telephone to call Carol.

"I know you weren't planning to come in 'til tomorrow, but this is an emergency! Is there any way you can get over here now?"

Carol agreed and arrived in a matter of minutes. My father would look at the customers' purchases, and write all the prices on a piece of paper, and take it to the check out. My mother's nimble fingers flew over the register keys, and I loved the jingling sound I heard hour after hour. Since school was in session, the customers all loaded their own purchases into the car, and no one complained at all. It was a crazy day, and I wondered what Saturday would bring. By lunch time, I knew just two things. One, I would need more help, and two, the Discount Nursery idea was going to fly!

That afternoon, several teenagers came to work after school, and we developed our strategy for the next day. The checkout would work the same way, but our crew of loaders would be standing by. Mother would assign a loader as the customer checked out to speed the process, and keep the parking lot from being gridlocked. Betty had made signs that said "Tipping Encouraged!" Our loading crew were thrilled with the money they made that first day.

My Dad was definitely the right person to write-up the customers. He was a charming, genteel, people-person who had a way of diffusing problems and putting people at ease. He would look over at mother and gauge how many people were trying to check out. If there was a backup at the register, Dad

Meadows

would begin a slow, friendly conversation, complimenting the customer's choices and dispensing bits of helpful how-tos he knew from his own gardening days. Other people in line would join in the conversation and ask questions, until Dad would look up and notice the line at the register was gone. "Oh gracious," he'd say, "We're keeping Maye waiting! Just take this ticket to her and we'll get you rung up."

Some time during the course of that first Saturday, Hy Johnson stopped by to wish us well. He stood with dropped jaw, shaking his head. "I said it wouldn't work, but darn it, it is! I don't believe this!"

Later, he sent me a plaque bearing a bumble bee, and an inscription explaining that the bumble bee had not been engineered to fly, but since it didn't know that, it flew anyway.

That night, we knew we had something really big, and we decided to head to the Holiday Inn to celebrate. It had been a day successful beyond our wildest dreams, and once again, we felt blessed beyond measure. By the time we put the children to bed and showered, I felt drowsy and content, though my mind was racing with the excitement of the day.

Turning out the lights, I felt Betty slide between the sheets next to me, silky and fragrant. As she nestled in close to me, I could feel her warm breath on my neck. I remember thinking that I was probably the happiest man on earth. And then, my silky, fragrant wife explained later, I went out like a light. Nothing, she said, could wake me up. Absolutely nothing.

*Farmer receives
the Entrepreneur of the Year Award, 1989*

Chapter Twenty-Eight

By Leaps and Bounds

"Come to bed, Bill! You've got to get up early tomorrow."

"I will as soon as I work out these last couple of plays."

"Plays? What exactly are you working on, honey?" I got out of bed to find my mysterious husband. After our first incredible weekend at the Discount Nursery, he was set to go on a buying trip early the next morning. He needed to get to bed. I found him stretched out in what we called our cave room. It was an area one could enter from two openings by dipping your head under the low-slung doorway. The floor was padded with six-inch foam rubber, covered with a soft, deep carpet. The walls were covered with fur, as was a swinging bed, suspended by ropes from the ceiling. In a corner, a fountain flowed gently, like a babbling brook. There Bill lay, enjoying some music on the magnificent sound system. What kind of plays was he working on, I wondered.

"Do you realize you told me you were working on plays?" I said, as I stood there noting he was pretty comfortable for somebody who was working.

"Did I?" he chuckled. "Come here, Betty," he said as he pulled me down to join him. "Maybe I am. Look at this."

I did, but I wasn't much further enlightened. On his yellow legal pad were a series of arrows and dotted lines, words written sideways and up the margins.

"Hmmm," I said.

"Now, over here are some things I learned in the produce business: Keep up with the money—I'll never lose sight of that again; treat folks right, employees and customers both ... "

I listened as Bill outlined some of the ways he would apply the same principles to the running and development of our Discount Nursery. I was so proud of him. We both shared such a passion for what we were doing, and it seemed that our success was inevitable. I recognized Bill's winning attitude. I had seen him do it in sports, and in produce, and then, our very own nursery.

"You don't want to be putting out fires all day," he was saying, "that would be really stressful. We want to anticipate the problems and prevent the fires. We want to cover all the detail ... "

"Keep talking, but let's start moving," I said, taking hold of his arm. "You've got to get to bed."

We continued our discussion about the business, and Bill, as he has many times, was able to paint me a word picture that left no doubt. I could visualize our future, our work force, our products, and of course, our success.

One of our goals was to be new for us—to be a leader in the field; to try new things ... and in our naïveté, we assumed everyone would welcome our enthusiasm and fresh approach. It turned out to be quite a while before we realized that the established nurserymen in the area preferred their prices high, and actually seemed to resent the fact that we were doing the same thing they were, but at prices everyone could afford.

Our biggest coup in those early months had to be the nineteen-cent azalea. One of the contacts Bill had made on his forays into the south, was a courteous southern gentleman by the name of Sydney Meadows. He was no relation to us, by the way. Sydney was with the Flowerwood Nursery in Mobile, Alabama, and we found him to be an ally and a friend. He really wanted us to succeed. He seemed to understand that we were looking for something different, and Bill and he brainstormed over the plants that were readily available on the market.

As the two men made their way through the huge and growing operation, Sydney showed Bill something called a liner. It was really not much more than a six- to twelve-inch sprig in a two-inch pot. These liners would be planted in one-gallon containers and ready for market in two years. Sydney explained that they were bundled in packages of five peat pots, all with the same variety of azalea, wrapped in paper, and bound with a big rubber band and had a picture tag showing the color.

They went a little further before Bill stopped and turned back toward the packaged azalea. "Could I buy some of these?" he asked.

"Well, you could, Bill, but it's not a real good idea. Everybody thinks they want to grow their own plants, but it's tougher than it looks. Besides, there's a lot of hidden costs involved in growing … "

"I don't want to grow the azaleas," Bill explained. "I want to sell them just like that. Cheap! What could I buy some of them for?"

Before long, they struck a deal in which Flowerwood would ship Meadows Farms a tractor trailer loaded with boxes of little packages of azaleas, and Farmer would be able to sell them for nineteen cents each, but sold in packs of five for ninety-five cents.

Bill returned from that particular trip brimming with excitement for his new promotion. "Think of it, Betty! A ten- to twelve-inch azalea for nineteen cents! Can you picture that in the Washington Post?"

"But a whole tractor load, Bill? I think that's going to be too many," I said. "Can't we mix some other things into the order?"

"Fraid not, Betty. Sydney said that price was only for a solid load of liners."

Later, in bed, just before I passed into the land of Nod, Bill shook me. "Betty! Betty!" he whispered loudly.

"What, honey?"

"Do you really think a tractor trailer load is too many?"

"No" I whispered back, "But it's a lot!"

The following morning, I was almost shocked when Bill switched the radio to the popular morning show, Hardin & Weaver. "Bill," I said, amazed, "you hate Harden & Weaver!"

"I do not hate them. You know I don't hate anything. I don't even use that word."

"Bill," I tried, "why are you listening to Hardin & Weaver?"

"Did I ever tell you about the teachers' lounge at school? They all thought Hardin & Weaver were the best thing since sliced bread. If you'll recall, I tried to listen to them once on our way to work, and I had to change the station."

"Right, that's what I was saying. So why now?"

"You know, I would sit in the lounge, listening to these other teachers, who seemed so old at the time, maybe thirty-five or forty years old, and they would quote these guys verbatim, rehash the show … I remember thinking that if I ever wanted to advertise anything, I would do it on the Hardin & Weaver Show. It would be a sure thing!"

"Are you saying we're going to advertise on there?"

"Maybe so—or at least we'll check into it."

The next day, Bill was on the phone to the station, getting rates and information. That kind of exposure came with a pretty price tag, but Bill had his heart set on it.

Meadows

The next morning, when we listened in, it was actually a pleasure to hear the men talk. They must have done a little research or had plants of their own, because when they spoke about the azalea, they knew what they were talking about. "These little guys look really healthy!"

"Yes, indeed, and here's one with a flower already! Can you believe that? A flowering azalea for nineteen cents."

Their dialog was so convincing that if I hadn't already had a truckload of them, I would have wanted to go and check them out myself! Well, I guess that's the mark of good advertising—it convinces even the person selling the product.

Evidently there were a lot of folks listening to Hardin & Weaver that morning. No sooner had I gotten to school and hung up my jacket, than a messenger from the office summoned me for an emergency phone call. I ran through the halls, my heart beating wildly as I imagined all manner of catastrophe befalling my little family.

"Hello? This is Mrs. Meadows."

My husband's voice was strained and his words fell out in an alarming jumble. "I need you here, Betty! This is an emergency!"

"What is it? What's happening?" I asked. "Are you hurt? Is it your dad? What?"

"They're everywhere! They're waving that nineteen-cent azalea ad all over the place. And they're scaring me! This is going to be a circus here!"

I felt panicked, but it really wasn't scary—it was just another of Bill's enormous successes in ideas and advertising. I left work on what I probably called a family emergency and arrived at the lot of our nursery. I felt a shiver of excitement zip down my back. It wasn't even 9:00 yet, and the place was packed! There were over one hundred cars in the lot. Bill met me halfway across the parking lot.

"Do you believe this?" he said, squeezing my hand. "Carol will be here in a few minutes and I called Mother and Dad, too. Hopefully, the five of us can manage."

That day passed in a blur, and when it was over, we had sold half of the load of nineteen-cent azaleas. No one bought just one pack, and most people wanted twenty or more packs. We wondered if we might run out, and whether we should put a limit on the quantity one person could purchase. By Monday morning, our little azaleas were gone, and Bill faced the new week with smug satisfaction, unaware that the "little azalea" would be a major staple in our spring marketing strategy for the next twenty years.

It wasn't long before Bill's dad decided to quit his salesman's job at Montgomery Ward and join Meadows Farms as a full time salesperson. We were privileged to have him, and as I watched his interactions with the customers, I remembered a younger version of the same man, greeting every customer at his little grocery store like an old friend.

"Dad definitely has a way with people. Not a day goes by that someone doesn't come in and ask for him by name!" I remarked to Bill.

"I know, and I don't want to lose that. It's really important to connect with the people so that they know you're glad they're there."

I thought for a moment. "You know, we say we're 'self-service,' but between Dad and Carol, most people can find out what they need to know. That's a pretty important part of service."

On weekends, we were staffed mostly with teenagers and were able to train some of the brighter ones to help customers and answer the most basic questions. We developed a test on plant identification and fundamental information on planting, watering, and landscaping. When a teenager passed that test, he became eligible to earn a commission on whatever he wrote up. Though we found it difficult to find the time, we tried to have employee parties a couple of times a month; usually one for adults and a second one without alcohol, for the young people. Naturally, our wonderful home was the best place to entertain, and the people who were working on Saturday evenings could come directly to the party as soon as their duty was done. It was a great way to get to know our people on a more personal level, as well as express our appreciation for the part they played in our success. Even as we grew and took on more employees, we all seemed to really enjoy the sense of family and belonging that pervaded our young company.

* * *

It was Betty's idea to get involved in some of the professional organizations in the area. "That's bound to be the best way to share ideas and learn new things," she reasoned. "These people who have been in business for thirty years will surely be able to teach us something." She spent days getting information and applications filled out.

But within a couple of weeks, we met with disappointment on all sides. Betty received several letters, all denying us membership in the professional organizations. Even the suppliers she had contacted for such mundane things as fertilizer and grass seed, responded that they supplied only to "industry professionals."

"What is that supposed to mean?" I asked, my dander up. "Aren't we professionals? Isn't this our profession? And these silly clubs you're trying to join—who do they think they are, anyway?"

"They're not silly clubs, Bill," Betty said. "But I will definitely find out why we've been turned down. Meanwhile, there's a new company just getting

Meadows

on their feet—they might be hungry enough to sell us fertilizer."

Not long after that, a Sterling Park neighbor named John Scanell, wrote up our first order, using tomato crates as his desk.

I was hurt and dismayed when Betty reported back to me that our membership applications had been denied because we were discounting prices. Evidently this was resented by the old timers who were not even remotely interested in our way of doing business. Even though we were not members, we decided to attend all of the meetings of the Northern Virginia Nursery Association and the Virginia Nursery Association, although I suspect it put a crimp in the members' plans to discuss us. It wasn't until a member named Charley Parkerson made his thoughts clear that things changed.

"What the hell is the holdup?" he demanded impatiently at one meeting. "We're sitting here saying they don't qualify to join this damn organization while Bill and Betty Meadows are laughing all the way to bank. What's it all worth if we don't listen to what they have to say? Any fool can see they're not suffering—and most of us are barely getting by!"

After the next vote, we were begrudgingly accepted for membership. But it wasn't an organization that we would ever get particularly cozy with, and neither Betty nor I could stomach some of the staunch, greedy old timers.

Business continued to grow, and one day, Betty's sister-in-law, Shirley, approached me about a job for her nephew.

"It's my sister's boy, Ted," she said. "They're out of New Mexico, you know, and Ted has just finished up college. He's thinking of coming east."

"We could probably come up with something," I said. "Let me think on it."

"Thanks, Bill. Anything would help."

We met Ted a few weeks later, and were informed that he had found a warehouse job with Woodward & Lothrop, a local department store. Soon after, however, we realized we were seeing quite a bit of Ted around the nursery, where he occasionally would pitch in as needed.

"Hey, Ted," I said, "I've been thinking. Would you be interested in making some deliveries for me on Saturdays?" Ted was a bit of a hippie, but seemed like an OK guy, and was fairly friendly. He didn't know many people in northern Virginia, and I thought if he came on with us, he'd assimilate a little faster.

"Thanks, Farmer," he said. "I'd like that."

Ted's quick acceptance suggested to me that he was a little lonely. Within a few months, I noticed how well he was doing, though. In between deliveries, he would lend a hand wherever he was needed, obviously not cowed by the physical nature of the job. He was quickly picking up the jargon used in the nursery, and knew the names of all the plants he was handling. And he seemed to like what he was doing.

"Ted, how's your job over at Woody's?" I asked one day.

"OK, I guess," he said. "It's a job."

"Does it look like a place where you could advance any?"

"Probably not. Eventually, I guess I'll have to find something else."

"Well, how about working for me full time?"

"I don't know about that. I don't think I'd wanna be driving all day, everyday."

"No, I don't mean as a driver. I mean in the nursery. I could use a little help. More like a manager is what I had in mind."

I had recently made the decision to move the then current manager, Ron Pietsch, into an assistant buyer position to give me a hand, and would need an adult to oversee operations. Thirty years later, Ted Zurawski is renowned throughout the country as a shrewd, straightforward, hard-bargaining buyer for Meadows Farms. He is one of my senior vice presidents and I believe I can count on him to be completely loyal and completely honest. Although he spends about twenty million of our dollars a year, he spends it as carefully as if it were his.

It was hard to believe that we were actually outgrowing our produce stand-turned-nursery. We had begun to organize our landscape division, and we really needed a little office space where we could work out of range of the effects of the weather. It looked as if the time was right to build a little office, and we began to brainstorm on it, as we always did when it came to new business.

"Bill," Betty said, "if we're going to build something, I think we need a little place for the cash registers, and maybe where we could store and display our gardening products."

"That would be nice, you're right, but I think the office space will benefit us more ... "

After a lot of discussion on it, we decided on a two-story building on the site of the original produce stand. The first floor, though, would be a full-scale garden center, and we would have our office space situated upstairs.

One end of the building was my office. I wanted it to be exactly right, comfortable, tasteful, plush, and elegant. It had to be perfect. We chose a rich burgundy carpet for the floors, and continued partially up the walls with it. Two of the walls were filled with a sectional sofa, covered in big soft pillows. Above the couch, the walls were covered with mirrors behind a shelf that held pieces of sculpture I had collected. It was an excellent room in which we could meet with our three adult and thirty-five teenage employees.

The other end of the room was virtually filled with the largest desk I could find. Its deep mahogany sheen picked up a glow from the lighted bookshelves behind it, where I displayed my favorite books and additional statues.

Beyond the sliding glass doors, my office was flanked by a wrap around deck, from which I could view my nursery, the traffic on the highway, and my home across the parking lot. It was an office befitting the commanding officer of a growing business, and it had my name on the door.

Life was nearly perfect!

About this time, we calculated that our sales were over a million dollars, and our net worth was about two million. I had become a multi-millionaire without realizing I had been a millionaire! I was thirty-eight years old.

Chapter Twenty-Nine

Whatever Happened to Stan?

I felt very much at home in my new office and developed a nice rhythm with the flow of business in the nursery next door and garden center be low. I had come to be able to predict the busy times and the lax times, but one day, there was a surprise in my routine.

"Stan! Come on in! Good to see you!" I was somewhat at a loss for words as I looked into the eyes of my old friend—one of my best friends in elementary and high school—and said, "Wow, isn't this great!" I must have said the same thing in a couple of different ways. Finally, I spread my arms out, indicating my office. "What do you think? Sit down, buddy! What have you been doing with yourself? Have a cigar?" I held the new box of imported Dominicans and watched Stan accept and light up. Strange how things turned out sometimes.

Seeing him sitting there took me back a few years.

"Mother, would it be all right for Stan to sleep over after the game Friday night?"

"Oh, I suppose so, Billy. Check with his mama, though."

I had had a few friends here and there whom my mother had not especially liked. But Stan had been a good boy, and everyone liked him. He was also a

Meadows

straight-A student, and would sometimes help me with algebra, which pleased my mother to no end. On top of that, Stan's parents went to our church and Stan when to the Baptist Youth Fellowship every Sunday afternoon with my brothers and me.

Stan loved sports—all kinds—and had already determined that someday he would be a sportswriter. I had admired him for already having his life figured out. I had so many things I wanted to do, yet I wasn't sure about any one thing I would do for the rest of my life.

"You don't know what you're going to do with your life?" Stan would tease. "Oh, come on, Bill, sure you do! You're going to marry Betty Lewis! And you're going to have a whole litter of babies. And you'll be stocking groceries down at the A&P. You'll be buyin' dented cans at a discount to feed your family, and borrowing from your families to pay the rent on a cold water cabin down by the creek." Stan would throw back his head and laugh good-naturedly. "Yep, you'll be quite the man about town, Bill! And when I come through these parts, I'll drop by in my big fancy car, and you and me'll shoot the breeze. I'll offer you a big expensive cigar and you'll be so proud to know somebody like me!"

Stan hadn't realized that I was already proud to know somebody like him. He was smart, ambitious and a great guy. At least I had *thought* he was a great guy. But one night, as we walked home from the Baptist Youth Fellowship, Stan gave me one of those "promise you won't tell anybody" spiels, and then confided that he had stolen the BYF money, over which he was the treasurer. I was stunned into silence. But my friend momentarily mistook my reaction as acceptance. "Yeah, I knew you'd be impressed! It was so easy!" he bragged.

I could hardly believe what I was hearing. Stan? Stealing? From the church? I turned to stare at him. "I'm not impressed, Stan! You're stupid! I can't believe you did that!" I had turned away from him and walked on quickly by myself.

Stan called after me, just once, but I didn't look back.

Things weren't quite the same between us after that. I didn't steal, had never stolen, actually, and couldn't believe a good friend of mine could talk about it so casually. What other things might Stan have done without my knowing it? I just didn't trust him anymore.

So Stan and I drifted apart just a little. We still walked home from church together, but I didn't ask him to sleep over anymore. I don't know if anyone even noticed we weren't as close as we had been.

When school let out that summer, we just kind of went our separate ways, and other than Sundays, we didn't really see each other until football practice started in August.

As I mentioned earlier, football was very popular in our town, and most young boys hoped to someday wear the maroon and white of the Woodrow Wilson Flying Eagles. That summer, I'd meet up again with old Stan, in his glory at last, ready to play some real sports. I had tried not to think about him over the summer, but seeing him kind of irked me, as I thought about his stealing that offering money, and getting away with it Scot free.

It was during the second game of the season when things changed a lot for old Stan. He got hit with a very hard tackle and fell to the ground like a lead weight. And he didn't get up. Man, I knew how it felt to get the wind knocked out of you and poor Stan was probably seeing stars right about then. The coach stood over him, then knelt down and motioned for his assistant and the team manager, who then ran off the field. Stan's mom ran onto the field, and knelt beside him, and looked like she was praying. She stayed like that until an ambulance arrived a few minutes later and Stan was whisked away.

I didn't know what had happened until his mother asked for prayer for Stan, who had suffered a seizure of some sort. That was the last game Stan ever played in. I knew it must have been killing him because he really had lived for sports, even though he was good at so many other things. Finally, I knew I had to go see him and try to give him some encouragement.

"Why, Bill, what a nice surprise!" his mother greeted me. "We haven't seen you in such a long time!"

"Well, I've been kind of busy, but I thought maybe Stan could use some company. How's he doing?"

"Pretty good! I guess you heard he can't play football anymore, but try keeping Stan away from sports! He's out back—you can see for yourself!"

I rounded the corner of the house just in time to see Stan do a string of cartwheels, ending in what looked like very painful splits. I moved to help him up, but he sprung to his feet with a big smile, his arms extended above his head like some Olympic pole vaulter.

"Stan! What the heck? Gymnastics?"

"Nope! Cheerleading!"

"What do you *mean? Cheerleading!* What are you talking about?" I was incredulous.

"I'm talking about cheerleading, dopey. You know—at the football games. I'm going to be a cheerleader."

"Stan, you're a guy. Cheerleaders are girls."

"Yep. Except me. I already tried out. I made the team. I'll be out there Friday night, cheering my little heart out!"

I couldn't believe what I was hearing. A guy like Stan didn't become a cheerleader in a town like ours. There were cheerleaders in college that were men, but somehow that was different. Stan would make a fool of himself, and be the laughing stock of the school. Didn't he have any pride? Stan must have read the look in my eyes as I saw his smile fade just a little.

"It'll be all right, Bill. I want to do this. That's how much the game means to me—I can't just sit in the bleachers waving a pennant. I had another seizure, and the doctors don't know what's causing them. I may never be able to play again. But I think I can do this."

I looked hard at my old pal, and wondered how well any of us ever really knew each other. Though we had been best friends, I never would have expected Stan to take that church money, and I never would have expected him to wind up as a cheerleader. You just never know.

"Well, good luck, buddy, I'll be watching you Friday night," I said, mustering up a cheer I didn't especially feel. And on Friday night, I did watch him. He was really good, and I was thankful that he didn't look girly or anything. Just different.

I saw him off and on throughout the rest of high school, but it seemed that our paths were veering off in different directions. We talked about our plans and it looked as if we were both headed for the military. Stan's seizures had increased in frequency and severity, but he was trying a new medication, and hoped he could still join the Air Force. He still teased me about marrying Betty and being poor hillbillies, who'd be impressed with his big car and imported cigars. We shared a few last laughs after we graduated, then went our separate ways and had lost track of each other until that day in my office.

That day, the badly broken man in front of me had once been one of my best friends. We had shared our dreams and our plans as younger boys, and there was a time when I had admired so much potential wrapped up in one boy. I had endured his teasing, and his dire predictions for my future. He had forecasted poverty for me, yet as he stood before me in that corporate office, where I presided over forty-two people in twenty offices, in a company of which I was owner with my wife. About the only thing he'd gotten right was that Betty and I had married—I guess that was one thing about which there'd never been any denying.

I waited for the feeling of smug satisfaction to settle on me, but it never did. Stan had made it to Sergeant in the Air Force. He had the telltale reddened nose and cheeks of a drinker, his grammar was poor, his clothing shoddy, and somehow, I knew he wasn't driving any big, expensive car. I had everything I wanted in life, and as I watched the smoke circle around Stan's face, I wondered why he had looked me up after so many years.

"Good cigar," he murmured after a few puffs. "Hey, this is a really swell place, Bill. You done good for yourself. Heard you done good, but I just had to see for myself."

"Thanks, Stan. Why don't you let me show you around," I replied, clapping him on the shoulder with a smile.

Like I said, it's funny how things turn out sometimes.

Willard Scott, spokesman for AAN and Farmer

Chapter Thirty

But Who Will Dig the Holes?

As we introduced more and more plants into the nursery, we phased out the produce arm of our business. I have always considered it very important to know when to hold and when to fold. It was good timing, too. Developers were rapidly turning the areas around us into suburbs. In those early days, the builder would completely clear a piece of property, leaving no vegetation whatsoever in order to make room for their heavy trucks and equipment. The result was stark tract housing, crying out for a few trees and shrubs to hide the nakedness. And there we were, just entering the market and almost forcing people to buy from us because of our low prices.

As time went on, we ventured into a more varied selection of trees, including Betty's favorite White Pines, and also Hemlocks. Both of which were in high demand as a screen between neighbors who had become situated just a little too close for comfort. We would bring a flatbed truck from Grandfather Mountain in Lenoir, North Carolina, full of evergreens, selling people five or ten at a time. Before long, people were asking if we could deliver and plant the trees, which were unwieldy and too big for the popular compact car of that period.

My brothers, all of whom had other jobs at the time (two were elementary

Meadows

school principals, one was a high official with the Department of the Navy, and one, a chemical engineer), helped me extensively in those early days, and a couple of them were willing to do a little side planting in order to make a sale. They would charge the customer half of the sale price to do the planting, and I allowed them to keep whatever money they made from the service. It proved to be a satisfactory arrangement over the following several years, and my brothers managed to pick up quite a bit of extra work if they wanted it.

But after a while, we all got busier, and I found I was occasionally turning customers down because no one in my family was available to plant their trees. I was not happy about it, and regretted the sight of any customer walking away without making a purchase.

"Oh, I don't like doing that at all," I grumbled to Big Al Pumner, a former student of mine who had begun to work for me full time.

"Then don't!" he said. "Anybody can dig a hole."

"True enough. I know *you and I* could. Heck, you're right, Al. Run and tell that man we can plant his trees after all!"

That very afternoon, Al and I took two of the other employees, some shovels, and ten White Pine out to the customer's house and did our very first landscaping installation. However, we were exhausted.

"That wasn't so bad, was it?" Big brawny Al boasted, grinning.

I gave him a thorough appraisal. "Well, not for you, maybe."

He laughed heartily.

"Is it something you'd want to do?" I asked him more seriously.

"I'm willing to give it a try," he said. "I think the rest of the guys are OK with it."

And so it was that Al and the guys formed my very first official planting crew, whom I called on as my brothers became less and less available.

Meanwhile, through the years, I had begun to gain quite a bit of knowledge about various plants, big and small. I had always appreciated the beauty innate to the natural landscape, the vast blue-green of the mountain country where I'd grown up. At first, the whole concept of landscape planting had been foreign to me. But as I found myself enjoying the rich variety of plants available, and seeing how they were used in the finer homes in nearby Great Falls and McLean, Virginia, and Potomac, Maryland, I began imagining how I might group them attractively. I had always had an artistic bent and ached to try my hand at putting my creativity to work. My chance came before long when a friend of mine proudly showed me his brand new house.

"Now I just need to buy some of your plants! What do you think I should get?" he asked. "Maybe some of those big Ligustrum?"

I cringed inwardly at the choice. "Tell you what, Jason. Let me figure out what you need to plant; I'll come out next week and draw you something."

He was delighted with the idea and I was happy for the opportunity to test my wings. The following week, I took a sketchpad and drove out to his house, parking across the street, unannounced. For the next hour or so, I sketched the house with the driveway, sidewalks, and so on, and jotted down observations about the neighborhood, and the direction the house faced. As I drew, I began to see the house five years from then. I drew in the greenery, not the way it would look just planted, but as it grew in and shaped itself. I drew curvy beds, shaded in to represent the dark mulch I saw used frequently. To the side of the sketch, I made notes about different possibilities for each area I would plant. I got out of the car to stretch my legs, leaning my sketchpad against the windshield.

Stepping back and looking at my work, it no longer seemed like a big piece of paper with pencil scrawling—it was a beautifully landscaped new home—the finest in the neighborhood. And I couldn't wait to see it fully planted.

Later that week, I took my crew and a pickup truck packed with an assortment of plants. I was still undecided on several of my selections and wanted to see what would look the best against the house. We set all the plants on the ground in the general vicinity of where they were going to go, then began rearranging things, shifting things a few feet in one direction or the other, and stepping back for a different perspective. After fifteen or twenty minutes of artistic license, I gave the order—Let's plant!

The transformation was immediate. The Spartan white siding was softened with the lush green silhouette of spreading yews. The austere corners seemed to mold themselves to the contour of the hollies I had planted at each end of the house. As various other shrubs went in, I found myself grinning. I had done a pretty fair job for my first time out—not bad at all!

Several hours later, Al knocked on the door and asked Jason to come out and see the completed landscape. My satisfaction was complete when I saw the look of approval on my friend's face.

"Wow! I can't believe the difference!" he exclaimed. "This looks great, Bill!"

Before long, friends were regularly asking me for my advice or for a landscape sketch, and I gladly went out whenever I was asked, knowing it would almost definitely result in a plant sale, if not an installation. Furthermore, with each design I created, my confidence grew. I tried new combinations that delighted my clients, and made me realize that I had a talent for design. Gradually, my time got taken up more and more as a landscape designer.

"Bill," Betty said one day. "You aren't going to be able to keep going at this rate. You've got a whole summer business to run, and you can't just do it part-time." I recognized the concern in her voice.

Regretfully, I had to agree. Designing had become my passion, and I enjoyed it fully. And though things hadn't degenerated to the degree that they had when I was working as a teacher and a produce man, I was getting overloaded. Besides, the business as a whole was important to me.

"How about designing two days a week?" Betty suggested. "That should sell enough to keep the fellows busy planting, and give you three or four days to get your other work done."

So that's how we worked it. In fact, we eventually needed to add on another crew. Together, the crews were able to install thirty-five thousand dollars worth of plants per week. Considering our low prices, that amounted to a lot of planting!

One of things I enjoyed most about what I was doing was the selling. In keeping with the play planning I had done on that yellow pad years before, it stood to reason that I counted a sale as a "win" and a decline as a "loss." Of course, I always wanted to win. The adrenaline would rush through my system as I prepared for a design session, in much the same way as it had before a football game I would be coaching.

As our business took shape, so did my vision of how I could impact the landscape industry. It had been my experience that professional landscape design and installation belonged exclusively to the well-to-do. There was certainly no dearth of money in northern Virginia, but there was also a distinct middle-class of folks who were buying nice homes in new subdivisions, and wanting a nice landscape package to turn their houses into homes. In general, these people could not spend hundreds of dollars in consultation fees and then have overpriced plants installed in their yards. They usually opted to do the job themselves and often regretted it. I thought I could change all that.

"I think we better get away for a few days to give this thing some attention," Betty suggested, with a twinkle in her eye.

"Hmm—I can't really think of any place we could go," I said casually, knowing exactly what was on her mind. Of course she was thinking Acapulco. We'd been there before in search of a getaway, and after a somewhat disappointing accommodation, we found ourselves a top notch hotel, the Acapulco Princess, to stay in and fell in love with the city.

We decided to take a trip out there again, and developed our nursery mission statement: We will design, plant, and guarantee a landscape for the same price you would pay for *just the plants* at another nursery.

Satisfied with our start, we decided on a second trip, a little closer to home, to further the planning with our key people. After working for several hours each day, we returned home with some solid ideas on what was to become our newly formed landscape department.

We knew that designing at no extra cost would decrease the cost overall to the homeowner. In fact, we were probably the first to put good landscape design and installation within the financial reach of middle class people. However, a concern we had was, how could we fairly compensate the designer?

"What about commission?" someone suggested.

"No one wants to work on commission—it's too uncertain," someone else said.

My research had told me that designers in our area had several ways of being paid. Some worked on straight salary, while others worked for a salary and a three to five percent commission on work they sold.

"I want to do straight commission," I declared. "That's really a better incentive, and there's no ceiling on how much you can earn. I believe in it so much that I will go against your advice and do it anyway."

The group considered the idea.

"OK," Al ventured. "Suppose I was a designer—how could I make it?"

"Well, let's see, Al. Remember that job we did the other day in Sterling? That job totaled fifteen hundred. If that had been your design, it would have taken you about an hour and a half to draw, and your share would have been two hundred twenty-five. That's fifteen percent."

Al considered what I proposed. "That's good money. One hundred fifty an hour!"

"Right!" I said, "And everything you can add on to that design is more commission for you! What do you think now?"

Heads were nodding in general approval.

"The foreman could make a commission, too," I added, seeing we were on a roll.

"Hold it, Farmer," said one, "that won't work for guys like us."

"Not so fast—hear me out." I quickly explained how a foreman could be compensated above and beyond his hourly wage. At that time, laborers made around five dollars an hour. I felt I could pay eight dollars an hour and add commission, based on meeting a production quota each day. It would be contingent on completing the job and bringing in any balance due from the client. A foreman could make well over one hundred dollars a day if he worked efficiently. I saw Big Al smile at the prospect.

Having determined that our primary marketing rested on the power of the free landscaping concept, we placed an ad, held our breath and waited to see the response.

We didn't have to wait very long. After only two weeks, we were swamped! There was more than enough work to keep our four designers busy, and the five crews we then had. Stress to get everyone accommodated had commenced—*good stress!*

Though my heart stayed in the design aspect of the business, I found I needed to cut back to only one day a week. The rest of the time, I was functioning as buyer, administrator, and customer relations.

* * *

That first year flew by, and before we knew it, we were cleaning up the nursery for the last time before putting the entire operation away for the winter. I was tired from the frantic pace he had kept up all year, working twelve or fourteen hours every day. I don't remember ever feeling so alive and so excited, but I looked forward to a couple of weeks off.

"I'd love to take a nice trip, Betty, but I feel that we have a lot of things to figure out before we open the gates again in March. I guess I'll be working this winter."

"Let's take the key people to Puerto Rico, Bill. If two heads are better than one, think how it will be with everyone there."

"True. There might even be a few problems I was never even aware of, and maybe Big Al or Chuck Trupe will know what needs to be done. Why don't we give it a try?"

* * *

The week in Puerto Rico turned out to be a godsend in more than one way. It gave Betty and me a chance to really know our thirty people who joined us. It also gave us a rest from the tough physical demands of the landscaping business, as well as a chance to take a mental rest and re-think things away from the fray. And most importantly, it gave us an opportunity to talk about what we had done right as well as what we had done wrong so we wouldn't repeat our mistakes.

On our first day of meetings, we simply listed our problems—such things as equipment failure, employee training, or damage to a mailbox or driveway—without engaging in any discussion about them. We asked that everyone think about the potential problems and think of solutions for discussion the following day.

Day two brought possible solutions. We tried to give each item on the list as much discussion as we felt it merited.

Then, by day 3, we were ready to start making decisions. I thoroughly enjoyed the process we had gone through, and appreciated all the input, but everyone knew that it wasn't a democracy. In the final analysis, the responsibility—as well as the decisions—remained on Betty's and my shoulders

We hammered out a lot of important things in those few days. We maintained that we were a residential landscaping business, and determined to avoid the extremes of commercial jobs as well as lawn maintenance. We wanted our landscape department and our retail department to complement each other, so that the average homeowner could come to us, no matter what they were looking for.

It was obvious that we would need more crews, more designers, and more equipment. That meant we needed more space. And strange as it might sound, we needed more overhead. I had very definite ideas about the way I wanted things done. I believed that if a landscape job bore my name, it was a reflection of me, and I wanted it to reflect quality. That meant I had to come up with a way to get everyone doing things the same way.

We developed a foreman's manual where we covered the basics like how deep to plant, and how thick to mulch, as well as some of the tricky things that might arise, like a customer who refused to pay, or getting to a site and realizing you didn't have everything you needed. We began to develop our policies and procedures, always bearing in mind our number one goal, which was *keeping up with the money!* We also focused heavily on our ability to maintain the terms of the guarantee that promised customers their cost for plants, landscaping, and installation would be equivalent or less than what they would pay for just the plants elsewhere.

And lastly, I wanted someone to head up the new department other than myself. I realized that the oversight of this new venture would be a full time job, and I already had a full time job. I began thinking of various people whom I felt had the organizational skills as well as the leadership qualities that would be needed. Before long, I thought of my brother-in-law, Bob Lewis.

He and I had grown up together, of course, and Bobby Lewis had been my best friend, let alone sharing long hours together in the pursuit of sorting tomatoes. By then, at the age of thirty-eight, he was retiring from the Air Force as a Master Sergeant. He had already begun looking for a new job when I approached him about managing my landscape department.

"Now, Bill," he said, "what do I know about landscaping?"

"Nothing, but you can learn. Meanwhile, try teaching somebody else what you *do* know—scheduling, managing, organizing, good work habits—you have the qualities I need in someone for this thing."

"I'll give it some thought," he said.

"OK, Bob," I said. But I was already sold on the idea.

Bob accepted my offer a few days later, and started down a ten-year path that got our fledgling landscape business on its feet and headed in the right direction. Bob's ability to manage left an impact whose success could long be seen in the running of our landscape department. He turned out to be the perfect man for the job.

We were several months into our second year, when our accountant finally gave us the word—our new department had lost somewhere in the neighborhood of three hundred thousand dollars that first year, but we had made about six hundred fifty thousand in retail. I was thankful we had met earlier to make some changes, and only wished we could have done it sooner. I was determined to do this thing right and make money doing it.

Betty and I did a lot of homework. We observed landscapers from the side of the road, asked to meet with people who were already successful, read magazines, and joined organizations. We were eager to learn whatever we could and were truly amazed when we realized that some people didn't want to help us.

"Why would I help you?" one business owner said. "You're competition, and you're undercutting everybody else. I learned the hard way, and you can, too."

"My gracious, that was a mean man!" Betty said as we drove away. I nodded, thinking of how freely I had shared information and ideas with other businessmen. Was I just being naïve, or was I justified in my belief that there was plenty of business out there, and the person doing it best would get the most money?

That was certainly one of my key philosophies; I firmly believed competition was good for everyone. I also believed that I could learn a lot from other people's mistakes.

My survival-of-the-fittest principle trickled down to the foremen and designers, too. I knew that there were many people who liked to be treated fairly, which they equated with being treated equally. It was a concept with which I found fault, having suffered at its hands as a teacher.

Nearly Perfect

One of the beautiful things about being in business for myself is that I could get *ahead* by doing a better job. Maybe that wasn't fair in some folks' eyes, but it certainly seemed right to me. I gave my most productive designers the best leads because they were able to turn them into the biggest jobs. I gave my most productive foremen the bigger jobs and the ones that were closer to the nursery, so that they could put in a full day on site. That enabled them to make the most commission, thus they were rewarded for their productivity. It may not have been fair, but it was the right thing to do.

Some of those highly motivated foremen voiced some concern that there were days when they couldn't even get off the lot until 9:30 a.m. because of the congestion. It took time for ten or twelve foremen and their crews to load plants and mulch, gather up tools and equipment, square away their paperwork, and hit the road. This was considered down time by the better foremen. We decided we needed another change.

After much discussion, we determined that the best idea might be to have a night crew that cleaned off the day's trucks and reloaded them for the next day. I chose one of my best full time men and offered him a little extra on the hour to head up a night loading crew, composed of several teenagers. The foremen viewed this as a big improvement, and we kept this practice for many years.

Though my foremen were making over a hundred dollars a day, and usually able to work ten to twelve hours overtime a week, and my top designer was grossing over one hundred thousand a year, which was a small fortune at that time, and we were still capitalizing on the phrase *discount nursery* in all of our ads. It seemed to somehow express that we sold below average quality plants. We were managing to get landscape jobs in some of the most elite neighborhoods in the metropolitan area, and eventually, we heard from one such client on the issue of our name.

"I contracted with Meadows Farms because I liked the plants I saw, and your prices made sense. But now there is a big red truck sitting in my driveway that says 'discount nursery' on it! I'm not buying bargain basement landscaping and I sure don't want my neighbors to think I'm cheap!"

I guess we thought the complaint was funny at the time, but she had a point. Our marketing truly was based on affordability, but certainly not on inferior or shoddy workmanship. Eventually, we took the words *discount nursery* out of our ads and off our big red trucks.

Though we maintained a pricing structure well below that of other nurseries and landscape companies, there came a time when we desperately needed to increase our prices. We were drawing very nice salaries, but company profits were small considering the tremendous amount of work everyone seemed to be doing. We couldn't grow anymore without turning a better profit. Several meetings later, we decided on our pricing for the following year, with more than a little concern that it might cause us to lose some business. Our fears proved to be unfounded, as we happily realized we were gaining a good reputation and a loyal customer base. The business grew, and so did our profits.

In time, Betty was to find out some new, interesting information.

"Look at this article," she said one evening as we sat reading together in bed. "It says here that Long Island is always a step ahead of our area. Who would've thought that? They say you can go to New York to predict what the trends will be here—but several years down the road! Do you think that's possible?"

"I guess it might be. But there's only one way to find out. Let's go to Long Island."

The article listed several renowned garden centers and landscaping firms in that area and Betty got busy on the telephone making arrangements for us to meet and talk to some other business owners. It proved to be an interesting trip. The landscapers in Long Island were, in fact, branching out into something new. It seemed that about sixty percent of the jobs included some sort of non-plant enhancement; walkways, patios, walls, decks, planter boxes, trellises, and gazebos.

"Why, you'd need to have carpenters, masons—this is more than a guy with a shovel can do!" I was bewildered by the prospect.

"It's not as hard as you think," we were told. "Yes, we have a couple of experts, but the crews are made up of laborers, just like the ones doing the planting. This is what the people ultimately want, so why shouldn't we be the ones to sell it to them?"

Although we didn't jump right on that bandwagon, we did see it become the wave of the future, and we were prepared to move in that direction when the time was right.

The next few years were exciting ones. We opened a second nursery in Annandale, Virginia, and continued a steady growth in the sale of landscape contracts. We planted six hundred cherry trees around the Tidal Basin, and also had the honor of landscaping President Gerald Ford's swimming pool. Although we were rather firmly requested not to use that jewel in our advertising, which I thought was wrong because we had not been alerted to that restriction when we bid, it was a feather in our cap within the landscaping community.

With business seriously on the rise, we sought someone to give Bob Lewis a hand. I found someone in one of the most unlikely spots.

"I'm not crazy about these Little League meetings," I complained to Betty one evening. "They don't start on time, there's no set ending time, and people blow off a lot of hot air about nothing."

"You have to go. You're a coach," Betty said.

"So I should be *coaching*," I pointed out, "not sitting in a meeting. Besides, I usually don't agree with them anyway."

"Go. You'll be late. I'll wait up for you."

Begrudgingly, I drove over to the elementary school in Sterling Park, where a board meeting would decide some policies for the fall football season. Attendance was good, and everyone seemed to have an opinion. I glanced at my watch and hunkered down for the duration.

Listening absently, I sketched football plays on my notepad, in between jotting down dates and ideas. I sat up and took notice, however, when I heard some ideas and decisions that sounded really bad for our boys. I wrote down a couple of thoughts, but before I could gain recognition, another man had the floor.

"With respect to the late hour, I hope you don't mind me getting right to the point," he said. "The decision you're about to make isn't realistic. Furthermore, it wouldn't surprise me if forty percent of the parents up and pulled their kids out of football if that becomes your policy. The league will suffer, morale will suffer, and next year, we'll be back in this same room trying to figure out how we can get participation up. Let's make the right call now instead of wasting a year."

A murmur of approval went through the room as the man quickly outlined an idea that was obviously superior to any that had been on the table, and to my amazement, much the same idea I was trying to work out when the man had stood to speak. Smart guy, I thought to myself.

"Who's that?" I asked the fellow beside me.

"Name's Sieber. John, I think. He coaches. Has a couple of kids in the league. Lives here in the Park, I think," my neighbor answered.

I surveyed the room of nearly two hundred parents and coaches, and wondered about a man who got up and told them what he thought. He cut a striking figure at six-foot-two and two hundred plus pounds or so, but it wasn't his size that got my attention. It was his self-confidence; his straight forward approach that got me.

"How was the meeting?" Betty asked later.

"Same old thing," I said. "But there was one interesting thing." I explained about John Sieber, and Betty nodded in appreciation.

"Not too many people like that out there are there?" she said, confirming what was on my mind.

"Maybe I'll give him a call sometime."

"Sure, why not? It's always good to know strong people in the neighborhood."

A few days later, I did give him a call. I wasn't sure what I would say, but I introduced myself and invited him to stop by the nursery. He seemed receptive to the idea and we arranged to meet, ostensibly to talk over the Little League situation. We did discuss that a little, but ultimately, I got around to what was on my mind.

"John, I'd like to offer you a job. I think you're the person I'm looking for to help out in our landscape division. We seem to be outgrowing ourselves!"

"I'm flattered, Farmer," he said, "but I don't happen to be looking for a job. And besides, I know nothing about plants!"

"I know about plants. My designers know about plants. My foremen know about plants. Tell me what you know."

"I'm in management. I make decisions, account for the money, work out the personnel issues, satisfy customers ... that's what I've been doing in restaurants, hotels, retail—but not in landscaping."

Yet, it must have sounded enticing to John, because two days later, he accepted. From the start, it was a good match. John worked with Bob Lewis for the next several years, maintaining the same type of order and discipline that Bob believed in. And then, when Bob resigned to live full time on the shores of the beautiful Shenandoah River, John was a natural to head up the landscaping department.

The transition occurred almost seamlessly as John took over the supervision of close to one hundred people in the department. He was tough, sometimes even mean, but he ran a tight ship and didn't take advantage of his people.

As we moved John up, we were happy to be able to move a young man within the company up to the position of assistant. His name was Dave Reed. He'd already shown his abilities quite clearly and we were confident in his capacity to take the next career step in stride.

In 2003, not only is John Sieber a senior vice president of the company, but so are both Dave Reed, and Ted Zurawski.

Back in 2000, with Dave Reed running it, the landscape department had sales of close to twelve million, after having moved to its fourth home, a twelve-

Nearly Perfect

acre site a mile or so west of our corporate headquarters in Chantilly, Virginia. As usual, we're already looking for more space for our huge inventory as well as sixty work vehicles and a fleet of employee vehicles, twenty-six designers, forty-two crews, and one hundred and sixty laborers.

Though the new location housed a nursery for many years, there had always been a problem with water, and we were concerned about signing a contract for something we might not be able to use. We agreed to a sixty-day feasibility study with the owners, during which time we began drilling a well.

At twelve dollars per foot, well-drilling was a risky proposition. At a depth of four hundred feet, we were bring up only one gallon a minute, and reluctantly began drilling at another site. The same thing happened again, and the equipment was set up at yet another spot. We crossed our fingers, but were disappointed to only get two gallons per minute at the same depth.

Jay held the contention that we should go for another one hundred feet. At five hundred feet, the rate was three gallons per minute, which was still a far cry from what we needed. At six hundred feet, it was just a trickle more.

It was getting hairy—should we cut our losses or go for it. Jay was adamant.

"I know it sounds crazy, but I just know there's water down there—go a few more feet!"

"It's your money," the driller retorted, grinning.

I raised an eyebrow, but held my peace. Jay was president by then, and that was due to my confidence in his decisions. He had made other important decisions, too, by then. Betty and I found ourselves thrilled with his fiancé, Doreen, whom he married in September, 1990. Their meeting had been chance, when Doreen's father had brought her along to our housewarming in 1987. Although Jay had taken his time to pursue a relationship with Doreen, it had been time well spent. The two made a wonderful match and have two terrific children. Good decisions were becoming something I could depend on my son for.

At the depth of six hundred and twenty-five feet, we hit a gusher of one hundred and sixty-five gallons per minute! The area just didn't yield that kind of water—we may as well have struck oil!

A year later, I listened incredulously as Dave Reed told the board, "This place is fine for now, but we won't be able to stay there forever."

It was a pretty stressful notion, but it was the kind of stress I could live with. *Good stress!* Ultimately, I guess the answer to my question is that just about *all* kinds of people will dig the holes.

Meadows

Long before we'd made all of those moves, though, and before we even decided to change the place that we called home, Betty and I would go through the most challenging experience of our lives.

Cindy, 1981

Love endures forever

Our Cindy

Chapter Thirty-One

The Longest Night

"*M*om!"

I awoke with a start, and looked around the dark room, feeling disoriented. I had heard her voice clearly as she called for me, but as my eyes grew accustomed to the blackness, I could only see Bill's outline as he slept beside me. The trailer was silent and I could just make out the numbers on the clock across the room. Two o'clock. The middle of the night. I whispered softly, "Cindy?"

Silence.

Normally, I was a sound sleeper, and was rarely awakened by a dream. But a feeling of dread had begun to creep through me. I tried to shake it off and hunkered back down under the covers, closing my eyes, willing sleep to return quickly. I thought of my sister, Mary Lou, and the problems she had been having with her husband, Gary. I wished that she wasn't so far way so that I could be there for her. I had missed her so much when she moved to Florida. She was hurting then, and my hands were tied. It was so frustrating not to be there. I vowed to call her the next day.

I went back over the conversation I had had with Cindy earlier in the day. She wasn't as far away from me as Mary Lou, but still, she was gone off to college and I missed having her around the house. That night, her new boyfriend had plans to go somewhere without her. It was an event, a concert, that had been planned before

Meadows

they'd started going out together. But Cindy, well, she wasn't used to be left out, I guess, and she was very upset. I had wanted to give her a hug and comfort her, and I had done my best. I knew I couldn't protect her from the bumps and bruises of growing up, but I still wished I could do more than just reassure her over the phone that everything would be all right.

I frowned a little in the dark. Was I experiencing the empty-nest syndrome, I wondered. I moved closer to Bill, wanting to wake him up right then, but I waited for the feeling to go away. It never did. I tossed and turned for the next several hours, and woke feeling tired, restless, and unexplainably sad.

Fumbling around the kitchen, I urged my fingers to wake up and act right. Turning on the oven, I prepared several pieces of chuck roast to slow-cook. They would make a nice lunch for the gang after a busy morning in the woods. Glints of sun made their way through the sheer curtains, and I pushed them aside to brighten the room. It was going to be a gorgeous day.

Taking my mug of steaming coffee, I stepped out onto the front stoop and sat on the stairs of the trailer. We had brought it down there as a nice place for us to stay on that beautiful land. The sky was clear, and meshed with the brilliantly colored foliage, all captivating in the spring-like temperatures that week before Thanksgiving. Such days never failed to fill me with joy. Except for that day. I pulled my robe close to me and shuddered involuntarily. I could not seem to shake the feeling of dread that had gripped me since I'd awakened at 2:00 a.m.

"Honey?" Bill called gently from behind. "You OK?" His face was filled with concern.

"Yeah, fine!" I replied in what I hoped was a cheerful voice. I stood and kissed his cheek, then moved my body into his warm embrace.

"We'd better get a move on, Betty! I told Berman we'd be out there around 8:00. I think I heard Jay moving around in there. Should we get a little breakfast?"

Bill sounded so cheerful that I think I envied him a little. We were meeting for a family tradition of setting up tree stands and various other preparations for the start of deer season the next day. Everyone else was staying at the family farm, an eight hundred-acre farm Bill's family had purchased mainly for weekend retreats for the whole family. As usual, though, we were staying on our new piece of property, adjacent to the farm. Bill was really in his element there in the country with his family and the beautiful scenery. He looked healthy and rested and happy. I felt a rush of love for him just then. Life was good.

We all headed over to the new 425-acre farm we had purchased at Mine Run. The air fairly snapped with excitement as people moved in various directions. Many people rode four-wheel drive vehicles, while others walked and visited at a leisurely *pace. The younger cousins ran around laughing and playing with the dogs, while the older ones compared their hunting stories, and boasted of what they would bag the next day. It was a perfect morning.*

"Look!" one of the little ones pointed eagerly down the lane. A state trooper's car followed slowly behind a car driven by my sister-in-law Margaret. My knees went weak as I instantly envisioned Mary Lou. I thought of my restlessness the night before. I was sure something terrible had happened to her. I knew that in that very moment, I would be forever linked to that complete stranger approaching me, whom I believed was about to tell me that my sister was dead.

The trooper stopped to talk to Bill and his brother, Berman for a moment, and I watched as the two appeared to collapse into one another, their faces defeated, looking small and weak. It was a moment of indescribable sorrow, playing out in slow, agonizing motion. The brilliance of that fall day had faded to sepia, and though I could see people seeming to fall with the same looks of devastation on their faces, my eyes were riveted to Bill. He moved to me. I willed him to keep the awfulness to himself. I was petrified of feeling the horror drawn on his beautiful face.

"It's Cindy," he choked out, his voice cracking. "Cindy's dead."

"No, that's not right," I said, shaking my head. I knew it had to be wrong. I had just spoken to her. She would be calling later. She'd said so. That would clear everything up. But even knowing that, my body had betrayed me. It began to shake, and I felt myself giving way to the many loving arms surrounding me.

I needed to get home, though. I needed to be there when she called. Hearing her voice would break the evil spell under which everyone had fallen. "Cindy will call, soon," I said, trying to reassure us all.

Bill squeezed my hand, but remained silent. We were in the back of someone's car, and I only remember sights and sounds in short, strobe-like pieces, everyone seeming to move in awkward, disjointed ways. I did see tears pouring from Bill's eyes. I leaned over and whispered to him, "None of this is true. She's going to call me later."

He responded by looking at me in a way I'd never seen him do before. Then he simply looked away, his grief separate.

I moved through the following days woodenly. I watched my world around me like that same old sepia-toned movie. It was drab and lifeless, strangely disconnected from me. There were kind people around me, like my sister-in-law, Margaret, who gave me some pills to help me rest, who took me through the day-to-days, like brushing my teeth, taking phone calls and giving me messages, and even cried for me.

I asked about Bill occasionally, and Jay, but in a formal, almost polite manner, as if they were someone else's people. Mostly, I stared straight ahead, focusing my mind on my beautiful eighteen-year-old daughter, who could smile and laugh so close in front of my face that my hand would fly out to touch her, but grasp only at the empty air.

I heard someone in Cindy's room, and for the briefest moment I was sure she was back. But it was only Margaret, opening the closet door and looking at Cindy's clothes.

"What are you doing?" I demanded. What an outrage, especially in light of all the madness going on around me! I ran over and slammed shut the doors to the closet.

"Betty," Margaret said as gently as she could, "I just wanted to find something nice for Cindy to wear, but I can do it later if you prefer." Her voice was so kind and compassionate. I looked at her in confusion.

"To wear? You said, 'to wear.' What do you mean?" But as soon as the words slipped out, I knew. It was as though a lead weight had been bouncing around inside me, but then landed solidly in the core of my being. Cindy was gone. She wasn't going to call. There would be no more calls. No more girltalk. No more planning, shopping, trips. Nothing.

Cindy had gotten into a car with three other teenagers, all of them students at her college—and all of them had been drinking. The driver was the captain of the football team. I guess Cindy felt she had to do something, not wanting to stay home alone, with her new boyfriend going out without her. But through all of our efforts, all of our constant reminders and talks about the dangers of drinking, Cindy hadn't distinguished the peril that night. The other three virtually walked away, but our baby was thrown through the windshield, ending up underneath the vehicle. The officials assured me that she had died on impact. It was the only comfort I could take. In so many ways, I, too, had died on impact.

The wake, the funeral, out-of-town relatives. Neighbors, employees, and family. My world was like a revolving door with people rushing in to squeeze my hand or pat my head, then rushing out again, unchanged.

Yet, for me, time would forever be marked as "before Cindy died," and "after Cindy died." Losing her became the pivotal moment around which every other element of my life revolved. My world grew small and dark. I stayed in bed long after I woke in the morning, drapes pulled, my head toward the wall. I would stay in my nightgown and sip coffee, then realize with a start that most of the day was gone.

I would catch glimpses of Bill here and there, yet there was a canyon of grief separating us. We would pass each other in the hallway and sometimes embrace silently. I would stroke his head as I passed him on the couch. He would pour me a soda when he got one for himself. We did not ignore each other, but we each had to lick our own wounds.

I would see him staring out into nothingness, looking bewildered and confused, and my heart went out to him. But I had no words to float across the canyon and touch my beloved's heart. Nor could he touch mine. It was the loneliest, coldest place I have ever been.

As the weeks unfolded into months, I began to go through the motions of living. I read the notes people had written, carefully noting those needing a response. I cleaned out the refrigerator, and returned people's dishes, with a little thank you tucked inside. I accepted a few phone calls, always feeling as awkward and at a loss for words as the caller. I missed my husband, as we shared our bed, backs to each other after a murmured goodnight. I missed sharing with my best friend, my childhood sweetheart. We would look at each other and smile sadly across our self-made gulf, feeling completely alone for the first time in almost thirty years.

Every day, as a part of my routine, I would go into Cindy's room where I had placed her cowboy boots after having them repaired. In those days, Urban Cowboy was the rage, and Cindy had looked terrific in her stylish boots. Just before she died, she had asked me if I could drop off a pair of them to be repaired, which I had done. On their return, I found that they gave me comfort; their scent, the feel of them. Somehow because they represented one of the final acts of love I had performed for her, they seemed to remain ever so slightly alive with her, and it gave me comfort to hold them.

Then one day, my friend, Eileen, coaxed me into having a day out together—lunch and a haircut. We had a nice time, at least on the surface, for I was becoming accustomed to living life on two distinct levels. At the one level, I listened to Eileen talk about the problems she was having; a separation and impending divorce, aging parents, and self-centered adult children. I nodded sympathetically. But on a deeper level, I tiptoed through a minefield of memories; Cindy's first day of school, Cindy in a school play, in her prom dress—everything was Cindy and me. Shadowy figures around us represented those who loved us, cared about us—Bill, Jay, Mary Lou, Margaret, and Mother. I had closed them out since that terrible day.

Eileen was saying, "You have no idea!" right about the time that my two distinct levels merged into one, functional level, and I became alive again—not kicking, maybe, but alive.

"Actually, I do!" I said, startling my friend, I think. I rose from the table. "But I really must go. Thanks so much for the invitation. You have no idea!"

I needed to go home and figure things out; where was I? Where did I need to be? I entered the house with renewed eyes and saw the pervasive darkness, the gloom. I began to open curtains and drapes, not so much with a sense of joy, but rather one of determination. I would pull myself together and go back to work. I would stop thinking only of myself and start looking for ways to do things for other people. I would get some professional help for myself so that I could get on with my life.

Looking out the side window, toward the nursery, I could see Bill on the balcony adjacent to his office, just watching, as men so often do. I could only imagine the painful thoughts that were his constant companions. I wasn't sure how we could reach each other, but I knew that we must. I had read that when couples lose a child, eighty-five percent of them end up divorcing. If I had read the same article a year earlier, I would have scoffed at the very idea. It seemed obvious that a tragedy of that magnitude would bring people close together. Yet, there were Bill and I—lovers, sweethearts, best friends since childhood—unable to be together even as we made our daily treks to the cemetery to spill our lonely tears on our little girl's grave. Was I in danger of losing my husband?

I grabbed a yellow pad, as Bill and I had done hundreds of times before, and sat down to make my plan:

"1. Return to a normal life as soon as possible." That was as far as I got.

I stared at the words, I felt the tears puddling in my eyes, then spilling down my face. Was the idea of normal even possible in the wake of so much pain? Where had God been when my daughter's life was snuffed out? If He were a loving God, I didn't need that kind of love.

I thought of my precious son, Jay, keeping his feelings inside, though he had left school temporarily to move into a house with his cousin and be close to us. He only had one more semester of school, and needed to go back and finish. I wanted to encourage him in that direction, and to assure him that Bill and I would be all right.

I took several days in that self-evaluation type mode, counting my blessings, making notes to myself, planning how I would reclaim my life. It looked like a big job, but I would take one small step at a time.

I looked for a psychiatrist who could meet my needs, and it was a frustrating search. The first doctor I laid out my heart-wrenching story to actually had the audacity to suggest that Cindy had wanted to die. But I must have already grown stronger, because if I hadn't, I think I might have melted back into a permanent pool of personal abandon. Yet, I knew he was either very poorly adapted to his profession or experimenting on his patients, and I moved ahead with my search. On my sixth attempt, I was able to find someone who seemed to be able to connect with me at some level. At the end of our session, he suggested a medicine that was new to the market at that time, called Prozac, and I was not enthusiastic.

"I don't think so," I said.

But he explained to me that the medication might help me to process information without the filter of sadness and grief through which I was seeing everything. Reluctantly, I agreed to give it a try. In a few days, I began to notice a little difference. It was an encouraging sign.

* * *

Although I find it nearly impossible to relate all of what went on inside my heart and mind at that dark time in our lives, I can try to describe some of the events I survived. Betty and I had not borne the burden together at the start, and much as anything, I guess, if you divide the base, you can't expect to find much strength in the individual parts.

By the day of the funeral, I was running on nothing but unspoken, unfathomed agony. Not long before, I had experienced being faced with choosing a headstone for Cindy's gravesite. And that being one of the things that is beyond description, I can at least explain that it was the worst experience I have had in my life. At the arrival of the funeral, I was expected, of course, but I never showed. Although the day I never showed up for Larry Fones's presentation was nowhere near as devastating, I subconsciously responded similarly on that dark day in November of 1981. I began to run—I didn't know where I was going, probably not even *that* I was going. And when I was finished, exhausted, I had run ten miles through Sterling Park. I came upon someone as I puffed to a stop.

"My daughter is dead," I told him. "Her funeral is today."

He patted me on the back. I don't know if he knew me. I don't even know who he was. I was still somewhere in my mind, running, feeling transported. I was in the clouds, high up in Heaven, and I had died, too. I continued, until I saw some beautiful flowers. They turned out to be roses. I felt I needed them, and began to pick some. A woman appeared from somewhere. It was her home, and I was picking her roses. But she knew me, and she knew what had happened.

"Take whatever you want, Farmer," she said, her voice emotional and full of compassion. "You just go ahead and take all you want."

Somehow, I still made it to the funeral. I had brought those roses with me.

The days that followed are a blur. I remember driving the full length of the Washington Beltway, over and over, drinking coffee, trying to find something. In retrospect, I guess it was hope. But I saw nothing. So I kept going. I ran the high school track day after day, drank more coffee, and drove some more.

Betty couldn't get out of bed. And we did not connect as we had for so many wonderful years before. We were both buried in so much grief we just simply couldn't lift an arm high enough to reach the other.

I did eventually write about Cindy, and our loss. I put the emotions into poetry that we wanted desperately to have performed by someone well-known enough to be able to create a living legacy for Cindy. But it wasn't meant to be, and we eventually set the idea aside.

It was only by the will of the Creator that Betty found and kept that article about family's being torn apart by deep tragedy. On that night that we finally talked about all of it, I felt as though I had begun to live again.

* * *

The most critical part of my plan to bring back normal living was to bridge the gap between my husband and me. I could not imagine my life without him. Nor could I imagine continuing on the course we had set between us since Cindy had died. We needed to talk.

"Bill? Can I talk to you about something?" We were preparing for bed, and Bill sat at the edge, his back to me.

"Sure, what is it?" he said.

Pulling the newspaper article out of my nightstand drawer that had offered the eighty-five percent failure rate statistic on parents who lost a child, I handed it to him. "I want you to read this, Bill," I said. "I'm really scared." Just like we had so many times, I would find articles that I felt he should read. This would be one of the most pivotal in our lives.

Bill slipped his glasses back on and took the paper from me slowly. "What is it?" he asked. The Washington Post article was titled "A Death in the Family." Bill grimaced at the name, but took the pages and sat back against his pillow.

I left the room quietly and slipped downstairs to pour us each a cold drink. When I returned, Bill's eyes met mine for the first time in months. "You're right, Betty. We should be scared."

Thus began a long overdue dialog. Words flowed, tears streamed, suspicions were quelled, promises were made, and plans were laid. We shared our pain for the first time, each amazed at how well the other could describe what we were feeling. It was as though our ball of clay had been ripped apart and now we were being blended back together again, two halves of the same whole. Smooth again. One again. When we had used all our words, we fell into each other's arms, exhausted. We made love, almost reverently, then, before we drifted off to sleep, cleared of the demons of insomnia, I remember whispering, "I am so glad we're married." Bill's smile was the sweetest response I had ever known. The long night was finally behind us.

Rocky and Katie, 1986

Rocky at age eighteen, 2003   *Kate at age eighteen, 2001*

Chapter Thirty-Two

A New Idea

The next day, we slept late and I made us a nice brunch when I got up. After we ate and showered, I suggested to Bill that we go to the cemetery together, for the first time since the funeral. We were almost timid with each other, each of us having developed our own way of being there. But when we got out of the car, I took Bill's arm, then wrapped my arm around his waist. Together, we made our way over to the simple stone, and stood silently.

"Remember how thrilled she was when we moved to the new house?" I asked with a laugh.

"She loved life. Just like you, Betty," Bill said.

"You mean just like you," I said with a smile.

"Well, regardless of where it came from, we did a good job with her, didn't we?"

We were both crying softly, but smiling through our tears and holding each other close. After a few more moments, we turned back to the car, having crossed another of the hurdles that separated us. There would still be times when one or the other of us might go to the cemetery alone, but for the most part it became one of the things we could now share.

Bill and I had begun exercising for two hours after work everyday at a health spa with an indoor track. Afterwards, we would grab dinner out and usually end up going to a movie. By the time we got home, it would be 11:00 p.m. and I

Meadows

would take a pill and go to bed. We were usually able to stay away from home except to sleep. Our fabulous dream home had become a mausoleum, sad and somber. We talked about that one night over dinner.

"The house hasn't changed."

"Of course not. But it seems empty now. Cindy was a big part of our life there."

We began to talk about our life together, the many shared events and adventures. We had seen and done so much since our West Virginia childhood. We had met important people, owned expensive cars, gone on luxury cruises, traveled all over. It had been a wonderful life, but we both agreed that by far the very best thing we had ever done together was the raising of Jay and Cindy.

"Sometimes I wish I could just turn back the hands of time," I sighed. "The children brought us so much joy."

Bill leaned over and squeezed my shoulder. "Want to go make another baby, honey?" We both laughed at the idea. At forty-seven years of age, I did not especially wish to become pregnant again! Still, I wouldn't have minded raising a couple more kids. "Remember when Cindy first left for college, and we talked about maybe taking in some foster children?" I reminded him.

He nodded thoughtfully. "Right, but didn't you do a little research and decide that there were too many problems?"

He was right. Some of the articles I had read were very negative, not only about the foster children having many serious social problems, but also about the children being assimilated into a family only to be suddenly removed and returned to their birth family. It had the potential to cause pain for everyone involved.

I began to think seriously about the possibility of adopting a child. Wasn't there someone out there who was right for us? I began researching, as any thorough ex-librarian would do, all the avenues that might be open to us. We could put our name on a list for a baby. Our name might move slowly up the list over the next several years, but when we made it to the top would much preference be given to a fifty-year-old couple?

On the other hand, we could probably get an older child without the long wait. A child who had mental or physical disabilities or was perhaps emotionally disturbed. But again, it seemed too great of a challenge at that stage of our lives. We weren't especially interested in a foreign adoption either. It was probably best to shelve the whole idea and wait for Jay to marry and give us some grandchildren.

Meanwhile, the pieces of our lives began to slide back into place. Little by little. We agreed to share our thoughts as much as possible, and carry each other's burden of grief. We talked openly and began to laugh again, and enjoy the company of our friends. Jay returned to school and started to put his own life back together. Life was different, but it was still good.

Then, one day, I felt the rain pelting against the bedroom window, and peeked cautiously at the clock on the dresser. It was 6:45 a.m. and Bill had already gone over to his office to get some work done. I pulled myself out of bed and threw open the curtains. It was wet and dreary. Feeling a chill, I grabbed my robe and headed down to the kitchen. I just didn't want to go to work that day. I felt that I had been doing great for a while. My doctor had cut back on the Prozac. I went to work everyday, ate right, and took care of my husband and myself. So why was I in such a funk that day, I wondered.

Hesitating for only a moment, I called Bill's office.

"This here's the Farmer," he answered in his usual upbeat way.

Disguising my voice, I stammered, "Mr. Farmer, I can't come to work today."

There was a long pause, then, "Betty? Is this you?"

We both laughed, but Bill seemed concerned that I didn't want to come to work.

"I'm fine, baby. Just a little down, and with the rain and all, I think I'll stay in. Maybe make us something nice for dinner tonight."

"Well, if you're sure you're all right. Have a good day."

For months, everyone had told me to keep busy, and I did exactly that. So much so that I was a little lost with a whole unplanned day before me. Well, the first order of business would be a cozy fire. Ever since I was a child, I have loved fires—the warmth, the glow, the crackle. Bill would probably tease me about lighting a fire in April, but it was perfect for such a raw day. I dragged a beanbag chair close to the hearth and dropped into it, my feet extended toward the warmth. Reaching for the remote control, I flicked on the television, and worked my way through the channels.

The Charlie Rose Show, a local presentation with a talk show format, was just coming on, and I left it there as I reached for a magazine.

The guest was a woman named Harriet Blankfield, who was in the business of finding surrogate mothers for infertile couples. I perked up and began listening intently as the woman described something that seemed to have come from a futuristic sci-fi movie, yet there she was, operating successfully out of a nearby Maryland suburb. The concept was incredible. Sperm from the future father was used to impregnate the surrogate mother. She carried the baby for the couple and then handed him or her over to the couple at the baby's birth.

It could be the very thing we were looking for! After the interview was over, I pulled on some sweats and headed over to Bill's office in the rain, my funk forgotten.

"Bill, you'll never believe what I just heard!" My words tumbled out as Bill sat there, grinning, bewildered.

"Now, honey, settle down a little so we can talk this thing through. It all sounds pretty wild to me!"

Some women might have considered that reaction discouraging, but I knew my husband. If he said something sounded "wild," it was practically the same as his saying, "Let's go!" I eagerly told him all I had heard, as he nodded thoughtfully. When I finished, he was smiling. "That definitely sounds like it has possibilities! Woman, you just might have something here!"

I ran back across the yard, hugging myself, and grinning the whole way. He liked the idea! I liked the idea! We had something to plan and anticipate together! For a moment, it seemed like old times.

There is nothing quite like the smell of a library—the paper, the ink, the smell of books. My years as a librarian had been wonderful ones, and I had loved the hours spent among the written word. It was much the same now as then, yet there were also differences.

"Card catalog?" the young assistant asked, confused.

Her supervisor came around the desk with a smile. "Of course we still have a card catalog," she said, "but most people find the computerized system more convenient. May I show you?"

The librarian helped me locate what I needed, and I spent the next several days reading everything I could find on Twentieth Century reproduction. The more I learned, the more enthusiastic I became.

It had been just four years since the world learned of baby Louise Brown, the first test-tube baby, whose conception occurred in a Petri dish before she was implanted in her mother, who carried her to term. Two years later, Elizabeth Kane had become the first publicized surrogate mother, after being inseminated.

I focused on the legal and ethical issues. What about a child born with disabilities? A mother who wants to keep the baby? The adoptive mother changing her mind? The whole issue of selling babies? There was much to consider. I had received a box of information from Harriet Blankfield, via the Charlie Rose show. There was so much to learn. When Bill arrived several hours later, I was still sitting at the table with a cup of tea, hungrily soaking in the possibilities.

"Anything interesting?" Bill asked with a grin.

I jumped up and hugged him "I really think this might work for us!"

We talked into the late evening. We discussed the cost, which was twenty-five thousand dollars per child, the commitment, eighteen to twenty years of full time parenting, Jay's reaction—everyone's for that matter, how the child might feel later about his conception, about the legal issues, and about us. We scribbled notes and ideas on a yellow pad as we always had, then agreed to sleep on it.

The next morning, I sat up in bed as soon as I heard Bill get out of the shower. My first words were "Let's do it!" to which he answered, "Let's!"

The next few weeks were very busy. We visited agencies in Kentucky, Michigan, New York, and finally right in nearby Chevy Chase, Maryland. As we drove to Mrs. Blankfield's agency in Chevy Chase, we reviewed our experiences with the other agencies. They had been very business-like, disinterested in our lives or motives, and careful to state repeatedly that the money was nonrefundable. Bill read my thoughts.

"Now, honey, let's not get discouraged," he said. "I have a good feeling about this place."

Bill turned out to be right. Mrs. Blankfield's agency had a completely different feel to it. She sat and talked with us at length, patiently answering all of our many questions. She explained her own interest in the surrogate process, after witnessing the devastating effect infertility had had on a woman who wanted children. Her questions were probing and sometimes personal, but we were at ease because of the obvious care she took in the interview process. She explained that hers was an awesome responsibility, the outcome of which had the ability to affect many lives.

"If you think I'm prying with you, you can imagine how I have to be with the surrogates!" I had wondered about that quite a bit myself. What kind of woman could do this? Was she altruistic beyond the bounds of reason? Was she cold-hearted and unfeeling? So greedy for money that she would sell her own child?

Mrs. Blankfield smiled at my questions. "You know, that could really put you into a quandary, couldn't it? I mean, if the very characteristics that made a woman willing to do this were character traits you wouldn't want your child to inherit?"

She went on to explain that the surrogates all had to be married and have at least one child of their own, living under the same roof with their husband. That made a lot of sense to me. The connectedness, which a mother feels with her newborn baby, can take on a spiritual proportion in some women. Only a woman who had already given birth would know whether or not she would have that almost overwhelming response to her baby. I remembered how it had been for me, yet I knew from the start that she was bearing a baby for another couple as the fulfillment of a contract. She would feel differently than a woman longing for a baby to fill her own empty arms.

The surrogates underwent extensive physical and psychological testing. They also signed an agreement that they would abstain from relations with their husbands during the insemination process. They seemed to have covered all their bases.

Bill and I drove home with mixed moods. We were fascinated and awed by

Meadows

the complexity of the entire process. We were anxious to know how Mrs. Blankfield felt about the interview. We were a little unsure about talking things over with people. It seemed to be a topic where emotions sometimes ran high. We figured the most important place to start was with our son, Jay. We agreed that although we wouldn't seek anyone's approval, Jay's feelings were so important to us that if he were strongly opposed to the whole idea, we would rethink things.

"What would you think about a little brother or sister?"

Jay laughed. "Mother! You're not!"

Caught off-guard, I quickly realized with some amusement that my twenty-year-old son was appalled at the idea of my being pregnant. "Of course not! But there is something we want to talk to you about … "

To our delight, Jay turned out to be one of the most agreeable people we talked to. As he had done with our other important decisions, he told us that if we wanted it, he wanted it.

Next, we talked to family, and like Jay, most of them expressed a friendly interest in what was being referred to as "the project." There was also some concern. One sister-in-law took my arm, and locked her caring eyes on mine. "You can never replace her, you know," she said softly.

I felt my eyes well up with tears instantly and gave her a quick hug. "Of course not," I assured her. "No one knows that better than I."

Our friends were a much harder sell than anyone in our two families had been. Many of them had been looking forward to their empty nests for years. They had saved up for great vacations, or great furniture, or a dream house, or just time alone together, and at last could put themselves first. Bill and I had always made time for each other and enjoyed many wonderful things both as a couple and as a family. Because we had developed a master plan early in our lives, we had achieved many goals at a young age. We didn't feel that a decision to raise another child would in any way delay the things we enjoyed, as it would for our friends.

Initially, we had decided we would carry out our plan in a year or two, to give ourselves time to be really sure. However, as we talked about it, it became evident to Bill and me that our minds were made up. It seemed unnecessary to abide by some arbitrary waiting period when that would merely prolong the time until we had another baby of our own. It was time to contact Ms. Blankfield to set the wheels in motion.

So it was that we sat nervously in our attorney's office. We desperately wanted him to find the contract "in order" so that we could begin the insemination process. We were not prepared for his opposition.

"Bill, Betty, we've known each other a long time. I can't advise you to pursue something like this. It's too … too new. They haven't even scratched the surface of the problems that can arise out of a thing like this, let alone come up with the laws to cover them. Forget about it."

I tightened my fingers around Bill's, but he was listening quietly and intently. He couldn't be reconsidering—not after all the plans we had made!

Our lawyer continued. "A private adoption is what you're looking for. In fact, I'll be handling one in a couple of months—an old family friend. Let me give him a call, it would be perfect for you!"

"Thanks, Tim," Bill answered. "I know you mean well, but today, we just want you to review the contract. We're prepared to go ahead with this, but we don't want to fall into any legal holes."

I felt relieved. We had talked about adoption, but it had faded as we considered a baby whose biological father was Bill, a baby who would truly belong to us.

"Well, at least have this outfit investigated, will you?" Tim advised. "You're talking about a lot of money, and a process which for now, is basically outside the law. You're going to give twenty-five thousand dollars to outlaws."

We all laughed a little at Tim's overly conservative nature, but agreed to follow his advice. Harriet Blankfield's organization passed with flying colors, much to our relief. Though our lawyer still didn't give us his seal of approval, he was a bit more comfortable knowing we weren't being scammed.

Driving home that day, we discussed the qualities we sought in the surrogate.

"Someone who loves to read," I said.

"Someone with good eyesight," Bill said. "I don't like wearing eyeglasses."

"A good sense of humor, too."

"Yes, but not silly."

"Blond hair?"

"Blue eyes! Definitely," Bill said.

We laughed at ourselves. We had long since agreed that one of the most precious characteristic a person could have was the ability to adjust and be happy. Bill and I took such pleasure in the daily task of living, and felt that to some extent this was an inherited trait. At least it couldn't hurt to choose a surrogate with a happy disposition, so that our baby would hear laughter and sounds of happiness while he lived in uteri.

"Anything else?" Harriet asked after we'd discussed it with her. Shortly after, Harriet brought us the five folders of the possible surrogates she felt would be good matches.

Bill and I smiled at each other. "This is it!"

Greedily, we read the files, swapping with each other pointing things out, until Bill said, "Listen to this, baby ... Why do you want to be a surrogate mother? And she answers: My little boy is three years old now. Raising Adam is the best thing I've ever done—kinda like us, huh, Betty? I loved being pregnant, not just physically, but emotionally. I can't describe the feeling but I know I'm a better person for having experienced it. I would love to feel that way again, but my husband and I can't really afford another baby. We want our son to have the best we can give him. I would like to take this money and start a college fund. To think that I could do this for my son, while giving another couple the chance to be parents, is a great prospect."

Bill's eyes met mine. "She's the one, isn't she?" I asked.

"Yep, she's the one."

* * *

Not long after that, we visited the medical team. Betty winced as the doctor spelled out the details of the insemination process.

"What is it, Mrs. Meadows?" he asked with concern. "Are you worried about something?"

Betty shook her head. "No, not worried ... It's just that it all sounds so clinical—'ejaculate into a cup,' 'inject the product,' 'fertilization and implantation,' ... like the hypothesis of a science project or something."

The doctor laughed lightly. "Well, you're close. It is pretty clinical, after all. Pregnancy without sex is cutting edge technology. I understand that until a couple of years ago, it had occurred only once, and that was two thousand years ago."

I smiled a little, but I knew my wife, and that was bothering her. When we left the office, she was quiet, her enthusiasm seemingly drained. We drove a few miles in silence, until I reached over and squeezed her hand. "Talk to me, Betty. What are you thinking?"

"I'm thinking about us. About our babies. We've had three children together, each of them a direct result of our lovemaking, and therefore a result of our love. This doesn't have the same feel at all."

"You're telling me! I don't know that I've ever made love to a Styrofoam cup!"

"And I wouldn't be involved at all. I guess I'll just sit in the waiting room 'til you're done. 'Til you *collect the product*. Ugh!" Betty gave a little shiver.

"Well, now, honey," I said, "we can figure something out. A hotel room in the area, maybe—we'll have a little mini-vacation, do some smooching—maybe I can make my collection while we're together, and then take it to the clinic?"

Betty was not to be mollified by my suggestion, and the rest of the trip home was marked with her sighs of irritation and resignation. When we pulled into our driveway, she smiled wryly. "I'm sure it will work out fine, Bill, but there's got to be a better way."

A few days later, I sat in my office staring out across the parking lot to our house, where I knew Betty was still fretting about the insemination. I thought of the wonderful "swinging bed" in our den, off the kitchen. It was a great conversation piece, and had been lots of fun for Betty and me, a great boost to our spontaneity. "That's what I need—a swinging bed in the back room of that clinic! That would set the mood for us."

I watched without interest as one of my employees walked a customer into the parking lot and stood admiring the man's new van. I could tell by his gestures that he was describing the van's features and incredible spaciousness. Then it hit me—we needed a van.

I jumped up from my desk and headed for the fellows in the parking lot, still talking. "How do you like that van?" I asked conversationally. "I've been thinking of getting one myself."

The owner showed me around.

"And you can sleep in it?" I said. "It has a built-in bed?"

In response, the gentleman flipped a lever and I watched as the backseat turned into a spacious bed. "Nice," I murmured, working out the details in my mind. Thanking the man hastily, I almost ran across the parking lot over to our home.

"Betty, Betty! I've got it! We're getting a van!"

Betty was setting the table for dinner, and glanced up just long enough to say, "Oh, are we? Won't that be fun!"

I knew she had no idea what I was talking about, but decided to keep her in the dark a little longer. "Yep, we'll have a ball! We're going to pick one out tonight."

"Well, alright," she said in good humor, "but we may want to discuss this. We have two perfectly good cars already."

"Well there's a switch!" I teased. But right after dinner, we hit the dealership less than a mile from our house. While Betty meandered around the cars, I slipped away for a moment to speak to a salesperson. "I want one of those fancy vans with the bed in the back," I blurted out without hesitating.

The salesman smiled slyly. "Going camping?"

"Right," I said ignoring the wink, "Camping. What do you have?"

He nodded and led me to a creamy yellow Starcraft, and unlocked the doors. "Top of the line," he said, "and here's the bed." With a flick of a switch, the bed folded down.

"Nice. Let me show my wife," I said dismissing him. "We'll call you when we need you." I showed Betty. "Wouldn't this be nice for a special trip?" I said.

Betty stepped up into the back of the van and I followed, closing the door behind me. When she turned to face me, I pulled her close for a long kiss. "Bill! What are you doing?" she said, laughing.

"So ... do you think you could be comfortable in here?" I asked, sitting on the bed with her.

Betty smiled, understanding. "Oh, I see what you mean," she laughed, hugging me. "A love nest! I think you're on to something, Bill. Can we buy it?"

With that, I stepped from the van and motioned to the salesman. "I think we're ready for that camping trip," I announced, pulling out my checkbook.

A lot of planning led up to the day of the actual insemination. Betty and I talked about it almost constantly, and read about it in between. Our doctor had agreed to let us take the sperm to the clinic in its condom, but insisted that it must be kept warm, and be presented immediately after it was released to insure the most viability. The surrogate mother had to be ready at exactly the right time in her menstrual cycle for the optimum chance of fertilization.

And, equally important for us, Betty and I had to be feeling romantic, which we were sure would be no problem in our Starcraft Love Mobile.

The stage was set for December 10, 1982, and, as usual, my wife hadn't missed a detail. The back of the van held a vase of flowers, and Betty had put brand new sheets on the bed. A little box held some of our favorite tapes. I leaned over and stroked Betty's neck. "You sure look pretty today, baby." It seemed years since she had looked so happy, and I felt full of emotion.

"Thank you, Bill. I sure feel pretty today." She gently squeezed my leg, the squeeze becoming a caress. It was going to be a great day.

I popped in a tape and began to hum along. A quick glance at my watch told me we had plenty of time. The procedure was to take place at 11:00 a.m. It was just a little before 10:00 at that point.

As we approached the clinic, I began to search for a place to park along the crowded avenue.

"Over there!" said Betty, pointing to a newly vacated spot.

"Great!" We pulled in and shut down the motor. I saw Betty with a beautiful smile on her face.

"Shall we make a baby?" she asked innocently.

Taking her hand, I led her to the back of the van, feeling very much in the mood by that time. Betty began kissing my neck, murmuring, "Honey, you smell very sexy ... "

And it was just about then that our interlude was shattered by the piercing clang of a bell. Betty and I pulled apart in alarm. "Fire?" she whispered as I moved to the window to peek out the slatted privacy blinds.

"Oh, my heart, Betty, you won't believe this!" I moaned, aghast at the sight just beyond the sidewalk beside us.

Betty crept up to the window, adjusting her clothes like a teenager discovered at Lover's Lane. One glance and her hand flew to her mouth in horror. "Recess!" she gasped.

And there it was—a full-blown midmorning elementary school recess unfolded as we looked on in dismay. Children streamed from the school like ants, as their teachers blew their shrill whistles and barked orders. Above the sound of yelling, laughing, and whistle blowing, I began to whisper amorous words in my lover's ear.

"What?" she said, her tone clearly frustrated.

I tugged gingerly on Betty's hand, urging her back to the divan. "I know it's early," I said extracting a hidden bottle of champagne, "but let's toast a successful day."

Betty lowered her face into her hands and I could see her shoulders shaking. The stress had obviously been too much for her, and then the terribly unromantic setting—at that moment, I just didn't know what I could do to salvage the day. I felt like crying myself. But then, Betty tilted her head back and I realized that she was actually laughing.

"This is absolutely crazy!" she said, her laughter peaking.

I felt the same sense of irony bubbling up in me, and started to chuckle as I poured us each a glass of champagne. I turned up the tunes and thanked the Lord for the healing power of laughter.

Strangely enough, in retrospect, I would say it was one of the most romantic times Betty and I ever had, and over far too soon due to the constraints of the clock. It was time to deliver "the product" though I hated to tear away from Betty at such an intimate juncture. It wasn't how we did things. But Betty was full of understanding.

"Go on, Bill," she urged. "You're supposed to give it to them right away."

After I'd gotten dressed, I took the condom from Betty, and remembering how it was essential to keep it warm, I tucked it discreetly under my armpit. "I'll be right back," I assured my wife, who was still stretched out alluringly on the bed.

There was definitely a spring in my step, despite the winter chill. At forty-seven years of age, I felt healthy and vigorous. My wife and I had just enjoyed each other thoroughly. Those beta-endorphins were being released throughout my body so that I had a total sense of wellbeing. And nested in my armpit was a latex balloon, brimming with semen to make our next child. I was feeling fine! I felt nearly perfect.

With a smile, I punched the elevator button. I hummed a little, as I remembered the tape we had been listening to in the van, and nearly danced a jig as I pushed open the door into the doctor's reception area. And it was at that point that I stopped dead in my tracks, staring into what seemed to be a sea of women. Without a doubt, every eye was on me. I had trespassed into that sacrosanct place where women talked freely of mammograms, pap smears, pelvic exams, and Braxton-Hicks contractions; men without female escorts had best be delivering the mail.

Well, I had a delivery to make, all right, and those ladies would just have to understand. I approached the receptionist with false bravado. "I'm Bill Meadows," I said quietly.

"Excuse me?" she said in what seemed like a voice that was unnecessarily loud.

I leaned in closer, careful to keep my voice from traveling far. "Yes, I'm Bill Meadows," I repeated. "With the surrogate mother thing. I have the, the … the product."

The woman's attitude changed from nonchalant to surprise, and then bewilderment, as I reached into my shirt and extracted the condom.

"It's in here," I said awkwardly. I extended my hand through the window, and quickly, she took it from me and whisked it into another room, presumably where our doctor and the surrogate mother waited. I thought about it for only a moment, my attention definitely given over to the fact that I believed ten to twelve women had just witnessed me dangling a full condom in front of a stranger's face. I felt their stares and glares boring holes in my back. I whipped suddenly around, but found that most of the women were sedately sitting, reading magazines or chatting among themselves, and it didn't seem to matter if I was there or not.

Then, suddenly, it didn't matter to me either. Something wonderful was about to happen, and I didn't care *who* knew! The spring had come back to my step, the grin back on my face, and Betty was in the van waiting for me.

Life was nearly perfect!

The trip home was a happy one. Betty smiled and laughed and talked the whole way. "Bill, I know this sounds crazy, but I just know it worked! I'm telling you, Honey, our baby is already dividing cells, and we are going to have a baby in forty weeks."

My wife was so optimistic that I couldn't help but believe with her. I thought of all the times she had been an encouragement to me over the years, helping me through college, coaching, and the early days of the business. I felt truly blessed to have a woman like Betty at my side.

Reaching over, I took her hand and gave it a squeeze. "I love you," I said simply. She looked at me almost shyly, and asked, "Do you love me enough to go through all this again tomorrow?"

Shaking my head, I began to chuckle softly. "Woman, I'd do just about anything for you, but this was pushing it!"

"We'll look for a different parking place tomorrow."

"Right. And I'll need something to put the condom in. I was pretty embarrassed in there, pulling that thing out in front of everyone."

Betty reached over and began caressing my neck. "You were wonderful today. I wouldn't trade it for anything."

That grin sneaked back across my face. "Same here, honey, and tomorrow can only be better!"

Early in the following month, January of 1983, we headed off to Snowshoe, West Virginia for a Think-and-Plan—and ski!—session with our top people. We knew there was a possibility that our trip would be cut short by a call from the agency, though we had tried to time things so that we would be back in the D.C. area for the surrogate's next ovulation. We knew that it usually took three or four times for a pregnancy to occur.

Sure enough, the phone call came in the middle of a heated discussion about advertising strategies for the spring. Betty's eyes met mine and she shrugged a little. We excused ourselves to the other room, as she whispered, "It's OK. We knew this might happen."

Betty took the call, and listened staunchly as Harriet gave her the news. She began to weep, saying only, "Tell Bill," and then she handed me the phone.

"Yes, Harriet?" I was stoic at first, but I, too, broke down in tears when I heard her words: "It's a go, Bill! You're going to be a father. The surrogate is one hundred percent pregnant!"

We must have hugged and kissed for ten straight minutes before we rejoined the group. They looked up at us expectantly.

I cleared my throat, trying to think of the right words. In the end, I simply announced, "Our surrogate mother is pregnant. We're going to have a baby!"

Everyone broke into applause and warmly shared our joy with us.

But we weren't finished yet! We had decided right at the start that we wanted to have two children, and have them as close in age as possible. Our thinking was that if something should happen to us, we did not want the child to face adulthood alone. Besides, we wanted to forge a strong sense of family, as we had for Jay and Cindy.

We had already selected our second surrogate mother. If it were possible to be any more excited than we'd been the first time around, I'd say we were. The anticipation, the van adventure, the unique circumstances all produced a good feeling for Betty and me, and we were ready to go for it again.

As was the case a few months earlier, there was a lot of paperwork and red tape to plow through. Our attorney had resigned himself to the idea by that time, so we didn't have to sell him all over again. At last the big day arrived, and Betty and I felt the pleasure of looking forward to another romantic interlude in the van.

It was a fine April morning in 1983 when we headed up the Beltway to Chevy Chase, Maryland. We laughed a little at ourselves for taking on such a major project in the middle of the spring. We had been in our crazy business for many years by then, and knew what a drain the eight weeks of spring were on everyone involved. Year after year, I had welcomed our managers back to work in our celebrated Spring Kick-off with the distinct message: Whatever you do, please don't take on anything big right now—it's not the right time to buy or sell your home, get married, or have a baby. But there we were, doing just that ourselves.

We talked about the first insemination, and how fortunate we felt that it had happened so quickly. We began talking romantically to each other, about love, and finally about making love. It was hardly necessary to set the stage, as Betty and I had been abstinent for the last week or so, in anticipation of this day. No sooner had we parked the van than Betty and I set about the task at hand. I delivered the specimen on time, and Betty and I smiled and talked all the way home, feeling as though we may have gotten lucky again.

Returning the next day, it seemed that our enthusiasm had waned just a little. We couldn't find a quiet parking place, and ended up by the playground at recess again. Knowing what to expect didn't seem to help matters. We felt pressured and distinctly unromantic, but determination won out and we did, albeit somewhat mechanical, the deed we had contracted to do.

Two weeks later we got a call from Harriet saying that the surrogate was not pregnant. We set up the next date to try again. We were a little disappointed, but we knew it would not always run smoothly. Before entering the program, I had undergone a sperm count, and the doctor assured me I had twice the number of live sperm than the average male less than half my age. We were certain the next time would be the charm.

Nearly Perfect

But the May effort did not end in pregnancy either. When June arrived, with steamy hot days, and we sat in traffic on the way to Maryland, the van overheated a little and we turned off the air conditioning. As we rolled down the windows, the stench of burning fuel and oppressive heat did nothing to lighten our moods. We arrived with little time to spare, our backs drenched from the car seats, our spirits low.

Moving to the rear of the van, Betty bumped her head and let out an uncharacteristic swear word. "I hate this van!" she spouted irritably, but I pulled her close and rubbed her head.

"It's OK, baby. Don't let this get you down. This time it's bound to work. Now, let's get started."

Betty glared at me obstinately, and crossed her arms saying, "Go ahead."

It could have been another humorous moment, and in retrospect, it sure paints a funny picture. But at the time, I, too, got annoyed. "This is not something I can undertake alone," I said. "I'm going to need a little assistance here."

Betty smiled a little and moved closer. We made love with grim determination, and we managed to produce and deliver on time. But the trip home was uncomfortable, each of us annoyed, discouraged, and maybe a little confused.

When we received our call two weeks later, we were not surprised at the negative outcome. Still no baby. Meanwhile, we had been getting encouraging correspondence each month following surrogate number one's doctor visits. It was exciting to receive the details of her sonograms, weight gains, the baby's position, and other details.

Meanwhile, Betty began to plan for our next visit to the clinic. "I'm not going through that again," she announced as we retired one evening.

"Oh?" I questioned, wondering how we were to avoid the inevitable.

"I'm not, Bill. Why should two people who know each other so well and love each other so much have to dread getting together for sex? There must be something … "

Betty's tone made me curious, and I turned toward her in time to see her pull something out of the night stand. It was a thick book, entitled *The Kama Sutra*. "Ever heard of this?" she teased, sounding like the cat who had swallowed the canary.

The book was some sort of ancient Hindu sex manual, and at first, I couldn't believe my eyes. "Betty! Where in the world … " But she placed a finger on my lips to silence me.

"Page ninety-one. Next Thursday. In the van. Be there."

She slipped out of bed and went into the bathroom without another word. Well, what could I do? I turned to page ninety-one. I was amazed, and shocked, and utterly thrilled that my wife had been doing some homework.

When she returned to the bed, she acted as though nothing had happened, switching off the light, and planting a chaste peck on my lips.

I moved toward her, nuzzling the back of her neck. "Why wait?" I implored, probably sounding like some lovesick teenager on a prom night.

She turned and kissed me again. "Thursday," she reiterated, and that was that.

The week seemed to drag by on its belly, and Thursday never seemed to get any closer. Finally it arrived, and I was up at the crack of dawn. "Betty, come on, it's Thursday!" I said, throwing open the curtains for the sun to pour in. "Can't be late! Let's get moving—you have the book?"

Needless to say, that session was most interesting. Betty had to practically throw me out of the van to deliver the sperm, and when I returned, I was heartbroken to see her sitting in the front seat applying her makeup.

"What a woman!" was the only comment I seemed to be able to make.

Betty smiled back at me smugly. "Tomorrow, it's page two hundred nineteen, but you'll need to bring some grapes along."

All the way home, I thought of grapes and wondered what I'd find on page two hundred nineteen.

Betty's new-found enthusiasm and creativity did wonders for our mission. We continued to be disappointed in the outcome, but we enjoyed our special times together with just enough spice added to give it flavor. She supplied unusual props and sexy outfits, and in general made herself irresistible to me. So I was concerned when she came home one afternoon and threw herself on the couch with a sigh, close to tears.

"What happened, Betty?" I saw that she had been shopping. "Did something happen at the store?"

"Well, I guess that depends on your definition of 'something.' Would 'something' include browsing the lingerie department and pulling this out," she held out a sensational black, lacy teddy, "only to look up into the face of Barbara Shenton, who actually had the nerve to say, 'Got a heavy date?'"

I coughed to disguise the snicker forming in the back of my throat. "Oh, Betty," I began, attempting to commiserate with her, but she held up her hand.

"Would 'something' include standing in line only to realize that Karen Graham was the cashier? Imagine! She said, 'Hello, Mrs. Meadows. How's Jay doing? Oh, my goodness!' to which I replied, 'He's fine, dear, I'll tell him you asked about him.' Or perhaps you would define 'something' as the fact that Carol Canty was in line behind me. She reached around me to *touch* this thing." She indicated the teddy. "She said, 'Ooo, that's nice, Betty! Is there a sale?' to which I replied, 'No, full price, dear, but worth every penny!'"

So, yes, Bill, I think it's safe to say that something happened at the store. By tonight, half of Richland Acres will think I'm a middle-aged seductress who buys the tools of her trade at the neighborhood K-Mart."

I tried to suppress another laugh, but Betty looked so thoroughly outraged, and that teddy looked so thoroughly beguiling, so I began to speak. "Oh, Betty," I tried again, but I failed. Dissolving into laughter, I picked up the errant teddy and rubbed it against my cheek. "Full price, but worth every penny!" I said in her voice.

She pitched a pillow from the couch in my direction with amazing accuracy.

I was glad she had fun with the whole episode, because I wanted to do nothing to discourage her shopping trips!

By the fifth month of no conception, our doctor had become concerned, especially in light of the great results we had had with our first surrogate, and my better than average sperm count. "I've got to think the mother isn't ovulating," the doctor finally concluded. "Of course, there are several fairly dependable drugs on the market that can bring about ovulation, but there can be some complications."

"Like what?" Betty asked.

"Well, the most common one is multiple births. There is more than a fifty percent chance that using the fertility drug will result in twins at the very least."

"Twins?" Betty was thoughtful for a moment. We had already made arrangements for her to have extensive help with the two babies, but could we deal with three?

"What do you mean at the very least? What else could happen?" I asked.

"Well, of course, triplets, quads, quints, and so on. It can't be regulated. Of course, occasionally a couple will decide to abort part of the batch."

Betty grimaced at that thought, and my stomach did a flip. I wasn't really prepared for a whole litter of babies, nor was I prepared to select some and destroy others. The doctor sensed our discomfort and cleared his throat. "I guess you need some time to talk this over. It's quite a dilemma. Let's talk next week, and we can decide then."

Twins, wow! Triplets—OK, I guess. Quadruplets? Hmm ... All the way home, we weighed the pros and cons and what ifs. We had a decision to make.

We had selected the mother carefully, and felt somewhat bound to her despite the lack of pregnancy.

We had definitely committed to a sibling for surrogate baby number one. There was no turning back. We knew we could change surrogates, and finally reasoned that if a pregnancy didn't result that time, with the fertility drug, we would switch surrogates. We would take our chances with the multiple births, but keep as many babies as we produced. It was a heady feeling, knowing that by that time next year, we could have anywhere from two to five or six babies to care for!

* * *

The day after Thanksgiving is always the biggest shopping day of the year. Unfortunately it was also the date that Bill and I had to travel to Chevy Chase for the insemination. It had been a hard year for us. We had lost Cindy just two years earlier, and we had taken some time off the week before Thanksgiving, as we had the previous year, in order to be alone together. It was a time of reflection and grieving and remembering, which we could share with no one but each other. Nevertheless, we managed to join the extended family for a truly joyous Thanksgiving—only two months earlier, our baby Kate Marie had been born. She was a beautiful, blond bundle, and it was love at first sight. On Thanksgiving, she was passed around from aunt to cousin to uncle to grandparents, as Bill and I looked on in utter rapture. She was perfect in every way!

* * *

And so we were heading to Chevy Chase for what we'd hoped might be the last time. We had exhausted all of our tricks for keeping the thing fun and upbeat. We were tired of the trip, the van, and the sex-on-command. Thoughts of Kate Marie kept reminding us why we were doing it, though.

As we made our way through the thick traffic, Betty looked anxiously at her watch. "We're fine," I assured her. "We have plenty of time."

It had started sprinkling a little, but before long, the drops of rain had turned into huge wet snowflakes.

"Oh great, snow." Betty was morose as we looked ahead at the miles of slow-moving traffic. Drivers seemed to automatically drop way below the speed limit when the first snowflake hits the windshield. That day was no exception. We chugged along for the next twenty-five miles, until the traffic eased up just a little.

I exhaled with relief. That was my chance to make up for lost time. It would normally have been a holiday at the clinic in Maryland, but our special circumstances had been given consideration. With the use of the fertility drug, and so many failures behind us, everyone involved had a stake in expediting this pregnancy. We couldn't possibly botch it by being caught in traffic on the interstate.

The snow was falling fast and furiously by that time, and was sticking a little to the road surface. But I was a confident driver, and had logged many miles in bad weather, not to mention the fact that the Starcraft was a regular Sasquatch when it came to snow. While other drivers were slowing down, and occasionally even pulling to the side to clear their windshields, I more or less had the left lane to myself, and let my speed begin to creep up. After a few minutes, I could tell we were in the clear, time-wise. If I could continue at that pace, and we didn't hit any more traffic snags, we would be in Chevy Chase with twenty minutes or so to spare. No sooner had I given Betty this reassurance than I saw the flashing blue lights in my rearview mirror.

Assuming there'd been an accident up ahead, I pulled quickly to the shoulder, and was momentarily dumbfounded when the flashing lights failed to pass me by. Betty looked over and asked quietly, "Were you speeding?" I glared in her direction then looked in my side view mirror. The sight that greeted me was formidable.

Approaching my van from behind came the quintessential state trooper. He was a powerfully built African-American man, looking every inch of six-foot five inches tall, with a firm, square jaw and dark glasses. His uniform was sharply creased and his boots shined. I marveled at his impressive appearance for only a moment, as his unsmiling face appeared at my window. "Good morning, Officer," I managed, before he began dressing me down like a drill sergeant.

"What the hell do you think you're doing? Did you happen to notice the speed limit signs or were you going too fast to read them? Are you crazy, man? It's snowing like a big dog and you decide to pick up the pace? Are you trying to kill us all?"

I felt smaller and smaller as he harangued me. My mind raced—the months of inseminations, the miles we had logged going back and forth to Maryland, the strain on my marriage, all leading to this day that was about to go down the drain with a big fat ticket and an unavoidable delay. Next to me, Betty began to cry.

"Well?" the trooper persisted, and I realized he expected an answer.

"We, uh, well, we're going to make a baby." No sooner had the words left my mouth than I wanted to suck them back in and start over.

The muscles in the trooper's square jaw began to work back and forth tensely. His burnished face took on an even darker hue, and I realized he thought I was being a smart aleck. He looked as if he were about to detonate—I dreaded being at ground zero.

"Can I explain?" I asked lamely.

The officer sputtered a little, and then conceded. "Try."

"We have an appointment in Chevy Chase. We got held up in traffic down I-95. We are going to artificially inseminate a woman who is going to have a baby for us. And we are going to be late." The words tumbled out as the officer stared at me in disbelief.

He then pulled out his ticket book, and demanded curtly, "License."

Betty began to sob more audibly, and though I was a proud man, I felt that it was one of those few times in my life I needed to beg. "Officer, please, you have to believe me." I knew it sounded trite, but I went on. "Officer, please. Call the clinic. They can vouch for us. This is a bona fide emergency. We have to get there."

The officer looked at us doubtfully. It was evident that he called on his sense of mercy only rarely, and was questioning himself as to whether it might be one of those rare instances. Turning briskly on his heels, he walked back toward his car, but stopped midway. He stood perfectly still for a long moment, and then turned back toward the van. Appearing at the window again, he shook his head.

"I don't know why, but I believe you. That story is just crazy enough to be true. Follow me, and I'll take you up there."

He returned to his squad car and switched on the lights, driving around us, he signaled for us to follow. He took us all the way up I-95, and onto the Washington Beltway until we entered Maryland. As he drove on, I flashed my lights in appreciation.

"Bill," Betty whispered, "this might just be our lucky day!"

We arrived at our destination with five minutes to spare. *Never* had I felt such pressure to perform, to say the least. "Betty, I'm not sure about this," I said as we headed to the back of the van.

"That's OK," Betty laughed. "I'm sure enough for both of us."

And so, despite the pressure and stress surrounding that day, we were able to produce the desired outcome and make the delivery on time. When I returned to the van, I gave Betty a thumbs up, at which she began to cry tears of relief.

"Betty, I have an idea," I said. "Let's hang around for a little while and see if we can see the mother!"

She was thrilled with the idea, so we sat along the deserted street, spying on the building's entrance, to see who might emerge. We felt confident that the people involved in the insemination were very likely the only ones in the building that day. We put in a tape, and had some coffee out of the thermos Betty had brought along. Warm and comfortable, I felt almost like I might doze off, when suddenly Betty grabbed my arm.

"That's her!"

Sitting forward, I let the wipers clear a spot in the snowy windshield, and caught a glimpse of the woman I hoped was now carrying my child. A perky, petite woman, she walked across the parking lot with a spring in her step despite the blizzard-like conditions. Her waist-length blond hair swayed back and forth until she gave it a twist and pushed it inside her collar. She looked to be in her early thirties, with an air of confidence and the joy of living we had been hoping for.

"It's really her. I know it is, and I'm sure she's pregnant." Betty's total confidence proved to be the panacea for the stress, the doubt, the frustration we had endured for so many months. I reached over and squeezed her hand. "I know you're right," I agreed.

Before we knew it, Christmas Eve was upon us. Baby Kate brought us incredible joy as we indulged ourselves with red velvet outfits and photos on Santa's lap. She was an easy baby and we felt blessed beyond measure that holiday season.

Once Kate was in bed, Betty busied herself with a few last minute things to take care of before morning. The house was perfect, wonderful smells filled the air, and in the morning, we would have Christmas with our two children.

"Betty," I beckoned. "I know you're busy, but come enjoy the fire with me for a few minutes. It feels so nice."

"All right, I'll be there in a minute," she said, just as the telephone rang.

We each picked up an extension, but in different rooms, saying, "Hello," in stereo.

"Well, hello to both of you, and Merry Christmas," came Harriet's friendly voice. "Good news! You have another baby on the way."

"I knew it!" Betty cried triumphantly, and left the phone dangling to join me in the other room. We threw our arms around each other, laughing and kissing, and finally sinking into the couch to watch the dancing flames. And very faintly, from across the room, we could hear, "I'm hanging up now. Merry Christmas!"

The Farm House

Chapter Thirty-Three

The Millionaire & His Wife

Gilven not only helped us start our business, but in the process learned that he enjoyed plants just as much as I did. More than that, however, he enjoyed the people. He was a lot like my dad in that respect; able to strike up conversations with anyone and make friends as well.

He had purchased a small piece of property tucked into a residential neighborhood along busy Backlick Road, in Annandale, but rather than build a house, he decided to build a garden center, which he called Gil's Gardens. It was a folksy neighborhood plant market, run by the man next door when Gil wasn't there himself.

Gilven purchased his stock through Meadows Farms, tacking on a small load of plants to our order from merchants in the south. He took a lot of pleasure in his nursery, but eventually, he lost interest in the project, and I leased out the land for fifteen years.

We opened the nursery in September of 1977, with a lot of fanfare, complete with a party and ribbon cutting ceremony. It was an immediate success, as our nursery in Sterling had attracted clientele from all over the metropolitan area, this site would be closer for a lot of people.

That year we had grossed over a million dollars and had a big celebration,

Meadows

thanks to my wife, who believes a day worth living was a day worth celebrating. We had turned a nice profit and were tempted by the many things money could buy.

"Just because we *can* buy things, doesn't mean we *should*," Betty said.

I knew she was right. We enjoyed the things money could buy, but the money itself was meaningless. We were so happy just being together then, enjoying Jay and Cindy and the extended family that were so much a part of our lives, and working in a fulfilling successful business. Was there really anything we lacked? After twenty-five years of marriage, my heart still fluttered when one Betty Marie walked in the door and her eyes found mine across a crowded room. I knew the feeling was the same for her. What else could a man want? Our life together was nearly perfect.

"How about another nursery?" I proposed. We had been looking over a thirteen-acre site on Route 50, on the west end of Fairfax. It was quite rural that far out, but ever the visionary, I could see future development, and I was certain the place would be a gold mine.

Our Fairfax branch opened on March 1, 1978, once again amidst grand festivities. I had paid three hundred thousand dollars for the commercially zoned real estate, and felt confident we would recoup that money in no time.

I was wrong.

The Fairfax venture proved to be unsuccessful, and we were really disappointed. We could not manage to turn a profit, no matter *what* we did. The sales just weren't there. Betty and I would play with the idea of unloading our White Elephant, even as we opened several other stores, since the payments were more than the store was bringing in.

"If I could sell it for six hundred thousand dollars, I would feel OK, even if it didn't work out as a nursery. I would have doubled our money, and we could buy a different piece of land somewhere else."

Betty frowned. "Who's going to pay that much money for thirteen acres? I'd say our best bet is to get what we can and get out!"

We half-heartedly listed our property with an agent, with an asking price of six hundred thousand, and were amazed when a realtor began showing the place to various clients.

"Why would anyone consider buying a place like that?" Betty pondered. Before long, we had our answer. Sewer and water were finally being installed along this remote corridor, in conjunction with a huge new shopping complex on the drawing board for a site not half a mile east of us, called the Fair Oaks Shopping Center.

"Well, that changes everything! We're not going anywhere! I bet I can sell that place for a million dollars!" I said.

"That's absurd, Bill, but if, by some miracle, you *are* offered a million dollars, take the money and run!" Betty said, laughing at the notion.

I found it amusing as well, until the realtor presented me with an offer of one million dollars.

"Oh my gracious, Bill! We'll be multi-millionaires! Just as you always said we would! I can't believe this is happening!" Betty hugged me fiercely, her spirits high.

"Not so fast, baby. If we can get a million, we can get a million and a quarter. I'm going to hold."

"This isn't a card game, Bill," Betty said. "Don't be greedy. Take the offer."

But I couldn't. Somehow, I just knew we could get more money for the land. Money to invest in the business or in retirement—I knew I had to wait.

Offers continued to come in, even though our land was no longer officially on the market. Each offer was for a little bit more money, and when we were finally offered *three million dollars*, I knew it was time to fold.

By that time, we had eight retail nurseries and had moved our landscape operation to a site two miles east of our original location in Sterling. Though we hated to lose one of our stores, plans were already in the works for another place ten miles west of Fairfax, just over the border in Loudoun County.

Though our company's net worth had grown impressively, the sale of the Fairfax nursery, as well as that of our original site in Sterling, catapulted our personal worth into the seven digits. After thirty years of marriage, we were multi-millionaires at last, just as I had promised my wife so many years before. In fact, we had a net worth of twelve million dollars. Betty and I joked back and forth.

"How in the world will we ever spend all that money?" But in fact, we knew that wouldn't be a problem.

First, we paid Uncle Sam, and swallowed hard when we realized that we were left with only a little over half of our fortune. We had always wanted to make some stock investments, and now felt, for the first time, that we could do so without feeling that we were tying up the money we needed for everyday expenses. We decided we could spend five hundred thousand dollars on stocks, and soon found out that we had our pick of brokers. Eventually, we connected with the right brokerage firm, and our five hundred thousand dollars amortized to the tune of three million.

Meanwhile, Betty and I had started our second family and were already thinking about raising them somewhere other than northern Virginia. Along the way, we had purchased that four hundred twenty-five acres in the Fredericksburg,

Virginia area. In time, we determined that this county was the perfect place to build a home and raise our second family.

By then, we'd had the wonderful experience of having our son, Rocky. On August 26, 1984, at 5:00 in the morning, the phone had rung.

"Hello?" I answered, startled by the early call, but already awake.

"Mr. Meadows?"

"Yes," I said.

"It's Mrs. Blankenfield," came the voice, "and I'm afraid it's time! You've got plenty of time, but you might want to head on over to the hospital pretty soon."

"We're on our way!" I said.

Betty and I had eagerly awaited that call. We had corresponded with our surrogate, and sent her gifts along the way, encouraging her to relax, knowing of course that that was best for both her and our baby. We even sent her off on vacation. We'd been through the experience before, so we were able to let the time pass at its own pace, but the moment of phone call was every bit as stirring and exciting as the first time.

At the hospital, it was a case of hurry up and wait.

"It's been three and a half hours, Bill," Betty said. "Do you think everything's OK?"

"I'm sure everything's fine," I told her. But of course I was just as nervous.

Then came the big moment.

"Mr. and Mrs. Meadows?" the nurse called. "Would you like to see your new son?"

And there he was. We looked at him as our hearts filled with love. All covered with mucous and fluids, Rocky was probably one of the ugliest sights we'd ever seen! In the birth process, his nose, which was enormous for such a tiny little one, was all squashed over to the side.

Betty's eyes were wide. "I know what you're thinking," I said.

"No you don't," she said.

"He's mine," I said. "Don't worry about that." I don't know how I knew, because he sure did not look at all like me back then.

"Honey, I just love him already. I don't really care if there was some kind of mistake." She looked at me imploringly.

Just then, the doctor came in. "Now, Mr. Meadows," he began, "as you know, this would be the point at which you would give us a little sample of blood and we would confirm the paternity. But this is just a formality, of course, and it's not necessary ... "

"Don't worry about that, Bill," Betty spoke up. "We love him already, don't we?"

I studied the little fellow through the glass, and I knew she was right. Still, I didn't relish the idea of living in mystery about the technicalities of the situation. "Betty, you are absolutely right. No matter what, I will love this baby, and be a father to him just as I am to all our other children. But honey, I think it's only right to get our facts straight. Don't you?"

Betty smiled. "You're right, Bill," she said. "As long as we love him all the same, you might as well have the facts."

The test revealed that he was biologically my son, which surprised us both. But even by the time we'd gotten the lab results, we had begun to see similarities between the two of us.

He turned out to be a wonderful, delightful baby with only one challenging habit—he never slept through the night! In fact, as he got older, he learned how to climb out of his crib, and into our bed, a practice that wasn't wholeheartedly received by us.

As the years passed, he began to look more and more like the Meadows children—especially with the signature blonde curls.

As we got on with the plans for building the home, I visited the acreage often. I enjoyed riding a four-wheeler around the property and it was a great way to oversee my country estate. The day before excavation began, I strapped Rocky and Katie into my homemade baby contraption and took them for a ride, making a last-minute detour up to the country store. Like any proud, indulgent father I bought ice cream for us all, unconcerned about the mess that two babies could make eating ice cream on their own.

While I was cleaning them up, Billy Goodwin, a fellow whose farm I was crazy about, managed to happen upon us.

"Will you look at that!" he said, amazed to see me in such a domestic posture.

"Hey, Billy," I said, "what do you know? Haven't seen you in a while."

"Hey, Farmer—so these are your little grandbabies, huh?"

"Nope—they're my children!" I said.

"Well, I think they're about the prettiest things I've ever seen!" he announced, scooping one of them up in each arm. I beamed in agreement, bursting with pride in my beautiful children. "So what's new?"

"Well, we're just about ready to start digging out our lake. We found a real nice site, but to tell you the truth, Billy, it's not near as pretty as your place. I can just picture these two little children growing up on that farm of yours, swimming in a lake, maybe riding a pony ... well, like I've always said, you let me know when you're ready to sell."

Billy and I parted with an amiable handshake and headed off in different directions.

Later that evening Betty and I sat on the floor playing with Katie and Rocky, when we heard a knock on the door. Betty went to answer it, and I heard Billy Goodwin's voice for the second time that day.

"Well, good evening, Betty. I saw those little cuties of yours up at the store today, and I just had to come by for another look!"

Betty laughed. "Come on in, Billy," she said.

When Billy sat down, he got to the real purpose of his visit. "You see, it's like this," he said. "When you asked me to picture your children growing up on my land, I really could see it! My kids are grown, and they're not like us—the land isn't special to them, so it doesn't matter to them what I do! But these two little fellas have a chance to enjoy the country while there's still some left. I want you to buy me out."

Billy stood up. "I know you've already gotten the ball rolling around here, and it's a nice place. But I know how long you've wanted my farm. It's a thousand acres and I'll let it go for seven hundred dollars an acre."

I jumped up and shook Billy's hand. "I don't know what to say! Can I call you tomorrow?"

"You bet!" he said. "Sleep on it, buddy. I'll talk to you tomorrow."

After Betty closed the door, she turned to me and her eyes sparkled. "Bill! It's just what you wanted!"

"What do you think, baby?" I asked her.

"You know, it's been a while—I don't really remember that much about his place."

"Well, let's ride on over there and take a look. You'll love it!" I told her.

Grabbing the children, we piled into our car and made the trip from Mine Run over to Locust Grove.

"You know, Betty," I commented as we disembarked, "I really expected to pay about one hundred dollars more an acre for this land. That Billy is quite a guy."

"I thought he seemed a little sad maybe."

"Well, he loves this place," I said. "I can't believe he's willing to sell it to me."

But I had lost Betty for the moment. She had strolled a little ways away and I could see she had caught the vision. A faint smile tugged at the corners of her mouth, and his eyes had that faraway look.

Moving in close to her, I tucked an arm around her waist. "The lake over there … "

" … and the house right there. I know. I can see it." She turned toward me suddenly, her face close to mine. "This is the right place, isn't it?"

We exchanged a sweet kiss, not needing words to imagine the years unfolding before us like those sculptured hills of the farm. Going on and on, better and better, more and more beautiful with the passage of time.

"IT'S BETTER IN THE BAHAMAS"

Nassau Beach Hotel

Farmer and Betty take 62 employees to Nassau

Chapter Thirty-Four

Time Flies When You're Having Fun

So there we were at the ripe old age of fifty, with a grown son and two little babies. When we got Katie, we moved to a townhouse in Reston, and then again to a house in Sterling, but we were spending most weekends at the double-wide trailer on our farm.

Kate was a good baby, and we were unprepared for little Rocky, who did not sleep through the night and could really stretch those tiny lungs with his crying.

Rocky was our fifth baby, but the first to really kick up a fuss when he wasn't happy about something. We had been delighted to receive the news that he was a boy, and prouder and happier than ever to have our new family together at last. And Bill had his Rocky Meadows that he'd foreseen so many years ago on the front porch glider! All of the efforts to make it happen were worth it many times over. But those two little blond bundles had definitely sent some shock waves through our peaceful lives! And it felt good. Good in that loud, unrestrained way that goes with fireworks, lighting up the dark, summer sky.

"We'll be all right, Bill," I said as soothingly as I could. The middle of the night is a tough time to try to be soothing to someone else. "This stage doesn't last forever. Now, tell me this isn't an absolutely beautiful baby!"

Bill reached for Rocky and was surprised to see the little fellow stop crying as his pretty eyes engaged those of his father. It was a wonderful sight.

Meadows

Life was invigorated within our souls after the long, sad winter of the years before. Bill and I were closer than ever, and when we lay on the floor, playing with the babies, it was as though we were young parents in our twenties—at least until we tried to get up off the floor!

Bill had begun to raise cattle, a love of his since childhood. It wasn't a particularly profitable venture, but it was educational and brought us a lot of adventure and journeys to new places. And by that time, we had also determined that we would build our home on the farm, facing the lake we planned to build. Bill loved everything related to building and machinery. He was fascinated with the huge earth moving equipment that dug our basement at the old house, and I knew he would feel the same way about the construction of our new house.

In addition to the house, we were building a twenty-five acre lake that we would be able to see from our living room. We both loved water so much, and we would name it Lake Cindy, a place of beauty, serenity and reflection. It would be a place our daughter would have loved.

We approached the building just as we had any business ventures; thinking, researching, and planning. I made a big scrapbook with all the different things we both liked—windows, wood, water, and so on. We jotted down notes every time we thought of a new twist. And we looked around.

It was important to Bill to always be an original. He loved for people to copy him, but of course he copied no one. Certainly he knew a good idea when he saw one, and was not at all opposed to borrowing something someone else had done well. His desire to be unique touched every facet of his life, and the building of our house was no exception. He wanted it to be different from any other house we had ever seen.

Because Bill and I had spent so much time traveling, we had an intimate knowledge of many hotels. We would immediately decide whether or not we liked the ambiance of a place when we first stepped in the door. I especially liked those lobbies that were set up for small intimate conversation groups. I thought of the various resorts where we had stayed—beautiful, inviting, comfortable, restful, yet exciting ... that was how I pictured our house—like a mini resort.

Bill summed it up another way. "Let's go for the three S's—soft, sexy, and sleepy. Isn't that what we're really looking for?"

I had to laugh. He was right, of course. That pretty well summed up the house we were looking to build. We took a lot of trips to model homes, toured the New England states, looking at the construction and style of what many consider the cream of the crop. Yet we didn't really see anything that truly caught our attention. Then, back in Virginia, we looked at what were called deck houses.

"You know, Betty," Bill said, "I love the whole deck idea. We have to have a deck or two on our place."

Nearly Perfect

"Definitely," I agreed. "Maybe someplace where we can sit and look out on the lake."

"These houses are kind of small, though, don't you think?"

"Not small, but I think we do want something bigger than this."

We returned to the deck house many times, always walking through thoughtfully, and talking to each other excitingly, but never really talking with the salesman.

"Back again?" he said amiably. "Guess it doesn't hurt to window shop."

"Not exactly. The house is terrific," Bill conceded, "but we were thinking of something bigger! This house might get lost in the middle of a thousand acres. It's too bad it doesn't come in a bigger size."

"We like it," I agreed. "The big open spaces. The great windows and sliding doors. We just want more."

"Then I think you folks need to talk to one of the architects. We can custom design and build a house to your specifications. You can keep what you like and change what you don't like. Why don't you give this guy a call." He handed us the card of Jess Goodman, a builder who agreed to meet with us the following week.

My husband, never one to leave things to chance, began to create a scale drawing of what he wanted so that when he met with Mr. Goodman, he could show him exactly how it should look. I enjoyed watching Bill's creativity and precision. It reminded me of his days as a landscape designer. I saw our house take shape as he laid it out on paper.

"This is some drawing, Farmer. It's going to be pretty useful in laying out the plans." Mr. Goodman seemed almost as excited as we were about the new house.

I remembered the house my parents built when I was young. "I guess there's two ways to do it," I mused. "You can pay as you go, like my father did, knowing it might take years to finish the house, or you can take out a loan and go into debt up to your ears."

"There's also a third way, Betty," Bill said. "We're in a position to pay for the things we need as we go, without debt, and without it taking ten years to complete. That makes the building process that much more enjoyable!"

We had always purposefully avoided being house-poor. We had seen what the stress had done to many of our contemporaries. Instead, like our parents, we had lived well within our means and always paid outright for things we wanted.

When Jesse turned Bill's drawing into an architectural plan, we were delighted to find that his drawings came to within six inches of Bill's. "Maybe I should be an architect," Bill mused.

I didn't say anything, but I knew that if he wanted to, he surely could.

Once the ground was broken for the house, it was just as I thought it would be. Bill couldn't have stayed away from the gaping hole in the ground if his life depended

Meadows

on it. I have to admit, it was a wonderful thing to behold. I would take the children over to their father's selected position for the day and listen to him explain what was going on. He would move a folding lawn chair from place to place, though he normally couldn't stay seated long enough to get much use from it. And though I loved watching the house take shape, I was even more fascinated with what we would do with the inside. Always keeping the three Ss in mind, I continued clipping ads and pictures of the kinds of things we would like. It was really an exciting time!

In late 1986, our new home was completed. We had thirteen thousand square feet of mahogany and glass, surrounded by gorgeous deck work on three sides. The floor-to-ceiling windows looking out onto Lake Cindy seemed to blend the outdoor and indoor space together. We had agreed never to put up a wall unless we needed one, so the rooms were light and airy and spacious.

And empty.

"Finished! At last!" Bill said.

"Well, the construction's done," I said. "But we've still got the inside—and sixty guests coming for Christmas! I'm getting pretty nervous."

We had made plans well in advance for the decorating phase of our new house. We interviewed five well-known interior decorators from the Washington, D.C. area and one from Fredericksburg. We had been given the name of Jerry Carranger, a local decorator from the Pavillion in Fredericksburg. We were told that he had just redone his own home with much the same philosophy we had about ours. We paid each of these decorators one thousand dollars for four hours of their time, just discussing our ideas and their ideas.

It was odd that most of the five decorators could not truly grasp the three S's concept, nor the "bring the outdoors in" concept. However, Jerry seemed to know just what we were looking for. We knew immediately that he was the right one for us. We worked together in selecting the furnishings and accessories. They were ordered from all over the U.S. and many were custom-made by furniture makers in Fredericksburg and North Carolina. By mid-November, all the furnishings were in the warehouse.

"There's just one thing," Jerry said with an impish grin. "The arrangement's got to be a surprise. You have to let me do whatever I want with your new furniture, accessories, and things, and I'll tell you when you can come in."

"Oh my gosh, Jerry! I don't know about that ... we have to get ready for Christmas and we have all the guests coming on Christmas Day. There's a tree to decorate—all the Christmas stuff, in fact, besides the regular things like furniture, and lamps ... "

Jerry nodded, smiling. "I know, I know. But I'm not going to let you down! I'll even put your tree up for you. Look, we have a budget. We have a philosophy. We have a deadline. Let me at it!"

Bill tucked his arm around my waist and looked down at me, reassuringly. "OK," I agreed. "But when can we move in?"

"I'll tell you what," he said. "When it's time for you to come over, I'll put a big wreath on the front door. It'll have a big red bow you can see from over at your modular home. When the wreath goes up, you come over!"

Reluctantly, I agreed to the arrangement. The time I had spent with Jerry assured me that he understood what we wanted, and my sister, Mary Lou, who was a bit of a decorator herself, assured me that it would be all right.

But of course the time dragged by. I had done all my Christmas shopping and wrapped them all, and done a little baking, but all I could think of was our new house. Besides, if we missed the deadline, we'd sure have one packed trailer on Christmas!

On the twenty-third of December, Bill was losing patience. "He should have been done by now," he said. "I'm starting to get very concerned."

"I believe it will get done, Bill," I said, reassuring both of us, "and I don't think we should even talk about the what-ifs."

"Baby, it's December 23rd! I'd say we've pretty much run out of time!"

By early afternoon the next day, I had almost given up hope myself. Then I heard Bill come inside.

"Betty! Betty! It's time! The red bow is on the door!"

I lost no time, quickly grabbing the overnight bag I had packed weeks back, grabbed a child in each hand and burst out the door with Bill.

"Let's go! Let's go!" Bill urged.

I can still remember the thrill of excitement as we crossed over to our new home. Unsure of how to proceed, we gave the big door a couple of solid knocks. "Jerry!" we called out, "We're here!"

Immediately the door opened. "Welcome!" Jerry greeted us, bowing, and motioning for us to enter. The four of us gasped, and moved slowly, mesmerized, through the foyer, as a single unit on eight legs. Our eyes were riveted to the twenty-six-foot Christmas tree in the corner in front of the windows. Jerry had decorated it entirely in red, with red balls, lights, and bows. The effect was dazzling! "Merry Christmas," he whispered.

The rest was just as wonderful; soft, sexy, sleepy—and ready! The children ran through the rooms, squealing with delight. Bill and I walked slowly, captivated, totally enchanted by Jerry's work. We loved it all.

"I'm sorry it took so long," he apologized. "I had a little mishap."

"Are you all right?" I asked.

"Oh, I'm fine, just my pride got hurt. I'm Jewish, you know, so my experience

Meadows

with Christmas trees is pretty limited. When I had almost completely finished, I leaned a ladder against the tree to try to reach up higher and brought the whole thing to the ground. I had to start all over!"

After thoroughly exploring the house we ate a light dinner, and put the children to bed, filling their heads with thoughts of Santa Claus.

"That's what I call cutting it close!" Bill said.

"I'll say. I have to admit I was getting worried," I answered.

"I'm so glad we're finished," Bill said with a sigh.

"I'm so glad we're married," I said, with a sigh of my own.

I leaned across our brand new bed in our brand new bedroom, and placed a kiss on the sweetest lips in the world. I felt Bill's warm embrace encircle me, pulling me onto the big, downy comforter.

"How about you?" I asked.

He didn't answer, but I knew exactly what he meant.

The next morning, when we awoke, a beautiful dusting of snow had fallen to the ground. Kate had run from window to window, squealing and giggling with delight. "Snow! Snow!" she called, pointing outside.

Rocky ran along behind, not to be left out, but wasn't quite sure what the excitement was. They got to the edge of our bed, both their beautiful eyes sparkling like diamonds. "I want to live here forever!" Kate said.

"Forever," I agreed. "Forever and ever."

Moving onto the farm was a wonderful, memorable period in our lives and really uplifted us individually and as a family. But, as with almost all great things, there was one drawback ...

Farmer's chauffeur, Steven Hodges, leading Meadows Farms champion Santa Gertrudius bull, Big Ben, in front of guest house.

Rocky Joe has fun with Farmer's personal limo

Chapter Thirty-Five

Wheels

"Are you going to Chantilly tomorrow?" Betty asked, climbing into bed next to me.

I stared at the ceiling for a long moment before answering. "I have to. Jay and I have a meeting scheduled at 10:00 and then we're going to look at some property after lunch." I knew I didn't sound enthusiastic, and I didn't want Betty to get the wrong idea.

"I'm excited about this property, Betty! It would give us a second store in Maryland."

"You don't sound very excited about it," she said.

"It's not the store," I said. "it's the drive. Three hours a day on the road, being away from the children for almost twelve hours. It's hard."

Betty squeezed my hand. "I know, Bill. Even when I know the children are in good hands, I just want to be with them. I know we don't leave them often, but I would rather not leave them at all."

Our beautiful life on the thousand-acre farm was nearly perfect. I spent less time in Chantilly by then because we had installed a direct telephone line between our two offices so that we could talk to Jay or our secretary as though we were using an intercom, rather than making a long distance call. As had always been our intention, we hired a wonderful nanny, named Brenda, who looked after the children as though they were her own. I would make the trip to our corporate office at least three days a week, with Betty joining me frequently, while Brenda looked after the family at home. It usually went smoothly.

Brenda would leave us in two years to get married to an old high school boyfriend. Her replacement was a young, beautiful school teacher from Alabama, Sarah Rankin, who had grown up on a dairy farm, so unlike most of the nanny applicants, was used to farm life. Sarah was with us for several years when she left us to return to her home in Alabama. She was a wonderful, beautiful, fine person and left an impact on all of our lives.

"Now back to the letter writing versus time problem. The one and one-half hour drive to work seems like wasted time. I could be using that time to do my work, and then I wouldn't have to stay so late."

Betty laughed. "I don't know how you could do that unless you hired a chauffeur!"

I laughed, too, but a tiny seed had been planted. A few weeks later, I was going by Moore Cadillac at Tyson's Corner when I decided to stop and look around. I would need a new car before long, and wanted to see what might provide a more comfortable ride for those long hauls.

I stopped in front of a long, black limousine. Limousines were for the very rich, for millionaires—like me. It was hard to picture myself driving a limousine, but then I wouldn't be driving it myself …

And so it was that the seed that had been planted, sprouted.

"I'm wondering what you'd be asking for a car like this?" I said as the salesman approached.

"You'd be surprised at how reasonable a car like this might be. It is, of course, a top of the line luxury vehicle. But this one has actually been on the road a bit. Technically, it's not brand new."

"It looks fine to me. How many miles are on it?"

"Just six hundred. We donated the use of it when Princess Diana visited a few months back. Of course, we can't sell it for the full price now. We're asking fifty-five thousand."

"Princess Diana? Where did she sit?" I asked. I knew it sounded like a crazy question, but what could it hurt to sit there myself?

"On the right side here, I believe."

I smiled as the salesman opened the door for me. I wished Betty was with me. I climbed in and planted myself in the very seat in which Princess Diana had sat. And then, I felt something—that tingling I had felt when I had stepped on the site of our first produce stand/nursery. Same as when I'd first stood at the crest of Billy Goodwin's thousand-acre farm, wishing it were my very own.

Maintaining my composure best I could, I climbed out of the limousine and shook the salesman's hand.

"Interesting. Would you have a phone I could use?"

"Certainly. Right this way, sir," he said very courteously.

I called Betty and talked fast. "Honey, it's another one of those feelings. I think we're supposed to have this car! I wish you were here with me, but can you trust me on this one?"

"Bill!" Betty exclaimed, "A *limousine?*"

"Betty, I got that tingling thing."

I could almost hear Betty's smile. "Then buy the car, baby," she said. "You haven't been wrong before."

Well, that's how we got that beautiful car. It was hard to convince Betty that it was a steal, but I know she really liked it.

"I think I'll ask Stephen Hodges to look it over," I mentioned to Betty. Stephen was our newest assistant farm manager, a recent Virginia Tech graduate.

"Stephen? I thought he was in animal science."

"He was. But somebody told me he's crazy about cars. Apparently, he knows quite a bit more about them."

I invited Stephen to take a look at the limo, and enjoyed his low whistle of appreciation. "Farmer," he said, "She's a beauty! I believe a car like that would be a lot of fun to drive."

"I think so, too. And hopefully someone else will agree, because we're going to hire a driver."

Stephen spent quite a while under the hood, checking things out. Then he sat in the driver's seat a bit longer, getting a feel for things.

"What do you think, Stephen?" I asked.

"I like it, Farmer!" Stephen answered, his southern Virginia drawl growing stronger with his enthusiasm. "You shouldn't have any problem finding a driver."

I sensed a little hesitation in Stephen's voice, and asked, "Stephen, do you know someone who might want to drive for us?"

"I would," he said quickly.

I was surprised and pleased at his response. Betty and I talked it over, and we agreed that we liked Stephen enough to be willing to spend time with him. We hired him on a trial basis.

Stephen rose to the occasion beautifully. He insisted on a chauffeur's uniform, complete with cap and gloves. I began to call him *Stevón* as a joke, thinking it sounded very aristocratic, and the name stuck. He took the job seriously, caring for the car impeccably, and drove with great care. He would study maps and plan out his routes efficiently.

Betty and I were truly amazed at the way people seemed to treat us because we had a limousine. We would do our normal things—go to McDonalds drive-thru, pull up at the grocery store—and people would fall all over themselves trying to be helpful and wait on us.

Stephen found the whole thing extremely amusing. He played it up, too. When people asked whom he was driving for, he would answer, "It's the senator," or "Paul Newman's brother." He would do his best, also, to create an upper crust type accent, but it was hard to disguise that strong drawl of his.

Even with a driver, a nanny, and working only three days a week, though, we still dreaded the drive at times. At those times, we would stay at a hotel close to the offices in Chantilly. We eventually zeroed in on the beautiful Ramada Renaissance, where we had a beautiful suite, a view of the airport runway, and the kind of attention that people with fancy cars are probably used to. With my big ego, I was absolutely loving it!

I knew my wife was happy living the lifestyle of the rich and famous, and I was a little surprised when she began to talk of semi-retirement.

"I love working, Bill. You know that. But I don't want to miss out on the children. I worked full time when Cindy and Jay were little, and it seemed like other people were sometimes telling me about the important milestones in my own children's lives. I don't want that to happen again!"

I took a long hard look at that incredible woman. She truly was a "Supermom." She'd played the role long before it was invented; she was lover, mother, business partner. If she wanted to take time off, she deserved it.

I began making fewer trips north myself, and Stevon began using his free time to return to his farm duties. We would still take trips in the limo, with Stevon at the wheel, of course, but our lives revolved more and more around the farm, and less around the nursery business.

"Are you ready to turn the nursery over to Jay?" Betty asked one day, seemingly out of the blue.

Though her question had caught me off guard, it was something I had given some thought to already. By then, I had become interested in raising cattle, which I'll tell you about next, and the excitement of raising Katie and Rocky was drawing us more toward the farm and further from the nursery business.

At that point, Jay was vice president, and doing a great job with the business. Betty had turned most of her duties over to my sister-in-law, Margaret, though I think at times she really missed her job.

Although we continued to attend meetings and pertinent seminars, and exchange thoughts and information everyday by phone with Jay, I began to think more about the farming business.

I was a different Farmer then. I'd done tomatoes and plants—were cows to be my next venture?

Farmer on cattle buying trip at the John Connolley Ranch in Texas

Farmer playing on his own golf course with friends, Roger Provencher, Jack Duncan, Farmer, John Sieber, and Bob Lewis

Chapter Thirty-Six

From Big Cherry Red Cows to Little White Balls

As a young boy of ten, I had already had a deep appreciation for nature—mountains, rivers, and lush green fields. I pictured myself as a farmer one day, with a beautiful spread of land and a fine herd of Hereford cattle. I loved their pretty white faces and dark, shining hides.

My grandmother had always had a cow, and my parents both loved cows and kept a few in on our small West Virginia farm, so it was easy to imagine cows playing a part in my life somewhere along the way.

When Betty and I bought our first property, the twenty acres in Chantilly, we also bought twenty cows and tried our hand as gentlefolk farmers. As usual, my brothers helped me fence the property in, and we gave the endeavor a decent shot, but the site was really too small. Temporarily, we shelved the idea of cattle.

As our business grew, however, we sought out larger parcels. But nothing gave us the feeling we were hoping for until we went to Mine Run. There we fell in love with four hundred and twenty-five acres of streams, hills, and creeks, and a sixty-acre field called King's Hill, where I could almost see my cattle

Meadows

herd grazing. We stood quietly on the crest, surveying the tract, and I felt a quiver in my knees and a slight bumping in my chest.

"What do you think?" I whispered, almost reverently.

"I think this is the place," my wife whispered back and squeezed my hand.

In short order, we had purchased the farm for six hundred dollars an acre and wondered if we were ready to try our hand at farming after an eight-year hiatus.

"I guess we should start out with Angus, like most other folks have here," I said.

"That sounds good, honey," Betty said, ever the librarian, "but let's do a little research. Maybe we could talk to an extension agent, too."

A few days later, Betty came in with an armload of magazines and dropped them on the coffee table. "There you go, Bill. Now we can make an informed decision."

I browsed half-heartedly through the magazines until I found a bull I hadn't seen before. The caption said, "King 34, King Ranch, Texas." The animal was huge by any standard, with a deep, cherry-red color. I read the accompanying article, and decided I would like to see the *Santa Gertrudis* bull for myself.

A few days later, I was shaking hands with a real live cattle farmer in Leesburg and touring his farm. Before I left, I had written out a check for two of the big red cows, gotten the names of some other herdsmen, and gotten the information on an upcoming cattle auction in Texas.

Betty laughed at the idea of our going to Texas for cattle.

"It'll be fun, Betty," I said. "There's a big barbecue for the auction!"

"We'll be like J.R. and Sue Ellen," she said. "Maybe we could even stay at *South Fork*."

But Betty ended up loving our first auction weekend. We flew to Texas, rented a car, ate barbecue, met the governor of Texas, John Connelly, on his ranch, and bought four cows from him.

We continued to travel, buying and researching for our new project and before long we stumbled across the concept of the embryo transplant.

"That should be easy for us to understand," Betty said smiling. "There's not too much reproductive technology we're not familiar with!"

We made an appointment to see Dr. Joe Lineweaver, an animal husbandry expert from Virginia Tech, who ran a transplant business on the side.

"You start with the best cow you can find, and you buy the best semen you can get from a polled herd. Now, you don't want to wear out your good cow by keeping her pregnant all the time, so you let a cheaper cow actually do the hard part. You give both cows a shot to bring their heat on every thirty days. You inseminate your good cow and let her put out her eggs—up to twenty at a time and you wait. After about two weeks, you flush the eggs out and put them in your cheap cow. She carries them and gives birth to them and there you are!"

"Like a cow factory," Betty said.

"Well, something like that, ma'am. But you figure a year-old bull could bring you ten thousand dollars, maybe twenty. You get this breeding thing going, and there's a lot of money to be made."

We were able to produce beautiful cows and they were worth the effort. We sold them in distant places like California, Kansas, and Connecticut. Ronnie, our farm manager, would load a few choice specimen into the trailer and head off on a five or six day trip to the auction site. There would be frequent stops for water and feeding, and Ronnie would arrive exhausted. Meanwhile, Betty and I would catch a flight the night before and arrive at the auction refreshed to watch our cows being sold or to bid on a new one.

Our best sale came from a bull we had no intention of selling. He was a show bull, and we took great pride in taking him to various rings. On one such occasion, we were approached by an Australian, who had set his heart on having that bull.

"That's quite a nice bull you 'ave there, mate! I'll give you twenty-five for him right now."

Behind me I could hear Betty whispering, "Twenty-five thousand?" and I quickly nudged her with my elbow.

"Thanks mate, but he's not for sale!"

Of course, the conversation didn't end there, and when it was all said and done, I had sold my prize bull. For forty thousand dollars. It was unthinkable, not to mention our buyer would pay another ten thousand to get him to Australia!

There was a down side, however, to the cattle business. As much fun as it was, we simply were not making money with it. It was a little disappointing. It didn't feel as if we were successful, and that was important to me. I loved the equipment, the smells, the whole farm ambiance, but it wasn't quite enough.

After eight years, we moved away from the transplants and switched to using Black Angus bulls.

In a way, I was glad I had spent time up in the haylofts, watching, and smelling the fresh cut grass, becoming addicted to the beauties of that wonderful but inefficient way of living. But it was sad, too, to know that such a glorious life would not produce a profit.

However, I was right on the edge of something very interesting, and any negative feelings were short-lived, as always.

Just to give you some background, let me tell you a little bit about my time in college. When I was a freshman, as a physical education major, I had quite a few friends. There were probably three hundred other guys there, but I was about the only one that wasn't on scholarship. So they were all fine athletes and although I was above average athletically, and what you would call a good athlete, I was no comparison to the student athlete on scholarship for his excellence there at Marshall University in Huntington, West Virginia.

One week, some of my friends wanted to go golfing on the upcoming Saturday, and that week they were hell-bent on my going with them. I was determined not to be made an ass of—I didn't want to go unless I could perform at least close to as well as them. Due to their insistence, I decided to go.

The event started off well and as my buddies all teed off, I found myself not too far behind them. Overall, in fact, I seemed to have played well for the duration. I was happy, relieved, and surprised to find that I had found a sport I hadn't realized I was good at. I started thinking about it as a sport that I could excel in. I came in all excited, telling Betty about it.

"I just got done with the golf game," I told her. "I think I did OK for not having any experience. Maybe this is what I've been looking for, and maybe, if I work hard enough in the next five years, I could become a golfer!"

Then, fast forward to me at the age of fifty-two. I thought, well, everything's going well for me in my life. I'm not only a millionaire, but a multi-millionaire. My business was going very smoothly, and at that point, boasting a net worth of twenty-eight million. It was also under the leadership of my son and the vice presidents. So, after talking it over with Betty, I decided it was time I devote a few more hours each week to recreational pursuits. And if I really wanted to start playing golf, I thought, maybe then was just the right time.

So I bought five hundred used golf balls and constructed a little driving range at home. This was pretty easily accomplished within the boundaries of our one thousand-acre farm. I had a driving pad, and I could drive the balls out into the fields area. I started driving and hitting two hundred balls every morning. Then, when Ray Wines, our gardener, would report to duty the first thing he would do, was go over and shag—pick up all the balls. And they'd be sitting there in the evening for me so I could go ahead and hit two hundred more balls before I called it quits for the evening.

I was using Shannon Green Golf Course at that time, to practice chipping and putting three times a week. It was about fifteen minutes drive from our home, and located in Fredericksburg, Virginia.

One day, my son Jay was visiting at the farm. He and my nephew, Kelly Lewis, were going to go down to Shannon Green to play. They stopped by the cattle barn and invited me to go along. Jay and Kelly hadn't known at the time just how hard I'd been practicing, although they knew I was doing some work on my swing.

"Sure, I'll go along with you," I said.

I addressed the goal of becoming a great golfer just the same as I address every other goal. I thought about it quite a lot, figured out the best way to go with it, and determined a strategy. I decided that the best way to go was to hit several thousand balls for a little while before I went to the course, and do some practicing. That would promote my success when I took the show on the road, so to speak.

I can remember the scores on that day—Jay and Kelly both shot one hundred and ten, and I shot ninety-eight. My goal was achieved my first time out to the course.

I played maybe four or five times there over the following couple of weeks. I began to realize that the course was not run well, and that maybe I'd like to have a more properly run, successful golf course of my own. The prices there were too high and the construction of the course did not seem too exciting to me.

I found out quickly that the management at the now defunct Shannon Green public golf course exercised a condescending disposition toward those with whom they were not familiar, or who did not exercise the same degree of pretension as those working the course. I could drive onto the lot in my eighty-thousand-dollar Mercedes, and somehow be made to feel as though I should be using the service entrance.

My brother-in-law, Bob, nodded as I described the feeling to him.

"Yessir," he said. "I know exactly what you mean. Like you should be *grateful* they let you play there. It's a public course with a country club mentality."

"Right! If I had a golf course, there'd be none of that! I would treat people like I was glad they were there. None of that stuffy, high-falutin' arrogance! I'd just want everybody to have a good time!"

Bob looked at me suspiciously. "If *you* had a golf course," he said. "Now that would be something."

Well, that was pretty much all it took to get that notion going. It *would* be something. I continued playing, but I also visited all of the golf courses within a few hours radius of our home. I couldn't seem to shake the idea, not that I wanted to, that I could build a better course.

Over the following months, I took hundreds of pictures and filled dozens of the infamous yellow pads with notes. I came to realize that some of the courses had no truly distinguishing characteristics. Yet, some were unique and memorable. I began to develop my ideas about what would work if I had my own golf course. Before long, I said, "Betty, I'm going to do it!"

"Uh huh," she said, "I know that."

"But I just now decided—how can you say you know already?"

"Bill, that golf course idea has been twinkling in your eyes for months now! We've been together far too long for me *not* to know!"

"It's going to be affordable."

"OK."

"And different! Unique."

"Of course it will!"

"I'm going to treat *everyone* like pros, you know?"

"I know."

I stopped short. "Well you're sure taking all this in stride!" I said.

"Honey," Betty said warmly, "I know you well enough to know that once you have the vision, it's pretty much a done deal."

I took her in my arms and gave her a hug, happy to have the support she willingly offered in every one of our new endeavors. I began to express my thoughts on planning. "I'll have to hire an architect. Or designer. Or planner—whoever you get to help you with a golf course. Maybe I can find some names in those golf magazines I've been reading."

"How will you know when you have the right one?" she asked.

"That's a good question. I guess I'll interview them and talk about ideas and see how they respond."

I realized I had about two thousand acres to work with, when taking into consideration the cattle grounds. The cattle business had been a pleasure but wasn't my most profitable endeavor, and I thought of the idea of building a golf course in those same terms. I wanted to have a lot of fun with it, and break even or maybe even make a little money.

So I looked over my farm lands, and there was one farm that was only about twelve or fourteen miles out of Fredericksburg. It was a rolling, contoured property. And it was interesting, with some fields, but also some woods, and adequate streams as well. I started visualizing how it could work as a golf course.

I knew that I did not know enough to pull the whole thing off myself, but I knew I had some great ideas that might be able to be incorporated into the work of a true golf course designer. So I decided I would choose five of the most interesting golf course designers that I could find, and offer them a thousand dollars each per day to come in and show me how they would put together my golf course. With a little luck, I'd find my designer in the group.

Of the first four, I had a couple that sounded good, but they weren't one hundred percent in line with my goals. One of them even went so far as to say, "I'm a conservative designer. If you want something too exciting and too different, I don't want my name attached to it." And I said, "Well, let me give you your thousand dollar check—you can go on home. Never in my life have I enjoyed doing anything that was right down the middle of the road. I want to be way out in left field. And I want to be someplace that's doing things that have never been done before."

The fifth guy that came in happened to be from Beckley, West Virginia. His name was Bill Ward. I knew of three courses that he had designed and I had visited all three. When he arrived, and I started telling him my objectives for the course, he seemed to approve. Right away, I got the feeling he would develop them in a new and exciting way. After two or three hours of conversation between Bill and I, we took a walk out on the course-to-be, and he started showing me how he could use the natural lay of the land.

It didn't take long after listening to him for me to make my decision. "When can you get started?" I said.

He was very excited about that. "I guess in a couple weeks," he said.

"You know, Bill," I said, "I think I'd like you not only to design the course, but also to be there when it's being constructed, and generally manage everything that needs doing during the entire process."

"That's an excellent idea," he said. "I would like very much to do that."

I explained to Bill that my three major objectives for the course were first, to be affordable for the golfers. I did not want a golf course that required the fees to be as high as they were at the nearby courses, in which the average person could not indulge himself on more than that rare occasion. I wanted that fee to sit at twenty-nine dollars or less, including the cart and everything else. Bill felt he could accomplish that. And we did accomplish it, as I was to find out later on.

My second goal was for the course to be unique. I realize that most golfers, especially as they get older, really prefer traditional, conservative-style golf course. They don't want excitement and uniqueness to deal with. But, in contrast to that, I told Bill, I wanted the course to be so unusual, that the golfer would come in and play the first hole, and when he went to the second hole, it would be as if he had just loaded everything into his car and started off on another course. Every hole would be like starting to play on a whole new course. I did not want any resemblance between the different holes. And this idea required that we were willing and able to get away from the traditional style of course.

Additionally, I told him that as the golf course got off the ground, I expected every person working at the course to treat every golfer coming in as if they were a pro. They had to be thanked when they called in to reserve tee time, and then when they paid, they would again be thanked. And then, when the starter took them out, they were to be thanked again and once again by the marshall, bringing the total thank yous to four. Then I'd have a big sign up as they leave the course, thanking them one more time.

Golf courses ten years ago had no use for the words *thank you*. The only people who were treated nicely were the veteran players, who'd been playing for fifteen, twenty years, and were really great golfers. So the idea of thanking the every day customer distinguished our plan for the golf course right at the start. However, it did seem to catch on. I like to think that my practice of employing manners with our customers and the use of thank yous revolutionized the golfing business etiquette. Now, when you go out to play a golf course in the D.C. area, you are thanked a couple times, and players are generally appreciated more than they had been before we started our practice of outwardly valuing the customer.

Once we opened the course, we started playing three hundred golfers on Saturdays and three hundred golfers on Sunday, and sometimes, as many as two hundred during the week. The golf course was the most played golf course in the D.C. area.

During my meetings with Bill Ward, I asked him what we could do to make the course different.

"Well," he said, "there is such a thing as a Par Six." He went on to explain to me how Par Sixes worked, and explained that there were only five other golf courses in the state of Virginia with Par Sixes, which added to the uniqueness.

"Bill, that's good. Let's do it," I answered before long. "But let me add something to it. Let's not only make it a Par Six, but let's make it the longest golf hall in the United States."

"Fine with me!" he said.

After checking through the records of all the courses in the U.S., and finally consulting the *Guinness Book of World Records*, I found that the longest one was eight hundred thirty-seven yards. So I made mine eight hundred forty-one yards, Par Six. Since then, there have been at least two or three articles in *Golf Digest* about it and several in other golf magazines. I believe the publicity of appearing in these magazines is one of the reasons why the course has been so successful.

Sometimes being the opposite of conservative can really help you—of course, sometimes, it can really hurt you, too. But I have had one business philosophy all along that in all my businesses I've been in, I've never wanted to have a partner. Naturally, whenever you're successful, you get folks who would like to buy shares in your business. Meadows Farms was no exception, but Betty and I are the only owners. I think that if you are a person who enjoys doing some crazy things, like these crazy golf holes that have put us on the map, then you better not have a partner—even if you think you've found someone crazy as you are.

To me, the enjoyment of business is diminished when you have to answer to a single person. Betty, naturally, owns this business as much as I do, and we discuss things and we talk about some things for a long time, and we have even had a few little arguments—nothing real serious—but a few. But when it gets down to the nitty gritty, and we still disagree, she'll say, "OK, we'll do it your way." She has never ever forced me to do anything that I didn't want to do in business, and I have always appreciated that.

Similar to my experiences in my other businesses, I had a few people who found out that I was building a golf course and wanted to come aboard. They'd offer investment money of course, and I would always say, "No." Even my brothers, who have worked in my businesses don't own any of it. I would be more likely to get along with them than with anyone else in the world, unless it would be my dad. And my dad would never have been successful being a business partner of mine because he was too conservative—he would not have shared my desire to grow.

With that idea in mind, the golf course is now twenty-seven holes. Eighteen, of course, is standard and I had eighteen. But within two or three years, it was completely overflowing with customers, and I opened up nine more. It is now twenty-seven holes plus the warm-up hole, where the folks that are rusty can warm up and those who are stressed out can settle down with a few practice strokes as well.

One of the holes, which I feel is quite unique, is a waterfall hole, in which the player hits the ball over a small pond. Just beyond the pond is a manmade waterfall on the far side, with about a thirty-foot flowing drop, about two thousand gallons a minute, dropping off the edge, making it look like a cliff, but beyond the waterfall, it's level. There are seven others in the United States that have waterfalls, but what makes ours so unusual is that there is a tunnel under the waterfall and back in under the green. You take your cart up there, and you can stop your cart when you get halfway up, then on busy days, you can have a drink at the bar!

Once you get your drink, you can pull your cart right on up the tunnel. The tunnel is built like a coalmining shaft. You come out close to the top, and on the back is another waterfall, which comes down with the creek to the left of the green. To get over to play your ball, there's a swinging bridge. As a kid, I loved swinging bridges where, in the mountains of West Virginia, they were actually functional. I played them by the hours. Having the swinging bridge at this unique hole has brought back many pleasant memories.

Most greens can be built for around sixty-five thousand dollars. But this one cost two hundred sixty-five thousand dollars, with all its unique features. But its uniqueness and appeal is something that stays with our customers.

Ironically, the idea for this hole came to me while Betty and I were in Acapulco, where we could swim out, under a waterfall, and then sit at a bar. I found the experience to be a pleasant interlude, and wanted to revisit it often—although not in a swimsuit in water up to the elbows!

Another of my favorite designs is the par three baseball hole where you go to the almost official-sized diamond, which has an in-field of sand, and all three bases. There's a pitching rubber and a plate that you throw to, and a grass outfield. A fence runs the length of the outfield, and there's a sand trap all the way around the inside of the fence, with the green situated right in the middle of the field. You hit the ball into the outfield, and then you play it. This is another nice spot where my childhood memories of many baseball games return to me.

Betty and I would talk and talk as the golf course began to take shape, and as our opening day grew closer. And on that first day, we *knew*. We could see the pleasure in the golfers' faces when we introduced ourselves to them and shook hands; when we invited them to warm up on our par-four warm-up hole; when they climbed into the brand new carts and headed out for a golf adventure; when they steered their carts under a thirty-foot waterfall and stood drinking sodas as they peered through the rushing water; and when they received a smile and a thank you from every golf course employee. We knew we were on to something good.

George Allen, Redskins coach, visits with Farmer

Redskin's coach, Joe Gibs, personal friend of Farmers, gives inspirational talk to all Meadows Farms employees

Chapter Thirty-Seven

Coaches

*I*t started one afternoon in 1969.

"That's Charlie Taylor!" my brother-in-law, Bob, hissed, poking me in the ribs.

"It sure is!" I said.

Standing there in line to pay, filthy from the rigors of football practice, holding two chrysanthemums, was the huge Redskins wide receiver, Charlie Taylor.

"Charlie!" I called tentatively, relieved when he turned to me with a smile.

"Hi," he said.

"Hi, Charlie! I'm Farmer Meadows. Thank you for shopping at my nursery!"

"Nice to meet you, Mr. Meadows. I thought I'd stick a couple of flowers in front of my house. It's brand new and totally bare."

"Maybe I could help you, Charley. We do landscaping, you know. I could come out and take a look—see what you need."

"That would be terrific," he said, "but the schedule's pretty tight right now." He indicated his football attire.

"Well, that's where I come in. I'll lay out a design for you and we'll get it

Meadows

all in the ground without you ever having to lift a finger."

Taylor nodded thoughtfully. "Tell you what. Come by the park tomorrow when practice is over and we'll run by my house together. After that, you're on your own."

I was one cool customer as I said goodbye to Charlie Taylor, but inside I was ecstatic at the thought of a personal invitation to Redskins Park. My love of the sport of football extended to all aspects of the game. I couldn't think of a better afternoon than one spent watching the Redskins practice.

Well, one connection led to many more as I began personally visiting the homes of the various Redskins players and drawing up unique designs for landscaping their million dollar homes. I extended them all fifty percent discounts as my way of showing my appreciation for the job they did for the Redskins.

I enjoyed meeting and designing for quite a few of them over the years, including Roy Jefferson, Mark Mosely, Joe Theisman (although it was Shari, his wife, that appreciated the landscaping), John Riggins, Pete Wysacki, Larry Brown, coaches George Allen and Joe Gibbs, owner Jack Kent Cook, and many others as well.

In 1969, George Allen was not only the Redskins coach, but a well-known personality in the Washington Metropolitan Area. A bit controversial, he was nevertheless a champ when it came to motivating his team and building morale. I believed we might have some traits in common when it came to innovation and notability, and I was pleased to make his acquaintance and have the opportunity to talk with him from time to time. His interests were varied, and I was surprised to learn of his insatiable interest in plants. And though he was a well-paid coach, George was also a man who loved to shop for a bargain.

In a town driven by football mania, it was no surprise that the customers at the nursery were always thrilled to find themselves shopping at the same time as one of the team members. There would be a general hum of excitement, and sometimes even a few autograph seekers. Word spread in the neighborhood that the Redskins shopped at Meadows Farms. On one Saturday morning, I was stunned to find an assembly of shoppers at the nursery an hour before opening, hoping to see some Redskins come in.

That spectacle gave me an idea. If that many would come to see a few Skins, imagine the response to a whole football team and their coach! Why sales would be through the roof! It was brilliant! I thought.

I decided to make a call. "George? This here's the Farmer. I'd like to ask a favor of you."

"You got it, Farmer. What do you need?"

By that time, George Allen and I had established a relationship that prohibited my being shy by any means when asking for something. The fact is, he'd already dropped all shyness himself that Saturday morning earlier in the season.

I'd been very busy in the nursery when I got the call from him, insisting I needed to drop everything and come right over to his Great Falls home.

"I need to talk to you about something," he said urgently.

I broke away reluctantly and headed for his place, convinced that something was terribly wrong. But when I arrived, he seemed very anxious.

"Come on out back, Farmer," he said. "I want to show you something!" He proceeded toward a tall, outwardly branching tree, stopping at the base of it. "Look at this!" he said, gesturing widely. "Have you ever seen anything like it? Look at those, those *things* hanging down! Incredible, isn't it?"

I stared hard at him. It wasn't incredible. And it certainly wasn't urgent. "George, it's a black walnut tree."

"A *what?* A walnut tree?"

"Walnut. And you'll find that when those *things* hanging down from it fall, you can crack them open and eat them."

His face wore an expression of awe. "Is it a rare specimen?"

I wanted to say that the *tree* wasn't a rare specimen, but perhaps the *man* ... I refrained, however. "No, George. The Black Walnut is indigenous to this area all the way up to New England and all the way out to Indiana. It grows wild."

His face fell. "Well," he said, "thanks for coming."

What? That was it? "Is that why you called me away from my busy nursery twelve miles away? To ask me about walnuts?"

"I guess so. Sorry. I'll save you some walnuts."

So when I called George that day with my idea, I didn't feel one bit shy about asking. "These folks are crazy about you out here George," I said. "It would be so cool to have eleven players and the coach here on a Saturday morning to sign autographs and talk to the fans!"

"I don't know, Farmer. I'm no good with personal appearances. Let me see if I can get some of the guys to do it, though."

"Come on, George, it wouldn't be the same without you. Hey! I'm doing that landscape job for you, George. A thirty-thousand-dollar job for fifteen! That oughta be worth something!"

George considered for what seemed like an eternity, then slowly relented.

"All right, all right. I'll do it. But just for two hours. No more. And nothing crazy. We just stand around and sign autographs."

"It'll be fine," I said. "Good for you, and good for me!"

Well, I took out a half-page ad in the *Washington Post*, headlined with MEET THE REDSKINS! ELEVEN PLAYERS AND THEIR COACH! We cleared a large area of the center of the nursery, and set up twelve pedestals, one for each player and the coach to stand on. I figured they would be more visible that way, and if they answered questions, they could be more easily heard. We were scheduled to begin at 11:00, but by 9:00 a.m., I knew it would be a different sort of day.

Cars were pouring into the parking lot, and when it was quickly filled, they began to park along Lakeland Drive and Route 7. It wasn't long before the police arrived and began directing people through the fray, and even waving some people on. Betty and I watched, fascinated as people nudged each other out of the way for their positions. We found, however, as we mingled in the crowd, that these people were really not customers at all. They were there to meet the Redskins—just as the ad had promised—and to heck with any trees we had on sale.

"At least it's good publicity," Betty reasoned. "You know, exposure ... "

"Exposure to what?" I had to wonder, as I watched the crowd grow.

By five minutes 'til ten, eleven football players stood ready in my office. But no coach.

"He'll be here," Betty assured me. "Look at this traffic. He's probably caught in it along with half of Northern Virginia."

By 10:05, the fans and players were interacting beautifully. Autograph signing, baby kissing, and picture taking were the order of the morning, but a long line of disappointed people stretched out behind George Allen's platform.

"I'm going to call his house," I told Betty. "Maybe his wife can give me some idea of when he left."

I exchanged pleasantries with his wife, then said abruptly, "He's not here, yet. We were expecting him fifteen minutes ago."

"He's here," she said. "I'll go get him."

George got on the phone as if nothing had happened. "Hey, Farmer!"

"George, what happened?" I asked. "People are here waiting for you!"

"Well," he said casually, "I got to thinking, and it's just not me. I just wouldn't have been that comfortable."

"Comfortable?" I said, shocked. "I'm not talking about *comfortable*. I'm talking about three or four thousand people waiting to meet you! I'm talking about the most expensive ad I've ever run! I'm talking about my business crawling with police, and my cash registers completely mute so that Northern Virginia and George Allen could get to know each other!"

"I know, Farmer," he said, "but I changed my mind."

"You changed your mind! That's fine, George. And I just changed my mind about fifteen thousand dollars worth of free landscaping. How's that sound?"

"Not so good. I'll be right over."

George made his appearance, to the delight of the huge crowd that had gathered. He apologized profusely for being late, and the people were most forgiving. And, of course, so was I. And despite the fact that we had record high crowds with record lows on sales, we still had no regrets. To this day, no one has ever had a full professional football team of eleven players and the coach to meet and greet since.

I continued my friendship with various players on the team. In 1978, Jack Pardee replaced George Allen, and then in 1981, we got Coach Joe Gibbs. By that time, I'd become good friends with Quarterback Joe Theismann. We both enjoyed unwinding with a game of racquetball, the game of style in the 1980s.

One afternoon, Theismann invited me to go to the racquetball court with him to meet Coach Gibbs for his first time. Gibbs was a bit of a racquetball champion himself, and I expected to watch a lively match between the two of them. The two players stretched and ran and dove for shots, sweating up a storm, but Coach Gibbs was undeniably the better player.

Then, at the end of their game, Joe Theismann astonished me by slamming his racquet so hard against the wall that the handle splintered. It was a side of him I'd never seen. I was horrified that he'd chosen to let it show in front of a man he was meeting for the first time. I shook my head but kept my thoughts to myself.

Gibbs graciously handed him another racquet and they played again. And by the time they'd finished, Theismann had destroyed three racquets! I knew I had to say something. After Gibbs left, I started in.

"Joe, you're an ass."

"Really?" he said, "what makes you say that?"

"Coach Gibbs is your new boss. He's apt to be around for a while. You get one chance to make a first impression and blew it. You were a complete jerk."

Theismann continued to walk and talk, unruffled. "You did a lot of coaching, didn't you, Farmer?" he said conversationally.

"Quite a bit, with the school and then the young people in the neighborhood—sure, I'd say I know something about coaching."

"How'd you feel when you lost a game?"

"I made it a point not to lose," I answered, "but if I did, I felt lousy. I couldn't sleep, couldn't think of anything other than what I should have done different. Nobody likes to lose."

"Did you ever have a player who didn't seem to care if they lost? Was just as happy either way?"

"Oh, yeah. I could name a few like that. It would burn me up. This business of being a good loser is for the birds!"

"Exactly," said Theismann.

"What's your point?"

"Nothing, really, except now my brand new boss knows how much winning means to me. I think he got the idea."

I looked at my friend differently, glad that I wasn't too old to learn something new. And as you probably know, Gibbs was the first coach of the Skins to effectively put Theismann into play—and end up going to the Super Bowl more than once.

Joe Gibbs and I hit it off right away. I was very happy when he extended me a personal invitation to come to practices. He loved the game, having waited seventeen years to reach head coach.

That was the year in which our Cindy died. It was a time of unfathomable sorrow for our entire family. I found myself isolated and solitary, unable to move in a healing direction. One of the few times I had any respite from my grief was when Joe Gibbs invited me to fly to Los Angeles with the team. I was hesitant at first, never imagining the trip would bring me any pleasure. I wasn't certain I should or could leave Betty either, but she urged me to go.

"It's all right, Bill," she had said. "Staying here won't bring Cindy back. Going on that trip won't show disrespect or indifference. It might help you. Go."

I will always be grateful for Joe's invitation. That simple gesture of friendship brought me pleasure and hope in the darkest period of my life.

Eventually, Joe decided to build a house at Fawn Lake, a beautiful, gated community not far from our Locust Grove farm near Fredericksburg, Virginia. It was an elegant design, and lent itself wonderfully to the view of the water. Joe's incredible popularity caused the local tradesmen to vie for contract work on his mini mansion, eager to be able to say they had installed the floors or windows in Joe Gibbs' house. The final result was breathtaking.

The community was baffled when Joe made a sudden career move just a few weeks after completing the house. He had decided to resign his coaching position in a blaze of glory, eager to turn his attention to NASCAR circuit racing. The beautiful new house stood empty.

"Bill, let's look at Joe's house again," Betty suggested on more than one occasion. "I just love those windows. And no stairs to run up and down."

I knew Betty couldn't be getting older, because I knew I wasn't, and we're the same age. But she was talking about one-level-living as if we were ready for the retirement community. She'd also been murmuring about how much work it was to keep up with the farm.

"Now, Betty," I said. "You have a lot of help already, but if you need more, I'll get you more." Nancy Wines is a great housekeeper, and her husband Ray does a great job as gardener.

"I know I have plenty of help, Bill," she said. "It's not that. It's just that it's so big. The children aren't home as much, and it seems empty. Besides, even though we have Ray to oversee the grounds, I still feel as though I have to always be planning and managing. I don't want to manage anymore. I just want to live, without feeling like the mistress of some plantation."

We would go back and forth, and we would look at the house that Joe built. Kate was excited.

But Rocky was just the opposite. "I'll never leave the farm," he said resolutely. "It has everything. I don't want to live in a neighborhood where people can look in the window and see whether or not you ate your broccoli."

"Just think about it, Bill. I know we're not getting older, but we're certainly not getting younger, either!" Betty said.

After a lot of consideration, we came to a crazy decision. We would buy Joe's house and we would live in both places for a year. We weren't sure whether it would be weeks versus weekends, or one month one place, the next month the other place, but I knew my bride needed to be happy, and there was a definite bonus in keeping Kate happy, too. Rocky was forlorn.

"I'll visit you, but I don't want to move," he declared, his emotion strong.

Betty and I wondered how we'd ever satisfy the whole family.

We made the move gradually. Betty worked with Mary Lou on interior designing, and we put the farm up for sale. At least one of us went by the farm everyday, but eventually, we all settled in—even Rocky.

They say there's no place like home for the holidays. And they also say that home is where the heart is. Our first Christmas Eve on Fawn Lake, in 1999, proved to me and the rest of the family that our house had become our home.

Betty following chemo with sister, Mary Lou Provencher

Chapter Thirty-Eight

Survivor

I was in July of 1997 that I felt a little knot in my left breast during a self-exam. I pressed on it gently, expecting it to move around. The doctor had told me that a lump that moved was nothing to worry about, and I had experienced that kind of thickening a time or two in the past. But this one didn't move.

I was due for my mammogram in just two months, but I called that day to make an appointment. I had my exam by the end of the week, and a few days later received a letter telling me the results were negative, no cancer.

The little knot, however, stayed in place, hard and unyielding. I touched it everyday, willing it to disappear. Then, in September, I went for my yearly exam and told my doctor the story of the lump. Her brow furrowed slightly as she examined it, and released a thoughtful, "Hmm ... it definitely does not feel like a cyst. I think I'll order a scan for you over at UVA. That'll give us a little more detail. If they see something suspicious, they'll go ahead and take a sample for biopsy while you're there."

"OK, good. That makes sense," I said, trying to sound matter-of-fact.

The scan did produce something on the screen and I was told they were taking a biopsy. "We'll have some results the day after tomorrow," I was told.

That evening, Bill and I sat down for a talk. "Don't mention this to the children," I said. "No use getting them upset for no reason."

Meadows

"No use in your getting upset either, Betty," he said, pulling me close. "We won't know 'til we know."

I smiled at my dear husband, and wondered how he could be such a comfort, even at the scariest times.

Two days later, the phone rang. "Mrs. Meadows?"

"Yes," I said, my heart stopping.

"It's Lauren from the Lab Center in Charlottesville. I'm so sorry, Mrs. Meadows. Your biopsy was positive. We're overnighting the results to your doctor … "

But that was all I heard. I went through the evening keeping the knowledge to myself. The following morning, I told Bill I had something to discuss with him.

"I heard from the lab yesterday. My biopsy was positive."

"Now Betty," he said, "that can't be right. You just had that mammogram two months ago, and there was nothing. Let's get a second opinion."

"Of course. I'll be talking to my doctor today," I said. "We'll get this whole thing straightened out once and for all."

Bill nodded and hugged me fiercely. I wondered if those strong arms could carry me through what I thought might lie ahead for me. Could any arms be that strong?

I called my doctor who gave me a referral to Dr. Moore, a breast cancer surgeon, who agreed to see me in a few days.

Dr. Moore wore an angry expression as she described my disease to me. Infiltrating lobular cancer is mean and sneaky and hard to detect. It has long skinny fingers that spread greedily through the breast, and it's hard to see on a mammogram. Only about ten percent of breast cancer patients have this form. It's a tough one."

Bill and I stared at each other in disbelief. She was confirming the cancer diagnosis, and already talking about surgery.

"Sometimes a simple lumpectomy is successful, and the breast remains intact. I don't think that will work for you, though. The mastectomy will remove the entire breast, but you will be amazed at how far this whole procedure has evolved."

"I think I'd prefer the lumpectomy," I said.

"As I explained, Mrs. Meadows," Dr. Moore countered, "that's probably not your best option."

Nevertheless, we scheduled the surgery. Bill and I rode home solemnly, holding hands and talking of inconsequential things. And we talked about the children.

"They'll worry so much," I lamented. "I don't want to put them through all that."

"We're a family," Bill reminded me gently. "That's what it's all about. We go through the hard things together. That will teach Rocky and Kate the best lessons I can think of."

"They're so young, Bill. That's a lot for them to go through." I tried to imagine Bill raising the children without me—proms, homework, drivers' licenses—while overseeing the business, the farm, and the house. My heart ached at the prospect. I simply had to beat the cancer.

"Lord," I whispered during a quiet moment alone, "can we make some kind of agreement?" My anger had long since dissipated after losing Cindy, yet I hadn't prayed in a long time. But I felt that in the stillness, God was listening. "I just can't die until I finish my job with Kate and Rocky. I need to see them start their adult lives, and then you can do what you want. But please don't take me now. I'll pay you back, God. I'll help others more. I know I could do more, and I will!" I pleaded and promised, then wiped my tears, resolving that the matter was in God's hands.

The surgery wasn't too bad, but Dr. Moore had bad news for us.

"I was afraid this would happen," she said. "I just couldn't get it all. I really feel that the complete mastectomy is the only way we can be sure."

Dr. Moore was joined by Dr. Cohen, a staff oncologist assigned to my case. He was kind and compassionate. "Mrs. Meadows," he said, "I wish it weren't so, but Dr. Moore is right. At this point, you still have cancer. We need to get rid of it. The mastectomy is how we accomplish that."

I tried to imagine the concept of breastlessness, and what it would mean in my life. My husband loved my body, including my two breasts, one on each side. Could his love for me overshadow the disfigurement we were contemplating or would my maimed body be repulsive to him?

"I want you to try again," I implored, holding onto Dr. Moore's hand. "I know you can get it. Can't we try another surgery?"

"We can't force the mastectomy on you, dear, but the longer we wait, the worse the disease gets. But, yes, we can try another surgery in a couple of weeks," she said.

I waited anxiously for the time to pass, eager to put this whole thing behind me and move on. I tried to bolster my confidence that the next surgery would be successful, all the while praying and promising, and wishing God would let me know that my deal had been accepted.

Dr. Moore came in after the second surgery and shook her head. I didn't even ask her what she meant. "Schedule the mastectomy," I said, as two tears rolled down my face.

Between the second and third surgeries, I read everything I could get my hands on that pertained to the mastectomy and breast cancer in general. I armed myself with bravado and optimism, and managed to keep the mood light around the house. We were approaching Christmas, and I managed to shop a little, decorate a little, bake a little ... and it was enough to give Kate and Rocky some sense of continuity and security. And it made me realize how much I wanted to live—not just for Christmas, but for graduation, weddings, grandchildren—and suddenly the breastlessness seemed insignificant.

After the third surgery, Dr. Moore entered the room smiling. "I feel really good about this," she declared. "Your lymph nodes look good, and I feel confident that we got all the affected tissue. I'm very pleased!"

I smiled weakly, wishing I could share her enthusiasm. A few days later, I was released, with drainage tubes connected to me and an armful of instructions on how to care for myself.

"I guess we'll be playing doctor," Bill said, trying to get me to laugh.

"Don't make me laugh," I said. "I ache all over!"

Bill patted my hand as he drove. "We'll get you situated in your own bed, and we'll treat you like a queen. You'll be back to your old self in no time."

Once I was in bed, I asked Bill to sit next to me. "I love you," I began, "and I know you love me. But I'll never be back to my old self again. Things will be different now."

"Not so different, Betty. Nothing could make me love you less. Or make me less attracted to you, for that matter. You are a sexy old lady and I have missed you madly." We talked and cuddled and dozed, and I believed it would be all right.

It took me two days to muster the physical strength and the emotional courage to shower and change my bandages. I had considered asking Bill to help me, but felt that I had to take that step on my own. I didn't tell him what I was going to do, so it was most disconcerting to him when he called home to check on me and could only hear my racking sobs. He was home in short order, and found me there, still crying and shaking all over.

"Baby, what is it? What happened? Tell me! Let me help you!" He sounded anxious and confused, and uncertain of how to offer comfort.

"This!" I wept, covering my chest.

"What? Let me see, sweetheart," he said gently.

I clutched my robe more tightly around myself. "No, you can't see. Not now, not ever," I said, knowing that it wasn't true, but too horrified to say otherwise.

"Betty, having you as my wife, alive, is all I care about. I swear to you, Betty, don't stop trusting me after all these years. Show me and let me hurt with you. I love you so much."

His words melting my heart, I felt helpless in my effort to protect him from the monstrous obscenity that had once been my left breast.

He ran his fingers lightly over the wound. Tears fell freely, but his voice never faltered. "It's OK, Betty, it's OK. I love you. You're beautiful. I wish you could see yourself the way I see you ... " His words were soothing, his voice calm, almost hypnotic. We sat for a few moments in comfortable silence.

"I've been meaning to ask you," Bill said in a tone I interpreted as serious, "could you still love me if I had ... if I had an appendectomy?"

I stared at him for a moment, not comprehending. Then all at once it hit me and I found a pillow to smack him with. "That's not funny, Bill. This is serious!"

"Hey, remember the one-armed coach in junior high school?"

"Bill, stop it!" I felt a smile tugging at the corners of my mouth.

"You know, Betty," he carried on, "I don't honestly think I've ever felt the same about you since you had that wisdom tooth removed. I loved that tooth, you know."

I fell into his embrace, laughing, realizing that his arms were strong enough to save me.

After a while, Bill had something else to say. "I'm hungry. Could you go for some Mexican?"

I dressed and put on lipstick for the first time in days, and shortly afterwards, we were sitting in Carlos O'Kelly's, drinking margaritas and talking as we had on any other lunch date.

"I feel nearly perfect," my husband announced, patting his stomach with satisfaction. "There's only one thing that could push it over the top."

He smiled expectantly, and I wondered if he was actually saying what it sounded like.

"You mean dessert?" I asked coyly.

"Well, yes, you might call it that," he said, helping me to my feet and draping my coat over my shoulders. "Would you care for a little dessert?"

"Yes, I believe I would, Bill," I answered as though negotiating a contract. "I believe I've gone without dessert for too long."

We laughed and held hands out to the car, where Bill gave me a long, passionate kiss. The trip home seemed to take forever, and we couldn't get into the bedroom fast enough. Our lovemaking was tender and unhurried, and I was still madly in love with my husband—a little more so, in fact. I was exactly where I wanted to be. And I was so glad we were married!

Six weeks later, it was time for me to begin chemical, or chemo therapy.

"Your incision is healing nicely," Dr. Cohen told me. "And now I have a little proposition for you. I want you to try a brand new drug. We'll use the two standard chemo drugs, then three or four weeks of the new stuff. It's called Taxol. Not only are you a perfect candidate, but your use of it brings us that much closer to a cure."

His last words hit home as I thought of Kate and Miranda and Monica. "OK," I said, "you're on. After Disney World." We had planned the trip months before. It included Kate and Rocky, Jay and his family, my nephew Bobby, his family, and us.

Meadows

"Of course, that's fine. We'll get started as soon as you get back."

I returned from the trip feeling both relaxed and energized and ready to face what lay ahead. Or so I thought.

"You'll be really tired," Dr. Cohen informed me.

"So I've heard," I said.

"No, I mean really tired. Immobilized. But you'll need to keep going."

"Well, naturally. I'll keep going, of course."

"You'll need to stay active, even when you'd rather sleep. You can't isolate yourself."

"No, no of course not." But I had no idea. The nurse showed me how to inject myself everyday to build up my red blood cells before the chemo wiped them out.

"Your digestive tract will be completely confused. You'll be nauseas, not to mention have either diarrhea or constipation. But we have medicines for all of that. We can make you pretty comfortable."

I nodded absently, already planning what I would do when all of this was finally finished.

Bill accompanied me for my first treatment. We found ourselves in a large room where twenty-five to thirty other people were already hooked up to IVs. There was a television and magazines and people talking in little clusters. Periodically, volunteers would offer juice or tea, or light snacks and sandwiches.

"Just getting started?" the woman next to me observed. She had big blue eyes, sparkling teeth, and full sensual lips. And a smooth, shiny head that nearly reflected the overhead light. Her smile disarmed me.

"Yes, my first time. How can you tell?"

"Your hair," she said. "It's still there."

I looked around at the assortment of hats, scarves, wigs, and bald or balding heads. I saw smiles everywhere I looked and heard words of encouragement and optimism. The nurses and volunteers had kind words for everyone, sometimes accompanied by a smile or pat. I watched and listened and talked to my husband for three hours as the bag of liquid hope emptied itself, drop by drop into my veins. A vague understanding began to dawn on me.

"Bill, the people here all look so happy."

"I know. I don't get it. What's to be happy about?"

"I'm happy for today," I said. "I'm grateful for each day I'm alive. I feel like I appreciate my life more right now, in this room, than I ever have before."

Bill nodded, his face serious. "I think I can understand some of what you're saying, because I can't say when I've appreciated your life more than I do right now, either."

We went home that afternoon, marveling at our day and the people we had encountered. With relief, I realized I wasn't at all nauseous, though I felt a little tired *after I cooked dinner and cleaned up afterwards.*

"Bill, I think I'll head on to bed. I'm fine, but just a little tired."

My head hit the pillow and I fell into a dark dreamless sleep. I didn't hear Bill come to bed, and I awoke on my own around 5:00 a.m. My eyes opened, but I felt almost powerless to move my limbs. Unfortunately, the chaos of my gastro-intestinal tract caused me great anxiety as I willed my frozen extremities to get me to the bathroom before I exploded from both ends.

I stayed in bed for three days, nearly comatose in my stupor, with only vague memories of Kate sitting on the edge of the bed, rubbing my arm. On the fourth day, I got up. I was still tired, but I longed to move back into the land of the living. I forced myself to wash, dress, and at least go through the motions. Gradually, I returned to somewhat of a normal routine, and much too soon, it was time for my second treatment.

Like my first trip, I was amazed at the joy around me. And like my first treatment, the second one left me completely drained.

A visit to Dr. Cohen offered me a modicum of comfort. "It gets easier. We start off with the hardest drug first. Meanwhile, you can't afford to indulge in perpetual bedrest. You need to push yourself so you can spring back just a little faster."

On my next trip, I told Bill I would go alone. And for the next four months I drove myself, administered my own shots, and cut my hibernation time down to a day and a half. I was still exhausted to the point of occasionally pulling over to the side of the road for a catnap, but I kept on going and was proud of each little accomplishment.

I was deeply touched by the support that I received throughout the treatment. Cards and letters and notes came, and many calls, many mentioning that they were praying for me. I was praying, too, and I believed I would get well.

Kate affected me profoundly during the difficult period. She was an angel, providing care and nurturing me through the rugged times. She would come in before school each day and talk to me, hold my hand and bring me everything I would need for the day. And best of all, she continued making plans for the future, confident that I would be part of it.

After about two weeks of chemo, my hair had begun falling out. It was no subtle process, as I had believed it would be. It was not a case of thinning hair, but rather mass exodus. A trip to the beauty parlor in Orange completed the process, removing a few wisps of stray hair and suddenly I had come to match my counterparts at the treatment center. I was devastated. There was no hiding the loss of hair.

"Come on, Betty," Mary Lou said. "We'll get you a cute wig. They have some really nice ones now."

"Wigs look like wigs. I want my hair back!"

"It'll come back—probably better than before!" she said.

"Yes, but right now, I'm bald." There was no escaping it.

I picked out a wig without enthusiasm, wanting only to lessen the trauma for the kids and grandchildren. In keeping with his earlier wit, my husband offered to shave his head so that we'd be a matched pair.

"Bald is beautiful, Betty," he said. "I don't care about the hair."

I believed him and loved him all the more. "Thanks, honey, but I think I'll stick to the ball cap when I go into town," I said.

"Fine," he said.

As any bald-headed woman will tell you, it takes forever for those first hairs to resprout. "Kate, look!" I called, pointing excitedly toward my head.

Kate moved close enough to see them and laughed, hugging me.

I wore my cap for a few more weeks, but when my head was covered with soft peach fuzz, I felt good. "Bill!" I called, excited, "I have hair!"

He smiled encouragingly, but I had a feeling he wasn't sure what all the fuss had been about.

When my hair began to grow back, it came in the form of snowy, white curls. The white color was startling enough, as I had been a honey blond most of my life. But I had never had curls! However, they eventually relaxed into a gentle wave, and I went in to my hair stylist to get evened up a little.

"How about color?" she asked.

"No, no color," I said. "I think I'll go au natural from here on out."

I took my last chemo treatment on June 22, 1998. It was a glorious summer as I celebrated each morning for another day stretching before me. The sky was bluer and the rain fresher, the sun warmer. The feeling was too big to explain, too magnificent to do it justice, too beautiful to describe with only words.

"Thank you, Lord," I would murmur, trusting that He had understood all I wanted to say.

On June 22, 2003, I woke up to breakfast in bed, five dozen yellow roses, and my whole family holding a big banner: *Congratulations! You did it! You have been Cancer-Free for Five Years!*

Farmer holding check for $3,300,000

Chapter Thirty-Nine

A Lucky Man

Lowell was a decent, hard-working man who lived in one of the trailers and farmed the little piece of property adjacent to our thousand-acre farm in Locust Grove. We always waved or honked our horns when we passed each other, sometimes stopping for a brief, neighborly exchange. One day, I had ridden my four-wheeler down to the road to check the mail and I saw Lowell coming out from under his pickup truck, which was pulled over to the side of the road. He was drenched in sweat and saturated with black grease on his hands, face, and coveralls. I rode over to the truck, as Lowell stood there, shaking his head.

"Drive shaft's busted," he said. "I'm gonna have to go into town and see if I can find what I need." He looked miserable.

I motioned for him to hop on my vehicle. "I'll get my farm manager to run you into town," I said.

We headed back to our property where several of the workers were finishing up their day.

"Hey Shiloh," I called, "would you mind running Lowell up the road to find a drive shaft? His pickup's dead in the middle of the road."

Shiloh nodded. "Fifteen minutes all right? I have one more thing I need to take care of."

"Fine. Meet us over at the house." I circled around to pick up the other end of our long driveway and rolled up in front of my thirteen thousand-square-foot home. Going in through the garage, I took Lowell through the mudroom.

"Why don't you wash up a little and we'll have a cold drink while we wait."

Betty met me in the kitchen with a tall glass of ice water as she had thousands of times. She smiled, happy to see me and gave me a nice hug. "Did I hear you talking to someone?" she asked.

"Yep, Lowell from across the field. Shiloh's gonna run him out to get a part for his truck."

Just then, Lowell came in holding his bedraggled cap in his hand.

"You look beat, Lowell," Betty said. "How about an iced tea or a Coke? Come on, have a seat."

"Iced tea sounds great, ma'am, but I won't be staying long. Besides, I'm filthy."

"Nonsense! Sit right down here at the table."

Lowell did have a seat, and Betty and I joined him there. We all sat and looked out on Lake Cindy, which glimmered in the late afternoon sun.

"Great view," Lowell noted. Then, after a long while, he said, "Could I ask you a kinda personal question?"

"Well, sure, Lowell," I said. "Go ahead and ask."

But then there was a tap on the door and Betty waved Shiloh into the kitchen, motioning him to join us at the table.

Lowell hesitated again before going on haltingly. "Well, you go by the name *Farmer*. We're both farmers, I reckon. But you didn't get this rich by being a farmer. I know that nice folks don't talk about their money, but I'm curious. I figure you inherited all this money and land, but I don't recollect my daddy ever talking about your daddy. What line of work was he in? I reckon he weren't no farmer!"

I studied Lowell briefly. I detected no anger or resentment. He was simply curious. He wanted to understand. Lowell was a man who had eked out an existence with his sweat and tears, plowing another man's field, and gratefully accepting hand-me-down clothes for his children to wear to school. By carefully squirreling away a little money here and there, he had saved enough to take his family to Washington, D.C., sixty miles away, where they stayed in a hotel over night, ate in a restaurant, and saw as many museums and monuments as they could pack into two days. It was their first vacation. It struck a chord inside me, as I remembered my trip to that same city in the back of a truck with the Baptist Youth Group. We hadn't even stayed over, and we'd shared drinks from a single thermos provided by the future Senator Byrd. Lowell needed to know the truth.

"Lowell, I didn't inherit this or any other land," I said. "My dad lived in a little house in northern Virginia and he didn't leave us anything that I could put into the bank. But I did inherit his self-discipline and ability to tell right from wrong. Betty and I have worked hard, and we abided by rules our parents had set for themselves—work hard, avoid credit, and treat other's with respect."

"Then maybe you won the lottery," Lowell said. "Callie don't want me buying lottery tickets. She says it's a waste."

"It *is* a waste," I said. "I've never bought lottery tickets. And I can tell you that we didn't get all of this from winning any lottery!"

"Well, then," Lowell said, shaking his head, "I reckon you're just plain lucky. Is that it?"

"That's it, Lowell," I answered. "And boy the harder I work, the luckier I get!"

Lowell rose to his feet and clapped me on the back, chuckling, "You're all right, Farmer! The harder I work the luckier I get! I gotta remember that one! Thank you for your help."

He and Shiloh departed then and Betty gave me a look. "Why'd you go and let him think we got this from luck? You worked hard, Bill, and you know that."

I smiled sadly. "Betty, how could I tell him that my hard work brought me this, and his hard work brought him that?"

I couldn't explain to Lowell why that was. Yet, I wished a little that he'd been able to stick around so I really could explain to him how we had arrived at our success. There were a lot of factors. When Lowell and I were very young, we had had to decide which path we would take to our futures. We had had to make decisions as to what kind of life we wanted in our futures. I made the decision (after much thinking) to go to college. I don't know how much thinking Lowell did, but chances are, he was comfortable on the farm and he just decided to stay there without giving too much thought to the future. I gave my future a lot of thought. I kept coming back to the fact that if I wanted to be really happy, and successful, I would have to go to college. But I did not like school, and I could hardly stand the thought of going to school for another three or four years. However, I knew this would be what I had to do, so my decision was to go to college—this with the full knowledge that I would likely be very uncomfortable, have to work hard, and not be very happy for that time period.

I had the patience and self-discipline to do what needed to be done.

Meadows

Lowell did what made him happy at that moment. As the years went by, there were other decisions that again required a lot of thinking, patience, self-discipline and planning. Lowell got married, had children, built a house, had huge payments on his house, cars, and farm equipment, and a career that did not pay much. I was patient, thinking through each stage of my life. Betty and I waited eight years to start a family, although we would have loved to have had children sooner. But we had a business to grow. We waited eighteen years to build a house and buy nice furniture. We purchased used cars and equipment for our business until we knew our business was successful enough to afford better.

The main thread was not only hard work, which both Lowell and I did, but rather, differences in our thinking, the decisions we made, and practices of patience and self-discipline.

There really is no such thing as luck. But it has long been my belief that when one is rewarded with good fortune, it is essential to show gratitude. I've watched any number of our employees from time to time—some are grateful when a opportunity comes their way, or a small bonus of gratitude, others simply take it in stride. I think the person who wants to be happy—and continue receiving—should show gratitude. I have always done my best to maintain this objective, and intend to do so in the future.

I believe that gratitude can be expressed best in some cases by passing it on—in other words, by being generous. As an employer, I apply that practice by trying to satisfy the individual needs of my employees; can I say "yes" when they need certain days off? Can I promote them? At the end of the year, can I give out bonuses, raises, trips, gifts? Betty and I have always found deep satisfaction in being able to help our employees. In fact, last year, when we were getting ready to give out two hundred thousand dollars in raises, I actually became a temporary insomniac, I was so excited!

Exercising generosity is an especially revitalizing thrill when it can be exercised out of the blue. I remember one year when things were going quite well for Betty and I that we decided to buy a sixty-five-inch projection television, which was the largest they had at that point, to watch the Redskins play-off game, and invite twelve of our key people in for a big party. I guess that's pretty nice, but I saved my big surprise for when they all were leaving.

"So, what'd you think Ted? Did you like that big TV?"

"Oh yeah, Farmer! That's terrific! You can really get a good view on that thing!"

"Well I'm sure happy to hear that," I answered, "because I'm having one delivered to each of your homes tomorrow afternoon!"

The shock that quickly turned to elation in their eyes warmed my heart and brought Betty and I unmeasured of joy. But sometimes you don't get to see the results of your efforts to be generous. Some say that makes it more special, and I guess in the long run it is. One of our first foremen ever in the landscaping venture, Big Al, developed a great desire to go to Maine and be a hunting and fishing guide. He'd wanted to do that ever since I'd known him, in fact. One day, we surprised him with the gift of a trailer up there in the wilderness for him and his family to get started in relative comfort. That trailer served to help him achieve his lifelong dream which he now lives everyday. We don't see him everyday, but we know he's happy.

Then, there's the compassionate generosity I believe everyone needs to exercise. We're not perfect, any of us, and when we make mistakes, we need to repair the damage as best we can. But we also need forgiveness. Betty and I employed a man who was a little down on his luck, but a good and honest employee. Yet, one day, for some inexplicable reason, he committed a crime that landed him in prison for probably the rest of his life. Our compassion leads us to try to make what's left of his life somewhat bearable. We are probably his only visitors, and I'm sure no one else sends him money every month. For that reason, we feel compelled to share a little of our good fortune with someone who, for some reason, made a terrible choice and must now live with the consequences of that move.

A lot of folks have made bad choices and some of them end up hurting only themselves. I guess I figure it could have been me, if things had been different. One morning I strolled the grounds of one of the very posh and beautiful hotels Betty and I frequent. I came upon three fellows in their twenties who had clearly spent the night outside, no doubt following heavy indulgence of alcohol the night before. They seemed to be at odds with the cold realities of morning, wondering where to go next and clearly without any means.

"Good morning," I said, startling the one nearest me.

"Oh, hi," he said, his voice gravelly and disoriented.

"This is for you," I said, tucking a twenty dollar bill into his shirt pocket.

He had no idea how to react. I think at first he thought he might be dead. I did the same for the other two.

"Thanks," one of them breathed, the scent of alcohol still very present.

"Have a nice breakfast on me," I said. "Go and get something good."

"Yeah, OK. Thanks!"

"Hey fellas, listen, the only thing I ask is that you don't waste the money on liquid refreshment. Get a nice breakfast, hear?"

"Sure, mister, thanks," said the first guy who'd found his voice.

Of course I don't know if they had breakfast or not, but I know they could have. That was what was intended.

I think it's also important to be generous with young people. They have a long way to go, and Betty and I try to encourage them to find the happiness in their lives early by offering what we call the Fun Award. It is an annually awarded three thousand dollar cash award for the senior who has had the most fun. The fun cannot be at the expense of others, but true, genuine fun. It is not awarded on the basis of income—the student can be the poorest or the wealthiest, or somewhere in between. It is offered simply on the basis of how much fun they had in high school. It's our hope that in this way, we encourage youngsters to develop a good attitude toward life from their earliest adult days.

In fact, it was right at that age that I began to see religion differently than I'd been brought up to see it. I had always believed in common sense and reasoning, and had seen the results in the lives of my parents. Adding to the fact that I had always been a philosophical person, it had become difficult to attempt to build my life totally around the simple faith and the Bible. It was at about that time also that I began to refer to God as the Creator, which settled better with me. Betty and I would discuss religion while on her front porch, and although my feelings about the Bible had changed, I still respected concerns it deals with and believe it to be a good tool to take mankind in the right direction.

We attended church together for a time after we were married, but even though we drifted from that practice, we maintained a closeness to the Creator in our efforts to do the right thing on a daily basis. It was difficult for me, particularly, though, to hear sermons weekly that dealt in what we should pray for, and how great things were going to be after we died, when I was already grateful for my life and all that was good in it and felt that thanking God in word and action deserved, instead, to be our focus.

We have raised our children to respect the goodness of the Creator, as well. In fact, we built a small chapel on the island contained by Lake Cindy. It was a place to visit surrounded by so much natural beauty and life that it virtually spoke of the Creator to our children in an unpretentious manner, allowing them to perceive the goodness of the Creator and feel gratitude within their own developing souls.

Loving also plays an important role in my philosophy of life. It has never been enough for Betty and I to only like our employees. We have always felt that we should know them well enough to feel genuine love for them; care about and for them as much as possible. Love begets respect of course, and as I think I've stated within earlier pages, it has always been very important to me to show the same amount of respect to the employee at the bottom of the salary range that I would to someone at the top level. The degree of respect a human being deserves should not revolve around how much or how little he or she makes.

    I say a prayer that the hereafter is half as good as it is here. I have so much to be thankful for in my life here on Earth. But when people ask me how I'm feeling, I usually reply, "Nearly perfect!" *Nearly* because only the Creator is perfect.

The Farmer Meadows Family

Chapter Forty

Living Nearly Perfect

Betty and I live a "nearly perfect" life now, in our golden years. I go to work every day, which I hope to do until the day I die. Betty joins me later in the day to do what she does now, take care of our personal life, running our household, and planning our family get-togethers. I play golf three to four times a week. We take great trips to Mexico, Jamaica, Puerto Rico, and many other islands in the winter. We talk to our wonderful children almost every day.

Jay is the man that every parent would hope his son would become. He exhibits all the important character traits that our parents taught us; trustworthiness, respect, responsibility, caring, doing the "right" things. As president of our company, which we love almost as one loves a child he has raised and nurtured, Jay demonstrates business talents I never had, but also the strengths and compassions I do have. He is a loving husband and father. We could never have asked for more from a child.

Doreen, Jay's wife, is the perfect partner for him. She is one of the most loving people I have known. When we first started to know her, I could tell how loving she was from the way she treated animals and children. She is extremely intelligent and runs their household in an organized and economical, yet selfless, manner. Doreen is a wonderful mother. She seems to know all

Meadows

the right things to do and say to our two granddaughters. Another thing I really like about Doreen is that she truly loves Jay and she always looks out for his comfort and keeps herself attractive and pretty. I believe their marriage is a lifelong commitment—like ours.

My wonderful, interesting, beautiful daughter, Kate, has made our last twenty years one of the most exciting times of our lives. Kate doesn't march to a different drummer, she marches to her own tune. Kate is a nursing student and she will make one terrific nurse. She loves and cares about all injured people. She wants to work with people who have mental or substance abuse problems. She will make life more bearable for many people, and the world will be a better place for them because of her.

Rocky Joe is one of those rare children that you really can describe as "nearly perfect." He is handsome, sensitive, caring, dependable, honest, a good citizen—always anxious to do the right thing. He and Kate have made every day of our last twenty years an adventure. He has been a good student and a really good sportsman, participating in football, wrestling, and baseball. He has learned some really valuable life lessons through his sports. He will be entering Auburn University in August, where he will study horticulture and business.

The "apples" of my eye are my sweet, beautiful granddaughters, Miranda and Monica. Miranda is now nine years old and well on her way to becoming a lovely, sweet, sensitive young lady. Monica is six and is a blue-eyed minx with a mind of her own. I love them both more than words can describe. I expect our next twenty years will be filled with their activities and I will love every minute of it.

Betty and I seem to be more "in love" than ever before. I could never have chosen a better life companion. We both are looking forward to another wonderful part of our life dressed in our fur coats and driving down the road in my Rolls Royce.

As we read and reread and wrote and rewrote our book, we regretted more each time how much we had to leave out. There were so many stories of our childhood, so many memories of Jay and Cindy's growing up days, so many good times with our family, friends and employees—all of whom we appreciate and love so much—just so many adventures and good times, and so many important, kind, and wonderful people who touched our lives. We know now that we must write at least one sequel to this book. The title would have to be: *It Was a Hell (or Heck) of a Ride*.

But in the meantime, our life really is—Nearly Perfect!

Appendix

> Farmer's Key Business Principles:
>
> 1. Keep up with the Money!
> 2. Always treat all employees right and with respect.
> 3. Always sell the best products at the lowest possible prices.

> Every Customer Deserves:
>
> 1. The best possible Price;
> 2. The best possible Product;
> 3. The best possible Service.

Most businesses can't do all of these, so choose the two you can do really well, and do those better than anyone else.

A Special Resource Section for Future Entrepreneurs

Our present net worth is seventy-two million dollars. Many people ask us how we have accomplished this. Many of these people think that if you have more than the average person, then you are really lucky. Twenty-five to thirty times a year, I hear youngsters and sometimes adults too, talk about hitting the lottery. The whole family plays the lottery. That's the way you get rich, according to them; that's the way to have a lot of money. They seldom think in terms of thinking things through, researching and planning, self-discipline and working, which are the efforts it really takes. If you tell them that you never play the lottery, their next question is, "How did your father make so much money?" It doesn't enter their mind that there are ways to have money other than inheriting or winning it.

They are constantly saying, "Farmer, how did you do it?" It causes Betty and I to think about how we did do it. I came to realize a long time ago—I might have been sixteen to seventeen years old at the time—that I was applying certain principles of thought and guidelines to follow in order to make the proper decisions that helps bring about happiness. Underneath the happiness, of course, you would list having money, because, in most cases, money helps one to be happier.

There are exceptions to all things. Sometimes money can get you in trouble. But whatever our problems are in life, on the whole, they tend to be just a hair easier if you have a lot of money, versus the identical problems but without any economic backup.

In most all of the major decisions in my life, I have applied basically the same principles, using the same guidelines that help me to evaluate each situation, whether it has been choosing friendships, going to college, buying a house, having a baby, or any career or business decision. The following is a listing of those guidelines.

Meadows

1. Thinking

To me, this is the most important step in the decision-making process. Many people, when trying to make a decision, say something along the lines of, "I have a plan. I know I'll have success with it." I think that's wrong. I think the first thing to do in this process is a lot of thinking about this decision you're getting ready to make. Now, this is a step you cannot have your employees do for you. Your wife or husband, or even family can help, but in most cases, it is so important and requires just the right type of concentration and you cannot pay money to have it done for you. The type of thinking you do, and your capabilities for thought, will determine the outcome. If you're in love with the idea, and excited, and enthusiastic about it, you will come up with better thoughts and better results than those who decide they will go into business and hire others to essentially do their thinking for them.

When you're at this thinking stage, consider all of the possibilities, all of the great things that can happen. But you must also consider all of the bad things that could happen. In other words, think about the pros and cons. See how this process applies to personal decision, such as marriage or having children, as well as business, such as expanding an existing business, or opening a new store?

Timing, too, can be very much a part of the thinking process. There are certain times when the economy is right for going into a business, and other times when it's terrible. A good example would be the restaurant business. Back in West Virginia, at a time when people really couldn't afford to eat out much, my dad used to say to his sons and daughters, if you ever want to go broke, just get in the restaurant business. But now, with all of us living in modern times, with a lot of economic strength, everybody goes out to breakfast on a Saturday or Sunday morning, two or three times a week for dinner and lunch, too. In this city, they could open up a restaurant every week for two years and still not have enough restaurants.

I happen to be in the nursery business. Most people can see the value of plants for their beautiful homes. A home cannot be completely beautiful without good landscaping. Of course, not everyone does the landscaping themselves. They use designers and planners when they are having their homes built, or when buying a new home. And although that is usually the last thing they do, they find the money somehow for landscaping because they recognize the necessity of it. So when I look at opening up another nursery, I look around at the homes. When I see the beautiful, expensive homes, I know that people are going to spend thousands of dollars each year, and probably start off with as much as ten to fifteen thousand dollars in their initial planting. When I see nice looking homes that probably cost around one hundred fifty thousand dollars, I know that the average person may spend six hundred dollars each spring for plants and two or three hundred in the fall, and it may be a stretch for them to part with as much as two or three thousand dollars to do the initial landscaping. These are examples of what kind of thinking you do at the first step.

Thinking is the most important part, and the most stressful part of making a good decision. So you should set aside time to perform this task, just as you would set aside time to cut the grass or shop for an important gift. I like to do this in the morning, after a hot shower and a cup of coffee. I just let my thoughts wander, as I settle myself in an environment that allows me to do this. I refer to this practice a couple of times in the text of this book. I get a good fire roaring in the fireplace, grab a six-pack of Coke (or even two), and a yellow pad. I crank up the rock and roll and see what I can come up with. If I have trouble, I play a little pool, which helps even more. Not everybody can start out with the option to go to the islands in the winter time, but that has become another great spot for me to thinking. I'll find myself out by the pool or ocean in the early morning, and try to put it all into operation. Once the gears start turning, you can find yourself coming up with ideas you never had even an inkling of before. I have taken many a vacation that culminated in two, three, even seven full legal pads of ideas. In fact, that's how Betty rates the extent of my thinking sessions—a three-pad or five-pad, or even seventeen-pad vacation.

For me, the end of a long day doesn't offer much incentive for thinking. That's when I'm ready to kick back. But it's very much the perfect time for others. You have to learn for yourself what suits your way the best. The main thing is, do the thinking, spend time with it, do it yourself, don't hire others to do it for you. Hold an open mind, and pay attention to what you come up with; listen to your instincts. You may produce an idea for something that hasn't been done before. That can be exciting, and it can be the thing that takes you to the top.

There are different ways of being successful. I always wanted to be the best at whatever I did. At first, I thought in terms of county, but then in terms of the state. After that, I might dream a little bit about being the best in the surrounding three or four states, or even in the United States. I think it's a good measure of success in entrepreneurship for one to be the best in the state.

In order to do that, you have to go and find out how everybody else is doing. This fires up the creative possibilities.

A huge percent of the people in business were professionals first. But in business, there is more room for the element of creativity than there is in the professional arena. This is actually often the reason professionals leave their fields to go into a different and more receptive business area. Lots of thinking is very good, but lots of *creative* thinking separates the successful from the very successful. In order to be a good creative thinker, you have to be born with just a little bit of it, which I imagine all people inspired toward entrepreneurship are, but you also need to plan a place to be, the conditions, and the right environment so that whatever creativity you are blessed with can flow freely from your head bone.

It's around this time that I ask myself some questions: Will this idea that I'm contemplating bring me more pleasure, joy, and happiness if I make the decision to go forward? Will it make my world a greater place to live in? And of course, if the answer is yes, that's one of the big things that weighs favorably on the overall decision. If not, I would need to indulge in a lot more thought to keep moving forward at that point.

I also ask myself, will this idea be financially satisfying? Will it make me stronger economically? What will I, personally, Farmer Bill Meadows, have to put into it? And how much time will be needed if I make the decision to go forward to make it successful? For instance, if the idea is a new business venture, how much time would I need to put into it in order to make it successful? Will it require that I work myself to death? Will it require a lot of physical strength, or is it more of a mental workout? I usually think in terms of wanting to work pretty hard for a couple of months in order to get the new business going, but I want the business to be such that once I have it established, I can step back and hire others to carry it out successfully. I can't be in more than one place at a time, so the idea is to find a business that can be run by others. I certainly don't want to increase the number of work hours on a long term basis, although I do expect to spend a lot of time in launching any new thing for a couple of months.

I then ask the question am I suited to this endeavor in a natural, sort of human nature way, or would it require that I act differently than my nature? I don't want to change my nature or take on things that go against the grain of Farmer Bill Meadows. Without a doubt, going in that direction creates a stressful situation.

One of the most important questions is will I enjoy this? Will it be exciting and interesting? Will it be an adventure? If I want to be super successful, I need to be able to live and breathe the idea, and allow it to become part of me. If I feel I can't do that, then I need to back away from it and try to find something that does produce that effect.

These types of questions need to have the right answers before I ever even consider the economic end of the endeavor.

So, when someone asks me how I did it, I have to say that I started out with a lot of creative thinking.

2. Research

This step is much easier than the thinking step. But it is very important. You need to find out all you can about the idea right at this point. All other signs are go, but you need to be sure that you can continue the plan. An example in the personal realm of researching decisions would be the question of having a child. Research would involve observing other parents in the midst of child raising, and asking them questions about the pros and cons of the process. Spend a reasonable amount of time observing—not just snapshots of the children at a picnic, or maybe a temper tantrum at the store. You should look at the finances, and the time commitment, and see if what is spent in these two areas in terms of time, money, attention, etc., are things that you are willing to part with to do the job right. When considering a business, you'd want to look at all the competition. Spot the weak points of other companies in the same business. Ask yourself what they are doing wrong that you might do better. Look at their strengths and see if you could at least equal their strong points. Then think of what you will do that will be unique and creative. Can you provide what they provide, but also offer something new and different on top of what they offer?

Sometimes, research even entails taking a job in that business for a few weeks, a month at the most, and then moving to a competitor for another job, and maybe a couple more over a period of a year. This will help you learn as much as possible about the business you are thinking of entering and give you a bird's eye view of what you need to do to get beyond the current state of it. It's OK to reach the same degree of success as your competitors, but with something new and creative, you will surpass their success.

In the process of researching, I like to write down everything that I see the other guy doing, and then put down what I think I can do to improve on the status quo. If I can't get a job there, I will sit in the parking lots for hours, counting cars. Lately, I let someone else do this. If I am thinking of purchasing a nursery for instance, I'll see how many cars are in its lot at a certain hour, then compare that figure with how many cars are in one of my nursery parking lots. If they are similar on the average, I know I can expect to get the same amount of business from that new store right from the start. Books that proprietors present to buyers often reflect a more optimistic picture than the real story. Counting cars is more reliable. This works also, by the way, if you want to check out the competitors' success. We count and then calculate the amount they would make in a one-year period, and arrive at how much better or worse than us they are doing.

Read everything; every business magazine and publication about the business that you are contemplating. Go to the county for information, too. For example, you can find the State Highway Department's traffic counts from the various areas. This information gives you a reasonable idea of your potential for success there.

In this phase, unlike in the thinking phase of decision-making, it is perfectly possible to enlist the assistance of others in the area of research. As long as you receive the end results of their research, you will have the research information you need to make a good decision.

3. Planning

I feel that a lot of successful planning has to be the result of a lot of thinking. The quality of the planning is only as good as the quality of thinking. My friend, Sydney Meadows, whom I've mentioned in the text of this book, has Flowerwood Nursery in Mobile, Alabama. Every year, I go down and buy twenty-five or thirty tractor trailer loads of nursery goods. And I will ask him, "What kind of year are you going to have this year, Sydney?" And he'll say, "I'm going to have a very successful year." And I say, "Well, Sydney, how do you know that?" "Well, because I've got a plan," he says, shaking his finger in my face. And I realize, with all he has to work with there, in my opinion, he is successful every year. But I felt that he wasn't as successful as he should and could have been, because he depended on everything to take place according to that plan.

I don't want to downgrade the value of planning in decision-making in business and one's personal life, but I think it's easy and exciting to do the planning compared to the thinking part of decision-making. As in the research area, planning is a part of the process in which you can allow others to help you.

Planning is simply how you figure out the best way to implement your good ideas born in your thinking stage. How can you make those ideas happen? It's not a bad idea to return to the yellow pads at this stage. When I'm trying to put together a good plan for success, I've taken as many as sixty employees on vacation to Puerto Rico. Each morning, regardless of what we all had to drink or eat the night before, we meet up for an 8:00 breakfast planning meeting that lasts about two hours, take a break, and then do another couple of hours. These planning sessions are fun as well as very successful.

4. Patience and Self-Discipline

I realize that success, for me, took a lot of self-discipline and patience. Most people, I think, always want to do what makes them most comfortable and happy at the time. And I remember that when I was ready to get out of the army, I realized it had been such an easy life and a nice life, that I had an important decision to make. Would I leave behind me the easy, nice life with a guaranteed income? Or would I go to college? I have to say I dreaded the thought of going to college, as I've said, because I knew I would dislike every minute of it. Yet, I knew that most likely going to college would help me to be a millionaire one day. At the time, that was a major objective of mine. In that case, making the tough choice to leave the military service and enter college took some strong self-discipline.

Over the years, I've had about fifteen thousand employees, and another four thousand students and football players, and I've had a pretty wide span of opportunity to observe the degree of others' self-discipline and patience. One thing I noticed, for instance, is when, say, an employee works as a landscape foreman for five or six years. He's installed thousands of plant jobs. He knows a lot about plants. He knows how to go out and successfully perform the installation for my customers. And often times, these employees will resign from my company to begin their own enterprises. I don't criticize them for that because I believe that if you have the right abilities, you need to go out on your own.

These employees come back to me to buy the plants for their customers. They have about two or three months of real good work. You can make some real good money, and you can make it fast. But the ones that have the least amount of self-discipline and patience will, around about the third month, show up in a brand new red 350 Ford truck. I think about my own vehicles when I started in business. Whenever I needed trucks, I purchased all used ones, and used equipment, too. I would never afford myself the leniency to go

Meadows

out and buy all new equipment and trucks, because I knew it was smarter financially to stay away from buying on credit.

Then, as the months passed, I have noticed that the young fellows who've gone into business for themselves would do well until winter came along. They've still got to make the payments, and sometimes they'd lose the truck, and often times, they'd give up the business. I guess about nine out of ten times, they end up coming back to me for a job. Of course I give them one right away. In their efforts at business, they've learned a lot, and have become better people. They appreciate an automatic check every two weeks.

But the point is, even if you do the thinking, the research, and the planning, but you don't exercise self-discipline and patience to overcome the temptation to go out and buy whatever you want or make other impulsive financial decisions, then you run into walls where you might otherwise find a wide open range of success.

Betty and I have always worked to maintain a strong degree of patience. A good example of this is our putting off having the family we wanted so much until we were twenty-six years old. We had degrees, and a couple hundred thousand dollars in the bank, and we certainly could have had new cars, but we didn't. And we didn't have children. We had nice clothes, but we even still bought used furniture. We waited eighteen years to have our first new house and new furniture. But at the time, we already had commercial property, with a net worth of over a million dollars. It was very difficult to wait eight years to have our babies, but we took self-discipline seriously, waiting for a time to have them when we felt we could be the best parents we could be to them.

To me, patience means know when to hold 'em, and know when to fold 'em. For instance, when we bought a piece of property in what is now the Fair Oaks Shopping Center for three hundred thousand dollars, and found that the nursery was not successful after two years, we decided to try to get our money back out of it. But we couldn't sell it—even for the price we'd spent two years before. So we held it. And then after another two years, Betty said, "Let's get rid of it, just cut our losses. We can't worry about getting the right price at this point." And I told her, "Honey, I believe in time it will be worth more money. Let's not fold, but let's hold." In business, Betty and I have had only a few arguments, and this difference of opinion probably falls into that category. "If I can sell if for six hundred thousand," I told her, "I will." A couple of years later, someone did offer six hundred thousand. But before we could complete that sale, another person offered a million dollars. "Well, that will make us multi-millionaires," Betty said. And I said, "You know, Betty, I think we still need to hold, not fold, just yet." And we had another one of those little discussions at that point, but at the end of it, Betty said, as she always does, "Do whatever you want to do."

Then, within a year, it was announced that Fair Oaks Shopping Center was coming in, and that it would be *the* place to shop for the region, the largest shopping center in the entire D.C. area. So I said, "Betty, I'm thinking two million is what we should let it go for, now." And before long, we had those offers, at which point Betty said, "OK, now I suppose you want to go to three million." And I said, "Yeah, but I promise you this time, I'll sell it for three." Within a year, someone did offer three and we ended up selling it for three million, three hundred thousand. And I think patience, and being able to determine when to hold versus when to fold, allowed us to make a three million dollar profit on that one piece of property.

5. Hard Work

As I think about hard work, I realize that my thoughts about it may differ from others' thoughts. I know they differ from Betty's. When I remember my time teaching school, I think of the three years of college preceding that time as very hard work. I worked Saturdays and Sundays starting early in the morning every day, and going 'til late many nights of the week. I knew what hard work was.

Then came teaching. It was so much easier, so much more fun—and there were only forty hours to cover. I jumped from something so difficult into something so easy and really, since then, I can't say I've spent any significant periods of time engaged in hard work. But this is because once I have decided I'm going to do something—open a new store, start a new department within a business, or even go into a completely new business—I am so excited by the idea and the process that the time I spend is fulfilling, exciting, and probably exhausting.

In reality, it's hard work. I've worked fifty and sixty hours a week on a job for periods of four or five weeks or more. But I don't realize that fact because I'm so thrilled with the prospect of making the new things happen that it simply does not feel like hard work. I never dread going to work—it's a pleasure. And if you can be in love with your spouse and children, which is pretty easy to do, and also like or love your job, then you will be a happy person.

Betty's thoughts on hard work in our lives is different from mine. Here are some of her thoughts on that subject.

* * *

My idea of hard work, as Bill said, is totally different from his. I believe we have worked really, really hard. When we were first teaching, he was teaching, working for the recreation department, taking graduate courses, taking Karate, and even got mononucleosis from being so run down. Then, when we started our business, he worked between twelve and sixteen hours a day, loading and unloading trucks on gravel, going to our tomato stands and selling until dark and then coming home, counting the money and getting deposits ready for the banks—and all of this after teaching school all day. We put in many, many hours when we were first starting our business.

If people asked me how did you do it? I like to say, well, we worked really hard! We certainly put in our years of hard work. We did not slow down or even take much of a salary from the business until we were forty years old. That was a long time of working that hard. And Bill still works eight or ten hours a day, but, as he said, he doesn't look at it as work. I've got a pretty cushy life now but I'm still going eight hours a day taking care of things that need to be handled around here. But we thrive on it, and I think that's what keeps us young.

I was telling a young girl what we had done, regarding the idea of hard work and patience. I said, "We didn't even have a house until we had been married eighteen years." And she said, "Oh, I could never do that!" So there's the difference in the way people do things. Some are patient and some can't be that way. In fact, most are not patient. I think most younger people today could not even think about working more than eight hours a day, even considering all the extra income and what they could do with it. Yet you can accomplish so much through hard work and being patient. You may not be as creative or savvy as the next person, but you can make up for it—as you can for a lot of things—with hard work.